D1236607

Global Signposts to the 21st Century

JOHN A. LORAINE

Global Signposts to the 21st Century

Foreword by Lord Avebury

PETER OWEN · LONDON

ISBN 0 7206 0538 5

PETER OWEN LIMITED
73 Kenway Road London SW5 0RE

First published 1979
© John A. Loraine 1979

Printed in Great Britain by
Daedalus Press Stoke Ferry King's Lynn Norfolk

To Lachlan Dempster Loraine (1888-1948) and
Alexander Bell Jack (1861-1942)

Contents

Foreword by Lord Avebury

'Prophecy is the most gratuitous form of error', wrote Goldsmith, and John Loraine is wise to have claimed only to describe signposts to the future, rather than what it will eventually look like if and when we get there.

Even over the shortest of time-scales, those whose job it is to see the shoals ahead sail blithely onto the rocks. At the end of August 1973, six weeks before the outbreak of the Yom Kippur War, which led to the quintupling of oil prices within a year, Mr Edward Heath, then Prime Minister, wrote to me saying, 'I am not as pessimistic about our future oil supplies as you appear to be.' And almost up to the date of the Shah's collapse, our Foreign Secretary, Dr David Owen, was still backing the loser.

Over the longer term, the mistakes can be even more spectacular. We had an astronomer royal not so many years ago who said that space travel was bunk. That well-known futurologist Herman Kahn managed to write a book on *The Year 2000* without mentioning Iran or Saudi Arabia. To pick an example nearer home, the electricity authorities in Britain massively overestimated future demand throughout the 'sixties.

The recognition of these errors will not prevent us from continuing to speculate about the future or even from trying to quantify it. We have to make informed guesses about demographic trends, for instance, if we are to plan long-term investments in maternity hospitals and schools. We need to think about trends in motor vehicle traffic so as to decide on road construction. We must take into account the trends in mortality if we are to provide enough old people's homes. More generally, by considering the directions mankind is taking, and the destinations they may lead to, we could take preventive action, in theory, to head off disasters.

Yet it is a remarkable fact that decision-makers frequently appear to ignore the most obvious pointers. The UK continued training the same number of teachers when the birth rate declined sharply, with the inevitable result that many young people went straight from the training colleges onto the dole. The West didn't even learn much

9

from the 1973 oil crisis: US oil imports have continued to rise steeply since then. A Washington taxi-driver told me recently that if there was an energy problem, it was entirely President Carter's fault because he had discouraged oil exploration by the domestic producers. He assured me there was far more oil remaining to be tapped in the US than in the Middle East, and that it could be produced cheaply enough to keep the price of gasoline below 80 cents a gallon indefinitely! It is this kind of thinking that leads to the use of force at gas stations rather than self-rationing and although the interruption of supplies from Iran may have penetrated the consciousness of the American motorist, his behaviour has not adjusted to it.

As to the major world catastrophes ahead, it is hard to avoid sharing Dr Loraine's frustration at the collective lack of will to use known technologies for their prevention. The essential feature of both the population explosion and nuclear proliferation is that political solutions are still lacking, the technical means being readily available.

Clearly world population is not actually going to reach 11 billion by the late twenty-first century, as it would do arithmetically if replacement fertility is attained by 2020. Mass starvation in parts of Latin America, Africa and Asia will have restored the balance between food supply and demand at an unimaginable cost in human misery and suffering. In Sao Paulo, for instance, which may have 25 million inhabitants by the turn of the century, the infant mortality rate shot up 45 per cent in the period 1962 to 1975, while malnutrition accounts for more than a quarter of the deaths of children up to one year old. Inescapably, this fearful toll will rise and the same phenomenon will be seen in Calcutta, Djakarta or Asmara.

While the world's inability to feed so many human beings becomes steadily more acute, so man's power to destroy his own existence grows inexorably. Dr Loraine shows that both the US and the Soviet Union could wipe out every city in each other's country many times over and that is alarming enough. But the acquisition of nuclear potential by countries which may have a greater readiness to use it could well become a far worse risk. It seems probable that it is only a matter of time before nuclear weapons are used by someone, and there is no way of pushing the genie back into the bottle. The painfully tortuous SALT negotiations between the Superpowers, and any future arms limitation measures, will only change the overkill multiplier – the number of times each side could obliterate the other using all the weapons at its disposal.

What can any puny individual do in the face of the vast impersonal forces pushing the world towards these disasters? In one sense a book like this answers the question, since it does make us more aware of the trends, and thus helps to create the political consciousness which has to be aroused before even partial answers can be given. In another sense, it leaves us at the beginning of the quest, making no suggestions of its own for a programme unless you take the hints expressed in Dr Loraine's concluding allegory.

I will give my own answer, for what it is worth. Professor Wilfrid Beckerman has written that 'In the absence of some transformation of human nature, the like of which has never been seen, in spite of constant admonition by powerful and inspiring religions over thousands of years, human nature has not abandoned the goal of increases in the goods and services that are enjoyed.' He sweeps away the teachings of Isaiah, Jesus and the Buddha in a single sentence, on the grounds that people find it difficult to adhere to them.

But this fanatical pursuit of growth and man's determination to grab as large a share of the world's resources as he can for himself, his family, tribe, union or nation, is the mainspring of the clock ticking towards Armageddon. The big businessman and the trade unionist, the Marxist and the capitalist, the media and academics are virtually all agreed that, as a recent Chancellor of the Exchequer put it, 'It should be the underlying objective of our economic policies to maximize the long-term rate of economic growth, since that is the only means by which we can improve the standard and quality of life in Britain.' It is through the pursuit of similar goals in all the nations of the earth that conflicts and scarcity arise, and it is only by overcoming the ruthless greed of mankind that we can leave a stable and inhabitable planet to our children.

Introduction

This is my fourth book of the decade of the 1970s dealing with global issues. The two basic themes of *Sex and the Population Crisis* (1970) were fertility control and overpopulation. In *The Death of Tomorrow* (1972) environmental pollution, destruction of natural resources, the menace of radioactivity and economics were major concerns. *Syndromes of the Seventies* (1977) endeavoured to present an account of the global dilemma as I percieved it in late 1976. *Global Signposts to the 21st Century* attempts the much more formidable task of peering into the future.

Forecasting and conjecture have traditionally been the province of astrologers, mystics, prophets and a myriad of soothsayers. Even today such people hold vast sway, affecting the expectations and aspirations of millions. Yet throughout the whole of the twentieth century there has been a subtle yet steady and sustained effort to make forecasting less of a mystery and more of an academic discipline and to effect a clearer delineation between scientifically-based projections on the one hand and unalloyed science fiction on the other.

To say that the human future is unknowable is, of course, a truism; only when the future becomes the present shall we really know and comprehend it. Nevertheless, futures research is mandatory. Keener foresight, combined with more responsible expectancy, has the propensity to enhance the chance of human survival and well-being. Futures research can provide greater insight into the possibilities for choice. Above all, futures research, through a rigorous examination, analysis and alembication of the past and present, can aid in the vital process of decision-making.

The opening chapter of this book looks back on the 1970s. It attempts to paint the global canvas with a broad brush, yet at the same time to fasten on abiding rather than on temporary and transient themes. Nuclear proliferation, the direct result of events at Hiroshima and Nagasaki in 1945 – the means whereby civilization was brought 'face to face with its own implications' – is the subject of Chapter 2. The next four chapters are concerned with energy futures in various parts of the world – in the OPEC countries, in the USA and

12

Canada, in the Nordic nations, in Britain, France and Federal Germany. Chapter 7 looks at the Soviet Union from two aspects – demography and resources – while Chapter 8, centred on food prospects, reaches the overall conclusion that worldwide limits to the provision of food need no longer represent a major human problem.

In Chapter 9 I return to the issue which has been my consuming interest for twenty years, namely overpopulation. After a general review of likely population trends between now and 2000 I concentrate on two main themes – problems posed by ageing populations in both developed and developing countries, and two ugly concomitants of overpopulation, excessive urbanization and joblessness, both of which are likely to dominate the history of the eighth and ninth decades of this century. The last two chapters have a distinctly medical flavour. The first is centred on birth control. Its importance in an overcrowded world is stressed; current and potential methods for curbing fertility are reviewed; the continuing need for innovative flair in this field of the medical research is emphasized. The final chapter is mainly concerned with the two illnesses – coronary heart disease and cancer – which are most likely to kill us in the next twenty years. It stresses the importance of environmental factors in their causation; it urges practitioners of medicine to give more thought to the chronology and evolution of disease processes and less attention to the ever-widening range of technological wizardry, however exciting and challenging the latter may be. The Epilogue is different from the rest of the book. It employs as its basis a zoo allegory and in so doing it compares and contrasts the highly divergent views which have been promulgated on world futures.

Any general work which attempts a broad synthesis of a massive field inevitably imposes upon itself severe constraints. The dominant one is compression. Each sentence, even each clause, is a distillate and as such is liable to asymmetry and even to distortion of the events and ideas it attempts to portray. Also the choice of themes is a matter of extreme difficulty. Which are ephemeral, the mere candyfloss of day-to-day living? Which are really important from an historical point of view? I shall undoubtedly be proved wrong in the selection of many of the issues. Nevertheless the allure and real excitement associated with the process of choice remains with me. We are all part of contemporary history. The endless, unpredictable and totally surprising twists and turns of events never fail to fascinate the global citizens of the 'seventies as they have from time immemorial. But now the difference is that the possibility is opening up for all of us to participate much more widely than in the past in the shaping of events to come. If this book has a major aim, it is to stimulate a healthy interest in what has been dubbed 'the rapidly proliferating art of anticipation'.

I wish to record my deep appreciation to Lord Avebury for writing the Foreword to this book. I am also grateful to individuals too numerous to name who assisted me through dialogue and conversation in the preparation of this book. Specifically, I desire to thank Professor John Erickson of the Department of Politics of Edinburgh University for helpful advice on Chapter 2, Dr Colin Davidson of the Department of Electrical and Electronic Engineering, Heriot Watt University, for scrutinizing Chapter 6, Dr Arthur Kitchin, Western General Hospital, Edinburgh and Dr C. R. Gillis of Ruchill Hospital, Glasgow for very useful comments on Chapter 11. Professor J. R. Williamson of the Department of Geriatrics of Edinburgh University provided me with invaluable and updated information which was incorporated in Chapter 9, while Dr Janet Higgs, Librarian of the Centre for Human Ecology at Edinburgh University, made a number of useful suggestions about the Epilogue and was at all times assiduous in providing me with important and relevant literature. The assistance of secretarial staff, particularly of Miss Marion Owen, Mrs Peggie Hunter, Mrs Sheena MacEwan and staff of the Reed Employment and Sheila Scott Agencies was much appreciated, and it is a special pleasure to record my thanks to my publishers, Peter Owen Limited, London and particularly to Mr Dan Franklin of that firm, for assistance, co-operation and unfailing courtesy. As in my previous books I wish to make it clear that the views expressed are personal and do not necessarily represent those of any of the bodies with which I am affiliated.

Many people have influenced my life – at school, in the practice of medicine, in professional research, in universities, in politics, in overseas travel to numerous countries. Yet two stand out, both schoolteachers – my father for his patience, his outstanding humility and above all for his veneration for history; my grandfather for his towering intellectualism and for teaching me from a very early age about nature and inculcating into me the principles of human ecology. I was indeed fortunate to be able to sup at the fount of all wisdom. The dedication conveys my gratitude.

Edinburgh, April 1979   John A. Loraine

Chapter 1

Retrospect on the Seventies

For me four issues have dominated the global scene during the 1970s –
continuing population growth, burgeoning nuclear proliferation, the
debilitating effects of energy shortages, and the recognition that
sooner or later the world must move towards a more sustainable type
of society.

In 1970 world population stood at 3,600 million. Each year during
the decade between 60 and 70 million people were added to the population of the planet and by 1979 it exceeded 4,200 million. The
'seventies have witnessed a welcome deceleration in the overall
growth rate – from 2 to 1.7 per cent per annum in nine years. However, there is certainly no cause for complacency. Although overall
contraceptive use has increased slightly at the global level during the
decade and by its end some 35 per cent of eligible couples are practising some form of birth control, unmet needs *vis-à-vis* family planning
remain massive.[1] The average family size worldwide is just short
of five children; 400 million women, mainly in the Third World,
are totally unprotected against pregnancy; archaic laws in many
countries make contraception and safe abortion difficult or impossible
to obtain; family planning's disenfranchised minorities – the young,
the poor and the rural dwellers – continue to encounter inordinate
problems in controlling their fertility.

The slow increase in contraceptive practice amongst young people
is especially worrisome; so is the apparent failure to change the attitudes of couples in the Third World to the size of family they want
to have. Educational programmes have lacked trained personnel,
have been feebly prosecuted and in many areas have never even got
off the ground. Amongst Western countries, only Sweden has made
sex and population education an integral part of all school curricula.
In the Third World the pace of change has been glacial. In Africa,
Asia and Latin America, 70 per cent of children under fifteen and 57
per cent of young people still have no instruction about reproduction

15

and sexual responsibility in schools or anywhere else.

In the developed world the fertility decline, first apparent in the mid-'sixties, has persisted and gained momentum. At least six countries – Austria, Belgium, the two Germanies, Luxembourg and the UK – have reached zero or negative population growth; others are rapidly approaching this situation. Ideology is having no effect. The lowest birth rate in the world in 1975 (10 per 1,000 population) was in staunchly capitalist Federal Germany, while across the Iron Curtain in the German Democratic Republic the figure was only one point higher. In 1978 birth rates below 17 per 1,000 were reported from countries with political systems as disparate as Bulgaria, Sweden, Finland, Japan, the USA and Switzerland. The geriatric tide has flowed strongly in the industrialized world during the 'seventies, a theme which will be further developed in Chapter 9. Europe, with 12 per cent of its 480 million inhabitants over the age of sixty-four, is by far the oldest continent, East Germany with a figure of 16 per cent the oldest nation state.

The population situation in the Third World has flickered like a kaleidoscope during the 'seventies. Longevity has been increasing in many countries. Death rates and infantile mortality rates have plummeted as infectious diseases have been further emasculated (or, as in the case of smallpox, completely eradicated) and as hygiene and sanitation have improved. There seems little doubt that a demographic transition, characteristic of the West earlier this century, is lapping on the shores of the Third World and that sooner or later the population pattern will alter from the high birth and death rates characteristic of agricultural societies, to one in which low birth and death rates are the norm.[2] Indeed, the large discrepancy in population dynamics discernible throughout the Third World during the last ten years merely testifies to the fact that the denizens of individual countries have travelled different distances along a road which will eventually culminate in a Western-style demographic transition.

Yet for the foreseeable future the developing world is destined to carry an enormous burden of population. The age structure with its high proportion of youth dictates this. In Africa 44 per cent of the people are under fifteen, in Asia 38 per cent, in Latin America 42 per cent. In some individual Third World countries – Algeria, Libya, Mali, Botswana and Iran are examples – almost half the population are in this age bracket. The parents of tomorrow have already been born. Birth control will reach a relatively small proportion of them;

as will be emphasized in Chapter 10, advances in reproductive biology and contraceptive technology have been limited and have in general lacked innovation and flair. At the World Population Conference in Bucharest in 1974, much rhetoric was devoted to the theme of socio-economic development. It became the modern version of Sir Galahad's holy grail, the epicentre for reproductive restraint, the only means of defusing the population bomb. Yet in a world decisively split between 'haves' and 'have-nots', development has been disappointingly slow and, as global resources dwindle in a finite planet and as prospects for economic growth continue to fade, there is no reason to believe that its rate will rise dramatically. In countries like India special value will continue to be attached to sons as tillers of the soil and as mainstays of aged and infirm parents; as long as this perception persists the dynamic for any reduction in family size will remain weak. Religious taboos and barriers to the acceptance of family planning continue to be dominant in many parts of the world. In Latin America Catholicism is still deeply entrenched and in many Islamic countries – Iran and Pakistan are typical – evangelical religions are resurgent and pro-natalist policies seem certain to hold sway for the foreseeable future.

By the end of the 'seventies about one-third of the earth's people were living in India and China. Increasingly these countries have come to occupy a pivotal position in the global population scene. Their approach to population control will be crucial for mankind and will do much to mould the history of the twenty-first century.

Undoubtedly the pyrotechnics with respect to population policy in the 'seventies have been provided by India. In 1976 the Indira Gandhi Government, faced with an annual increase of about 14 million people, decided to ride the population tiger. The Government first raised the minimum legal age of marriage from 15 to 18 for girls and from 18 to 21 for men. It then began its fateful flirtation with that pariah in the birth control armamentarium, compulsory sterilization. The movement of events was swift. Maharashtra became the first of four states to pass a law compelling sterilization in families of over three children. Forced vasectomy in India became increasingly widespread as the whole government infrastructure was mobilized to pressure people to be sterilized. The medical profession had perforce to join the imbroglio; it was overwhelmed by the demand and its standards plummeted. There were reports of vasectomies being performed under grotesque conditions – on office desks, on railway platforms, on street corners, in the fields, several times in one individual. The programme reached its point of culmination in September 1976 during which it is estimated that two million people were sterilized.

But Mrs Gandhi had read the political signposts wrongly. She had failed to take into account one of the eternal verities – that, of all forms of human activity, reproduction is the least susceptible to external coercion. She might have profited from reading John Stuart Mill's classic essay of 1859, *On Liberty*, in which he proclaimed, 'If there be an ethical doctrine which more than all others requires to be taught . . . it is that love of power is the most evil passion of human nature; that power over actions, power of coercion and compulsion . . . is a snare and a curse both to the possessor and to those over whom it is possessed.' She ought to have realized that, although compulsory sterilization might have been enforced by someone as barbaric as Hitler, as sadistic as Stalin, as paranoiac as Idi Amin, twentieth-century India, nurtured in the gentle non-violence of Mohandas Gandhi and in the progressive democratic socialism of her father, Jawaharlal Nehru, was manifestly inappropriate terrain for such a programme.

Nemesis for Indira Gandhi's Government was not long delayed. At the General Election of March 1977 compulsory sterilization was the crucial issue; indeed the integrity of the *vas deferens* seemed to have become the hub of the campaign. Wholesale disapproval for 'compulsionism' was registered in the vote. The Congress Party, in power since Independence, suffered a *dégringolade* of considerable proportions, its major defeats occurring in northern regions of the country where the sterilization campaign was it its most intense. Cabinet ministers favouring compulsion lost their seats by decisive margins. These included Mrs Gandhi herself, her notorious son Sanjay and the Defence Minister Bansi Lal. The collapse of Mrs Gandhi's Government was a serious matter for it could have long-term demographic consequences for India. Family planning had received a severe setback; its image was degraded, tarnished and defiled. The most striking immediate effect was the fall off in sterilizations, only 800,000 operations being performed in the twelve months up to April 1978 as compared with ten times that total in the previous year.

Meanwhile in 1979 India's intractable population problem remains. It has 2.4 per cent of the world's land, 1.5 per cent of the global income; but in contrast it contains 14.6 per cent of its people. A new baby is born every 15 seconds, numbers are growing at a million a month, towards a total well in excess of 1,000 million by 2000 AD. Will the present leadership of the Janata Party – geriatric and already showing signs of fissiparity – have sufficient political clout to reinvest birth control with the cloak of respectability and put the family planning movement firmly back on the rails? And can this be done without further recourse to coercive measures? These crucial questions remain unanswered. But population-wise the immediate prognosis for India can scarcely be regarded as favourable.

China is the world's most populous country. Precise demographic data are lacking but numbers almost certainly exceed 900 million. When Mao Tse-tung seized power in 1949, he had no doubts about the supreme task facing his fledgling People's Republic – to feed a large and growing population at a reasonable nutritional level. That he achieved his goal and did so without placing undue strain on global food resources is a testimony to the political will which he demonstrated in carrying through his country's population policy.

Throughout the whole of its tenure of office, the Mao Tse-tung administration showed great interest in and concern for the reproductive proclivities of its citizens. Late marriage was advocated – for men not before 26, for women not before 23. The two-child norm in marriage was favoured; by exercising restraint in reproduction, the couple were seen to be 'serving the fatherland' and to be showing a 'raised political consciousness'. Divorce and illegitimacy became rare in Mao's China. Premarital virginity is still a rubric of society while sex remains singularly non-commercialized in the People's Republic.

Paramedical staff, particularly the celebrated 'barefoot doctors', continue to be the spearhead of China's family planning programme. They deliver the services and they are especially active in rural areas where about three-quarters of the population live. Barefoot doctors also give overall instruction in methods of birth control and when necessary they can perform relatively minor surgical procedures, including vasectomy and early abortion. They are also an important element in providing pressure and encouragement at the neighbourhood level for reproductive restraint.

A striking feature of China's birth control programme in the late 1970s is its eclecticism. According to a recent report from the International Planned Parenthood Federation some 40 per cent of married couples in the People's Republic practise contraception in some form. The Pill is the lynchpin of the programme. Oral contraceptives have the same chemical composition as in the West; they are made locally and circulate widely through all strata of society; 'once-a-month' pills and injectable contraceptives are becoming increasingly popular as their reliability increases. Female sterilization is now gaining ground as a method of fertility control. Abortion is available on request in China; no stigma attaches to the procedure and the vacuum suction technique which the country pioneered is routinely employed. Other methods of birth control – intrauterine devices, condoms, diaphragms and vasectomy – are also represented.

Undoubtedly the widespread participation of women in the Chinese political and economic system continues to exert a profound antinatalist effect. Mao was determined that under his suzerainty female emancipation and women's rights would become dominant historical forces. In a much publicized speech in the 'fifties, the Great Helmsman proclaimed that the Chinese man carried on his back 'three mountains' – feudalism, capitalism and imperialism, but the Chinese woman carried a fourth 'and the fourth was a man'. Male chauvinism had been a prominent and odious feature of pre-revolutionary China. Mao now used the women's rights issue as an integral part of the regime's campaign against Confucianism. Male chauvinism was depicted as the archetypal manifestation of a reactionary past, and he declared that it must rapidly be consiged to the dustbin of history. Instead it was *women* who 'held up half of heaven'; and it was high time they rose up and smashed 'the thousand-year-old chains of male supremacy'.

By the late 'seventies there is little doubt that an unprecedented fall in Chinese fertility has taken place. Figures for natural increase as low as 1.4 per cent per annum are being quoted and these are, of course, very much lower than those obtaining in China's Asian neighbours like India, Pakistan, the Philippines and Indonesia. In some urban communes in cities such as Shanghai, Hunan and Changsha, phenomenally low birth-rate figures (less than 10 per 1,000 population) are being reported, suggesting that contraceptive use compares favourably with that in North America and Europe.[3] At the time of writing there seems no indication that the new regime in China will alter the population policy initiated under Mao; indeed, the new Chairman Hua Kuo-feng endorsed it enthusiastically soon after taking office. The success of the Chinese programme is such that other Third World countries, labouring under the debilitating effect of acute population pressures, might well be advised to emulate it and give it free rein.

Closely related to the population theme is that of women's liberation. The twentieth century has been a slow, painful and arduous climb for women up the ladder of social, political and economic emancipation. The 'seventies saw a definite acceleration of this process, especially in developed countries.

International Women's Year in 1975, with its slogans, 'equality, development and peace', focused attention on the women's movement. When the women of the world assembled in Mexico City in June of that year for their UN-sponsored conference, they showed that they were in no mood for compromise. They demanded that discrimination against women in employment and education must cease forthwith; the shackles of illiteracy which so effectively fetter huge numbers of women in the Third World must be fractured. Women were an integral part of the development process. Their political awareness had to be raised at both local and national levels: no longer need they fear to scale the commanding heights of world diplomacy.

The Conference demanded that women must have much greater control of their destiny as far as sex and reproduction are concerned. They should not be 'mere instruments of demographic policies' drawn up by soulless bureaucracies dominated by men. The dreary catalogue of reproductive performance in which one pregnancy succeeds another with monotonous regularity must be abolished. Within family life, women must have access as of right to the full panoply of decision-making. In particular, they must be enabled to make free, informed and responsible choices on age of marriage and number and spacing of children.

In *Syndromes of the Seventies* I wrote that female emancipation seemed like a growing tree about to burst decisively into leaf. But at the end of the decade this seemed less likely, especially in the Third World. The high hopes of Mexico City have not been fulfilled. Glaring inequalities persist between men and women in the poor countries. In Africa young girls are being sold into prostitution and the mutilating operation of clitorectomy, which removes forever orgasmic satisfaction, is being practised. In Moslem countries polygamy is still permitted; female sterility is regarded as a crime; male dominance is firmly entrenched and male *machismo* a continuing focus for adulation. Men are still too heavily involved in decisions regarding pregnancy termination; contraceptive methods directed towards males remain unpopular and poorly researched.

In industrialized countries, however, women are faring better. Radical changes in their status and expectations are taking place and more prolonged periods of education and training for women are being actively sought. The striking increase in the proportion of women in the labour force, first noted in the 'sixties, has continued. The institution of marriage is tending to lose some of its societal rationales. In particular women are increasingly questioning a situation in which they continue to offer their child-bearing proclivities and domestic skills merely to secure the dubious advantage of the security provided by a man's income and status. Certainly cohabitation in the absence of marriage has very definitely been on the increase in the 'seventies. In Denmark, 25 per cent of women aged between 18 and 25 are living with men to whom they are not married; in Sweden, 12 per cent of all couples living together (aged from 16 to 70) are not married. Yet in industrialized countries too, there are clouds on the horizon of the women's movement. Joblessness is on the increase *pari passu* with automation, and the view is being expressed that the second Industrial Revolution spearheaded by micro-electronics might put the clock back for women's liberation by preferentially favouring men in the labour force.

An issue whose imprimatur seemed greater early rather than late in the decade was the struggle between the world's 'Rich North' and 'Poor South'. By 1970 what Adlai Stevenson once called 'the revolution of rising expectations' was in full swing. North-South relationships were changing dramatically, Third World nations moving away from postures of deference, venality and sycophancy to attitudes of opposition, intransigence and outright defiance. It was becoming blatantly obvious that the opera glasses of the affluent would have to be focused to an ever increasing extent on the misery and degradation of the poor.

Developing nations had meantime enshrined their aspirations in the New International Economic Order. They demanded that the poverty curtain which divided the world philosophically and nationally be rent asunder, and the asymmetrical economic relationships currently in existence destroyed. A situation could no longer be tolerated in which *per capita* consumption was twenty times greater in industrialized countries than in developing ones. The Third World would no longer be prepared to live in thralldom and peonage, totally at the mercy of market forces which it had not shaped, could not control and which actively discriminated against it. The intransigence of industrialized nations *vis-à-vis* their trading practices was pushing the world ever closer to the rim of catastrophe and could only threaten global peace and security.

At the end of the decade, however, the North-South confrontation seems to have lost some of its dynamic. The sea is becalmed; a new wind is needed to stir it. Few doubt that such a wind will arise and could be blowing with hurricane force well before the end of the century. Unparallelled affluence cannot exist indefinitely with unprecedented inequality. Redistribution of global wealth and resources is vested with an aura of historical inevitability. The trend cannot be reversed: to try to do so would be as useless as attempting to stay the descending blade of a guillotine with an appeal for mercy.

World food production took a sharp turn for the worse in the early 'seventies. Monsoons failed in India, China and South-East Asia. The Soviet harvest of 1972 was poor and led to the 'great grain grab' during which the USSR clandestinely purchased the bulk of the US and Canadian grain supplies to feed to its livestock. Food problems were further compounded by the quadrupling of oil prices following the Arab oil embargo of 1973. Fertilizers, pesticides and herbicides, all manifestly oil dependent, tripled in price in one year, and the cost of agricultural equipment soared. The hardest hit of all were Third World nations without indigenous oil supplies. The rising cost of fuel imports presented them with an almost unsupportable burden; development schemes had to be postponed indefinitely; millions of people were brought to the brink of starvation and catastrophe.

The OPEC countries, rich beyond the dreams of avarice by the middle of the decade through soaring oil revenues, soon became a dominant purchaser in global food markets. During the 'seventies *per capita* food consumption rose spectacularly in countries like Iran, Saudi Arabia, Iraq and Venezuela. However, by 1979, with several of these countries running marked balance of payments deficits, this trend is less marked. The population giants of OPEC, Nigeria and Indonesia, will soon be able to flex their muscles for an assault on world food supplies; the precise date for such an onslaught cannot at present be predicted. Meanwhile the world has become far too dependent on the granaries of North America. The US hegemony in food seems unshakeable, and there have been unpleasant hints – particularly during the Nixon-Kissinger era – that food might be used as a political weapon. All in all it seems grossly unfair that the future of great numbers of people throughout the world could be placed in jeopardy by the arcane manoeuvring of American domestic and international politics, not to mention the vagaries of that country's climate.

At the end of the decade the dimensions of human hunger and malnutrition remain formidable. Hunger is thought to affect about 1,000 million people, mainly from lower socio-economic groups in developing countries. Protein-energy malnutrition has its highest incidence in infants and pre-school children of whom ten million are thought to be severely affected and 100 million moderately affected. Deficiency diseases are still rampant. Xerophthalmia from Vitamin A deficiency is a major cause of blindness in South-East Asia and Latin America; rickets and osteomalacia due to inadequate intake of Vitamin D are prevalent in infants, pregnant women and elderly people inhabiting the shanty towns in many Third World countries. Goitre due to iodine lack is common in women in mountainous areas of Asia, the Middle East and Latin America while iron-deficiency anaemia afflicts millions of people, with its highest incidence in infants and in women during the child-bearing period.

I suspect that, when historians come to review the events of the 'seventies, they will give pride of place to nuclear proliferation at the global level. Nuclear proliferation has seemed to have been in the process of fracturing the delicate and fragile web constituting the world balance of power. It has been presenting humanity with the awesome prospect whereby individual nation states will be in a position to fabricate atomic weapons on a mass scale like washing machines, refrigerators, television sets and motor cars. It has been bringing nearer the day when one country, by the use of its nuclear arsenal, will be able to reduce a neighbouring or distant state to absolute subjugation, to inflict upon it a Carthiginian peace beside which twentieth-century treaties like Brest Litovsk and Versailles will seem almost virginal in character.[4] The deadly game of nuclear leapfrog has persisted during the 'seventies. The laws of physics have been put to fiercer and fiercer torture. Both Superpowers now have a gargantuan investment in military hardware; each has been trying to outpace the other in the race for weapons superiority, the whole process being buttressed by doctrines such as 'deterrence', 'overkill', 'counterstrike' and 'measured escalation'. The Strategic Arms Limitation Talks have remained a touchstone of East-West relations, the lynchpin for détente. But SALT has not prospered during the 'seventies, largely because the ceilings put on nuclear weapons by the superpowers remain absurdly high. Moreover the thrust of technological change has become so rapid that any agreement reached through SALT is likely to be overtaken by events, so that any political benefit is quickly dissipated. There are some who have argued that SALT, far from limiting the arms race, has actually stimulated it because each agreement has provided inducements to exploit loopholes in the system, to compensate for apparent inadequacies by developing yet more lethal weapons, and to retain the existing armoury in the form of a bargaining chip.

A major event of 1974 was India's accession to the nuclear club, bringing the number of states definitely in possession of atomic weapons to six. The 15-kiloton device which she exploded in the Rajasthan Desert and which utilized plutonium supplied by Canada for the construction of atomic reactors was disingenuously described as 'peaceful'. But undoubtedly the detonation has had the effect of raising the global nuclear stakes considerably. For it demonstrated with considerable clarity that even an impoverished, grossly disadvantaged Third World country could become a nuclear weapons power if the political will existed to take this road. In the case of India, the situation was especially ironic because just twenty years previously the then Prime Minister, Jawaharlal Nehru, had been the first head of state to propose a surcease to all nuclear testing.

By the late 'seventies, many other Third World countries are in possession of technology sufficiently sophisticated to enable them to 'go nuclear' if they so desire. Nuclear materials can also be obtained clandestinely on the black market (the analogy with drug trafficking is highly apposite here). The nuclear restraint which has operated since Hiroshima and Nagasaki is visibly crumbling and denuclearization seems as dead as last week's mutton. The UN Disarmament Conference of 1978 was a major disappointment. Its final document was full of platitudes; the proliferation of nuclear weapons was only briefly discussed, and instead the delegates expressed the view that all nations must have access to nuclear technology and freedom to acquire it if they so desire.

May 1977 was an important month. The newly-elected US President, Jimmy Carter, made his first trip overseas to attend a Western Economic Summit in London. He brought with him practical and

imaginative proposals about nuclear energy. The US would not for
the present proceed with its programme to construct fast breeder
reactors; there should be a moratorium on commercial reprocessing
and on plutonium recycling and, in the meantime, the international
community should re-examine carefully the basic assumptions behind
the plutonium economy.

The President's vision was noble; but the practice would be in-
credibly difficult and his suggestions had a chilly reception. The
French President and the Federal German Chancellor could scarcely
be expected to welcome them. For during 1975 and 1976 – a time
which future chroniclers may come to describe as 'the years which
the locust hath eaten' – Paris and Bonn, finding their domestic
nuclear industries ailing and debilitated, were determined that commerce should clink its purse. In so doing, they gave a galvanic jerk
to global politics as they began to launch atomic reactors on seas
which future hurricanes could lash into a frothing fury. During these
years the President and the Chancellor permitted nuclear deals which
caught the world's headlines – between France and Libya, France
and Iran, France and Pakistan, France and South Africa, and biggest
of all (described in the press as *le marché du siècle*) between Federal
Germany and Brazil. All this time Paris and Bonn were paying due
obeisance to the London Club – a group of industrialized nations from
East and West which were holding their meetings in semi-clandestine
conditions and whose avowed aim was to halt the spread of atomic
weapons. Yet *pari passu* with these negotiations, the French and
German Governments were indulging in the very special form of
double-think which affects all aggressive arms vendors and which
flows fundamentally from intense commercial rivalry.

The US President made little headway in London. He could claim
a minor success in the establishment of his International Fuel Cycle
Evaluation Programme which would study the proliferation issue in
depth and report back to him in 1979. But the really substantive
nuclear issues have foundered on the rock of European intransigence.
The suffocating ectoplasm of international diplomacy has seemed to
engulf them and the gold of good intention has been swiftly changed
into the sand of reality.

The portents of the 'seventies have been that governments, irrespective of ideology, will embrace the nuclear option as a means of
generating electricity. Only in this way, it is thought, will material
living standards be maintained and policies of economic growth

fostered. However, the decade has also seen mounting public protest about this course of action, presaging the politics of confrontation on a massive and alarming scale.

Even as early as 1970, the US had a vociferous anti-nuclear lobby. In 1976 the issue had become of such importance that seven states held referenda on it. In all, supporters of atomic power triumphed. But nuclear critics have no reason to be disheartened with the results. They garnered a sizeable proportion of the vote; above all, they greatly raised the salience of the issue, and their actions could well have been a significant factor in the Presidential *démarche* of 1977, already referred to.

Australia, a major uranium supplier, has become increasingly involved in the nuclear debate. Miners have made it clear that they are reluctant to extract uranium from the ground lest it exacerbate the proliferation danger. In 1975 at a mass rally in Canberra, environmentalists joined with trade unionists, academics and pacifists to demand that the Government use all the *gravitas* at its disposal to establish a nuclear-free zone over the South Pacific and Antarctica. The paradigm, they said, should be the Treaty of Tlatelolco, signed in 1967, and prohibiting the manufacture of atomic weapons anywhere in Latin America. The Australian Government of the day bowed to the public protest and established the prestigious Fox Commission chaired by a celebrated lawyer. The Commission gave due credit to the skill, ingenuity and resourcefulness of Australia's nuclear physicists and engineers. But such adulatory comments did not prevent it from concluding that the industry was 'unintentionally contributing to the increased risk of nuclear war'.

Elsewhere in Oceania an ecologically-based organization emerged during the 'seventies. The Values Party in New Zealand claims to be the first 'post industrial' grouping in the world, and its main aim is to formulate policies which will be suitable in an era of resource depletion with inevitable shortages of raw materials and energy. The Values Party is predominantly orientated to the aspirations of individuals. It is also strongly anti-nuclear, and it takes considerable credit for the fact that the New Zealand Government has postponed for ten years the decision to introduce atomic power into the country.

From 1975 onwards Europe has been riven with politics of radioactivity. In the Swedish General Election of the following year, the Social Democratic Party, led by Olaf Palme, and having been in office for forty years, was toppled on the issue and a Centrist Coalition led by Thörjbjorn Fälldin took power on an anti-nuclear ticket and with the avowed aim of halting the construction of atomic plants in Sweden (see also Chapter 5). The coalition was never an easy one. In particular, the Conservatives and Liberals did not share the Centre Party's strong aversion to nuclear power. In October 1978 Mr Fälldin resigned and, with the likelihood of the return of the Social Democrats to office at the election this year, further nuclear expansion in Sweden seems probable.

Meanwhile resistance to proposed reactor development has been mounting in France, Federal Germany and Austria. Ecological parties sponsoring 'green' candidates have emerged in the first two countries and begun to capture a significant portion of the popular vote. These parties consist mainly of young people, but they have aroused concentric ripples of sympathy throughout society at large. 'Green' candidates have been staunchly anti-nuclear: like the Values Party in New Zealand, they are deeply concerned to preserve the quality of life and to protect human rights. Undoubtedly their electoral difficulties in France and Germany have been and will be great. For pitted against them is the full panoply of State power with its commitment to raw and unfettered economic growth and its dedication to ever-expanding consumerism and acquisitiveness.

In Austria nuclear politics have taken a different twist. In November 1978 the Chancellor, Bruno Kreisky, called a referendum on whether to commission the country's first nuclear power plant. He indicated that a vote in favour would be a vote of confidence in himself. But he was narrowly defeated and his Government will now have to give urgent thought to Austria's excessive and expensive dependence on imported energy – now running at over 60 per cent of total consumption and likely to rise to 80 per cent within ten years.

Three events have dominated the British nuclear scenario during the 'seventies. The first was the decision to replace the ill-fated steam generating heavy water reactor with the advanced gas cooled reactor as the prototype for future development. The second was the Report of the Royal Commission on Environmental Pollution published in 1976. This Report, undoubtedly the classic contribution of the decade, sounded the tocsin of alarm about the whole concept of the plutonium economy. It took very seriously threats of nuclear terrorism and sabotage, cogently arguing that fissile material in storage or particularly in transit could readily fall into the hands of irresponsible, fanatical or criminal groups. The Report argued that for something as important as energy, the country should not rely on a process which produced large quantities of a by-product as dangerous as plutonium. The Commissioners believed that undue dependence on the fast breeder reactor would be unwise, and that before there was any question of introducing it on a commercial scale, a wide-ranging public discussion should take place.

The Report of the Windscale Inquiry published early in 1978 had a quite different tone. Its stance strongly favoured the nuclear establishment, and it gave unequivocal support to the request of British Nuclear Fuels to build a new Thermal Oxide Reprocessing Plant in Cumbria. The Report has come under bitter criticism from environmentalists and others on the grounds that it is biased, misleading and full of specious arguments. Certainly it seems particularly weak on the proliferation issue, when it maintains that by building the plant and so encouraging national reprocessing of spent fuel global dangers in respect of proliferation will be reduced. In the past Britain has tacitly acquiesced in a global non-proliferation policy. The Report is worrisome because implicit in its wording is the suggestion that the UK might be changing its stance and might in the future become a 'nuclear hard-liner' like France or Federal Germany.

Throughout the 'seventies the world has floundered in a nuclear bog. There has seemed no way out of it, no path which might eventually lead to denuclearization and control of atomic energy at a supranational level. Instead everywhere the signals have been set for danger, the red lights flashing through the mists of contemporary history. Rebottling the nuclear genie seems a well nigh impossible task; it would require a level of statesmanship undreamt of even by the most idealistic in our midst.

Energy policies were forced on reluctant politicians following the Yom Kippur War and Arab oil embargo of 1973. Global oil prices soon quadrupled and it was slowly recognized that OPEC, far from being an ephemeral nuisance, was here to stay as a major global force.

As will be seen in Chapters 3 to 7, hard-energy proponents, favouring oil, gas, coal and particularly nuclear fission, hold the stage all over the world. Alternative energy pathways – from sun, wind, waves, tides and the earth's core – are still not taken seriously, although due obeisance is made to the possibility that they might have a minor role to play in the twenty-first century. Yet for reasons which will be discussed in subsequent chapters, the chosen energy pathway for industrialized nations could well turn into a *via dolorosa*. The thrust is overwhelmingly short term; Panglossian optimism about technological fixes is rife; the needs of future generations condemned to live in an oilless and nuclear-sated world seem to be receiving scant recognition.

During the era of cheap energy which has lasted for most of this century, the world has been outrageously profligate with its most precious patrimony, oil. Yet the writing has been on the wall for several years. As early as the 1950s, prestigious geologists like the American M. K. Hubbard were warning that oil was a finite resource, that global oil production would reach its peak in the 1990s and that thereafter, as demand exceeded supply, oil would become scarcer and much more expensive. No heed was paid to such forecasts, and they were written off as the croakings of eccentric and petulant Cassandras. Yet through our neglect, we have given a plethora of hostages to fortune and the Nemesis which is already overtaking us is largely of our own making.

Even now most people refuse to believe that the twilight of the petroleum era is well advanced. Immediately after the Yom Kippur War when the prodromata of the looming energy crisis were clearly visible, rational therapy was instituted. Energy conservation became respectable overnight; talk of petrol rationing was in the air; speed limits were enforced, and even the semi-regal status accorded to the motor car was being challenged. But very soon people convinced themselves that the malady had remitted and would not recur. Governments were all too ready to encourage this mood of *laissez-faire*. The motor industry continues to turn out cars in huge numbers and to build new plants to facilitate production. Yet the oil on which the entire edifice of the car industry rests is being used up fast and is unlikely to be available in adequate quantities even ten years from now. Petroleum products continue to dominate Western economies and Western-style agriculture. They have been woven into the warp and the woof of national life; they remain the lynchpin of the consumerist society, the spearhead of policies designed to stimulate economic growth. Their replacement must soon become a matter of acute concern and urgency.

The image of cornucopian economics has faded in the 'seventies, particularly in developed countries. For years both individually and collectively we have been demanding more from the economic system than it could deliver. The manipulation of aggregate demand, the proliferation of public works – the bedrocks of Keynesianism which had been successful and electorally advantageous in democratic countries for almost thirty years – have become progressively less efficient, and by the end of the decade seem incapable of steering Western economies off the reefs and shoals to which they are heading.

Between the end of the Second World War and 1973 the global economy expanded at about 5 per cent per year. But in 1974, in the wake of the Yom Kippur War and the massive rise in oil prices, growth rates plummeted to 2 per cent; in 1975 they were down even further to 1 per cent. 1976 *did* see a rise to 5 per cent, but this was not sustained; the figure for 1977 was 3.8 per cent and those for 1978 and 1979 are likely to be even lower. A change of major historical import has been taking place during the decade. The relationship between the earth's population on the one hand and its natural systems and indigenous resources on the other is deteriorating. The formidable troika of overpopulation, resource depletion and widespread capital scarcity is ineluctably propelling the planet along the road to greater sustainability. No feat of technological legerdemain can now reinstate the epoch of unfettered economic growth: the ecological imperatives imposed by a finite planet will increasingly have to be taken into account.

Lenin once wrote that the best way to destroy the capitalist system and overturn the existing order was to debase the currency. He would no doubt have derived great satisfaction from the progress of inflation during the 'seventies. Inflation has reached unprecedented heights in many industrialized countries and has frequently been associated with recession and joblessness. It has created great anxiety amongst political leaders because of its penchant to distort economic and social values, aggravate divisions within society and increase the likelihood of violent political change.

This is no place to probe the causes of inflation. To say that they are multifactorial is a truism. The currents which flow to generate inflationary pressures are numerous and diverse; they approach one another, meet and eventually coalesce to produce a flood, the waters of which no political leader has succeeded in holding back for any length of time. Yet what the 'seventies have demonstrated with great clarity is that global as well as purely national factors have become a potent new cause of inflation. In the past, plentiful resources could be substituted for scarce. Now, with oil wells running dry, natural gas at risk, accessible high-quality mineral reserves much less readily available, easily cultivable crop land in short supply and world fisheries increasingly depleted, the general outlook is much bleaker. During the 'seventies the demand for scarce resources has manifestly begun to outstrip supply. This has been mirrored globally in a number of ways, mounting inflationary pressures being one of the most persistent and obtrusive.

In the last ten years the world has become a more perilous place in which to dwell. Conventional politics, whether of Right, Left or Centre, seem increasingly ineffectual in dealing with a series of intractable and closely interconnected problems. J. M. Keynes once wrote that the only way to alter opinion was to set in motion new forces of instruction and imagination, to change the hearts and minds of men, to dare to venture onto fields of politics hitherto untrodden. Our planet badly needs such innovative forces but unfortunately at the end of the 'seventies there is no evidence that they are in the ascendancy.

NOTES AND REFERENCES

[1] See *People* (1978), 'Unmet Needs'.*

[2] Basic to the entire demographic transition has been the change in the economic value of children – from a source of income in Afro-Asian societies to an economic burden in industrial countries. See C. F. Westoff (1978) for discussion of this theme.

[3] In 1977 the birth rate in Kwangtung province was quoted at 18 per 1,000 and in Szechwan at 14.7 per 1,000. In 1977 nine provinces of China – Hopei, Hupeh, Kiangsu, Liaoning, Shantung, Szechwan, Peking, Shanghai and Tientsin had population growth rates of less than 1 per cent (R. Ravenholt [1978], *The Washington Post*, December 28). Ravenholt commented: 'We are witnessing one of the great demographic events in human history.'

[4] At the Treaty of Brest Litovsk in 1918 Soviet Russia lost to Imperial Germany 34 per cent of her population, 32 per cent of her agricultural land, 85 per cent of her beet-sugar land, 54 per cent of her industrial undertakings and 89 per cent of her coal mines. (See Sir John Wheeler-Bennett (1953), *Brest Litovsk: The Forgotten Peace, March 1918*, Macmillan, London, p. 227.)

For an appraisal of the terms of the Treaty of Versailles I recommend A. J. P. Taylor (1965), *English History 1914-1945*, Oxford University Press, and James Joll (1973), *Europe since 1870: An International History*, Weidenfeld & Nicolson, London.

* Where a shortened form of reference is employed, please refer to the Bibliography for full details.

Chapter 2

The Nuclear Imbroglio

Once upon a time the animals in the zoo met to discuss the question of nuclear proliferation. All agreed on the risks involved. Other weapons were infinitely preferable to atomic bombs. Lions, tigers, leopards and a host of cats extolled the virtues of teeth and claws. The rhinoceros, supported by the buffalo, was all for horns, the bear favoured hugging, the shark bared his teeth, the elephant pawed the ground, the eagle demonstrated its swoop, assorted snakes testified to the potency of their venom.

Then arguments erupted. Polemicists held the field. Claws, teeth, horns, feet and poison were all very well. But if man mounted a concerted attack on a species and was determined to exterminate it, would they be adequate? The answer was a resounding no. One thing and one thing only might deter him from his nefarious purpose and that was the threat of nuclear retaliation. So why shouldn't the zoo animals immediately make their own plutonium and fabricate their own weapons? After all, such a course was definitely *à la mode*; indeed it was only what individual nation states controlled by humans were already doing in increasing numbers. At this point the keepers appeared. The animals were still quarrelling fiercely about the *modus operandi* of their nuclear policy; however, they had no option but to return meekly to their cages.

This 'nuclear fable' is based on a speech made by Winston Churchill to his parliamentary constituents in Epping in 1928. The zoo allegory which he utilized to depict the political climate of the day towards disarmament is highly germane to the state of the world fifty years later when nuclear proliferation is gradually coming to overshadow all other global issues. Jacques-Yves Cousteau, addressing the UN in 1976, reflected that atomic power had 'reshaped what we may fear, what we may dream, how we live, and how we may die'. His elegant and prophetic oratory stressed, as many before him had done, that since 6 August, 1945 when the 14 kiloton bomb, 'Little Boy', was unloaded over Hiroshima and the nuclear Pandora's box thereby unlocked, mankind had acquired a fiendish potential for self-destruction. The beat of war drums, so penetrative and pervasive throughout the sweep of history, has assumed an altogether novel tone. The human condition has altered abruptly and irrevocably; *homo sapiens* is now an endangered species, living on borrowed time and with the sands of survival rapidly running down in the glass.

In 1956, Sweden's 150 years of uninterrupted peace was commemorated by the establishment of the Stockholm International Peace Research Institute. Since then SIPRI has become the recognized global watchdog on the armaments race, and in recent years it has been proclaiming with ever increasing urgency that the spread of 'peaceful' nuclear technology throughout the world is opening the floodgates to the manufacture of atomic weapons of mass destruction. The transcendent anxiety is, of course, the relentless accumulation of devices for nuclear war by all and sundry – by rich and arrogant nations, by young and immature states, by peoples of opposing ideologies, different colours and diverse creeds, by unforgiving leaders with paranoid mentalities and with the barren logic of vengeance as the only rubric of their diplomacy. Each year the nuclear market-place becomes a little more anarchic. Two decades ago, when the situation was still manageable, it was neglected; now, when it is generally recognized to be thoroughly out of hand, the remedies are much more difficult to apply; indeed, some would say that no remedy exists.

Since 1954 about one country a year has installed atomic plants. SIPRI estimated that at the beginning of 1977 180 reactors were shared by 20 countries and that 78,000 megawatts* of electricity were being generated in this way.[1] The projection for 1981 was for 365 reactors in 28 countries with a production of 234,000 MW. Between 1976 and 1981 the reactor score in the EEC is projected to rise from 54 to 134, in the Eastern bloc from 26 to 60, in North America from 64 to 124, in Asia from 17 to 39. Looking further ahead to 1985 the SIPRI forecast is for 450 reactors in 35 countries and a production of 300,000 MW of electricity. By 2000 AD, if nuclear migration is permitted to continue at anything like its present rate, fifty countries could be generating more than three times this amount through atomic fission.

The first atomic bomb to be dropped over Hiroshima had an equivalent explosive yield of 20,000 tons (20 kilotons) of conventional

* 1 megawatt (MW) = one million watts.

TNT explosive. According to SIPRI the tens of thousands of nuclear weapons in the world's arsenals in 1978 had a total explosive force equivalent to about 1 million Hiroshima-type atomic bombs. Harold Urey, the discoverer of deuterium, once commented, 'The next war will be fought with atom bombs and the one after that with spears.' If the arms race continues at the present speed his forecast is likely to be substantially correct.

The diversion of plutonium from a peaceful to a military programme – the classic example being, of course, the Indian atomic detonation of 1974 – remains the most sinister milestone on the road to nuclear war. And the more atomic power plants which a nation state acquires, together with ancillary reprocessing and enrichment facilities, the greater is the peril to mankind of an eventual holocaust. However, as has been repeatedly argued by authorities in this field, elaborate facilities are not mandatory if a country is determined to acquire a nuclear capability. Such a nation could readily obtain nuclear material clandestinely. Or if it so wished, it could use the 'small reactor' route to the development of atomic weaponry. Fissile material could be manufactured at quite low cost from, for example, a 40 megawatt plant. Twenty kilogrammes of plutonium could be produced per year in this way and this would be quite enough for the manufacture of at least two 20 kiloton bombs. Uranium enrichment facilities could also be quite small; little more than a few centrifuges would be needed to produce enough uranium in a single year to establish a modest nuclear weapon force.

Regarded in quantitative terms, the nuclear arsenals already accumulated by the Superpowers are gargantuan and their overkill capacity can only be described as mind-boggling. For example, the USA has enough strategic nuclear weapons to destroy fifty times over every Soviet city with a population over 100,000, while the USSR could raze American cities of comparable size twenty times over.[2] Both nations have in their possession huge numbers of weapons – land-based intercontinental ballistic missiles, submarine-launched ballistic missiles, advanced ballistic re-entry vehicles,[3] fractional orbital bombs, anti-ballistic missiles, surface-to-air missiles, sea-, surface- and air-launched cruise missiles, to mention only a few. Both Superpowers have strategic bomber forces the striking force of which is exceedingly formidable; both have immense stocks of tactical nuclear weapons, the majority of them infinitely more potent than the bombs which ravaged Hiroshima and Nagasaki.

Since the end of the Second World War the capabilities of large numbers of talented US and Russian scientists and engineers have been harnessed to the production of nuclear weaponry. These individuals have been provided with secure and lucrative career structures; their research has been vested with a patriotic aura and has been continuously lauded by their governments and other branches of officialdom. It is, therefore, a matter of no surprise that innovation has been dazzling, that the spark of originality has burned brightly and that advances in military technology have been spectacular, sprouting like trees in the ever thickening forest of the nuclear arms race.

The letters MIRV stand for Multi-warhead Independently Targeted Re-entry Vehicle. This is a strategic missile system with a powerful rocket launcher; it carries a large vehicle called a bus into space, the latter containing anything from six to twenty separate nuclear warheads. MIRV systems are very versatile. Once over hostile territory the bus can begin discharging its load of warheads according to instructions provided by a ground-based computer. The bus also has several radar decoys which can produce misleading signals on enemy radar screens. MARV stands for Manoeverable Alternative Target Re-entry Vehicle. It resembles the MIRV System with one vital difference – each MARV carries its own computer and sensors which control its flight. MARVs are exceedingly manoeuvrable and can take avoiding action as long as their fuel supply lasts out. By the mid-'seventies both Superpowers had completed research and development on their MIRV programmes. By the early or mid-'eighties MARVs should be fully operational and by that time the USSR and the USA between them will house over 20,000 strategic nuclear warheads.

Of all the qualitative advances in nuclear weaponry which have taken place in recent years pride of place must undoubtedly go to the increasing accuracy with which warheads can be delivered. Accuracy is generally measured in terms of Circular Error Probability.* The B-20 bomber which delivered the bomb on Hiroshima had a very large CEP but since then improvements have been spectacular. For example, the current US Minuteman III ICBM, fitted with MIRVs, is said to have a CEP of only 350 metres at a range of 13,000 kilometres. And much greater precision is on the way. Indeed, it can be

* CEP can be defined as the radius of the circle centred on a target within which half of the warheads aimed at the target will fall.

confidently predicted that before 1990 both Superpowers will have developed warheads the CEP of which is less than 30 metres. These could hit almost anything at their first attempt and they would be so manoeuvrable that they could readily take evasive action against missile defences.

The tactical device known as the enhanced radiation warhead or neutron bomb came into considerable prominence in the late 'seventies.[4] It is important to stress that there is nothing new about the notion of a neutron bomb, the possibility of developing a tactical nuclear weapon of this kind being recognized soon after the invention of the hydrogen bomb in the 'forties. The neutron bomb merely represents the latest development by the US military in the search for a 'cleaner' and more usable type of atomic weapon. When detonated the fission reaction is the trigger for fusion and a large number of fast neutrons are released. The yield of the neutron bomb is relatively low (below 10 kilotons). Its lethality results from radiation rather than from blast or heat and some version of it could be available for deployment by 1980 if not before.

The main attraction of the neutron bomb to military strategists is that it immobilizes and stops tanks by killing the crew inside the vehicle.[5] Unlike other tactical nuclear weapons already stockpiled in huge quantities by the Superpowers, the neutron bomb can produce its effects without necessarily damaging buildings, ravaging the environment and sterilizing huge tracts of territory as a result of fallout. Proponents of the weapon see its greatest usefulness in the defence of Western Europe by NATO forces following a blitzkrieg launched by the Warsaw Pact countries. Opponents of the neutron bomb argue that its production in peacetime might encourage the spread of nuclear weapons to nations not currently possessing them, that its deployment might dangerously and precipitously lower the nuclear threshold – the so-called 'firebreak' – and that its use in wartime would be likely to result in an all-out exchange of strategic weapons.

Possible effects of neutron bomb radiation on military personnel have been much discussed recently.[6] They would, of course, be very variable depending on factors such as dosage and distance from the blast. Some soldiers would die at once, others within minutes. At a dose level of between 3,000 and 8,000 rads men might survive for as long as a week and might even regain their fighting ability for a short period of time. The medical effects of neutron bomb irradiation would be protean. With doses over 8,000 rads the central nervous system would be irreparably damaged and death would be rapid. With 3,000 rads diarrhoea and high fever would be prominent, coma and death supervening in a few days. With 500 rads bleeding from skin and gums would be profuse and death would follow within a month. Although a dose of 100 rads would cause prolonged incapacity as a result of damage to bone marrow, death would not be inevitable.

An event in January 1978 reminded us that we could be preparing for the kind of war which H. G. Wells conceived many years ago as a scientific fiction. A Soviet spy satellite got out of control. It was orbiting the earth 150 miles up, carefully monitoring the movement of ocean-going American warships, including submarines. Cosmos 954 was equipped with a nuclear reactor to provide electricity for its radar system. It had been launched from the Cosmodrome near Tyuratimin in Kazakhstan in September 1977. Three months later the satellite began to sag and lose pressure; then it fell out of orbit and plunged downwards into the frozen wilderness of Northern Canada near the Great Slave Lake. The world's nerves jangled as the story unfolded. How much radioactive fallout would there be? Was this the beginning of the nuclear nightmare? The fears turned out to be groundless for by sheer good luck the satellite's eventual destination was in empty pine forests. But had it had the strength to limp once more around the earth the outcome could have been very different, for then it could have landed close to New York City between 9 and 10 on the following morning.

The proliferation of atomic-powered space vehicles is one of the most worrisome aspects of burgeoning nuclear technology. The celestial garbage dump is already considerable, some 4,500 man-made objects currently orbiting the earth. Many of these are relatively harmless pieces of ironmongery, representing the detritus of more than twenty years of space technology. But they also include some 950 satellites, 460 of them Russian and 392 American. The presence of these satellites orbiting above us is a portentous omen for the future. Not least among the awesome possibilities which they present (and this was well illustrated by the saga of Cosmos 954) is that space technology is acquiring its own dynamic, that it is slowly yet ineluctably slipping away from human control and that in the future national leaders, however dedicated they may be to the preservation of global peace, will be powerless to shape the course of events.

It is salutary to record how rapidly space is being militarized. The Outer Space Treaty, signed in 1967 and designed to establish space as a zone of peace, has egregiously failed. The members of the military space club have been continuously increasing; in addition to the two Superpowers they now include the UK, France and China. SIPRI estimates that of the total number of satellites launched during 1977 more than three-quarters were military.[7]

Reconnaissance satellites already abound. The Superpowers utilize them to observe each other's land masses, to check their compliance with SALT and to monitor the space programmes of other nations with ambitions in this area. The USA has now developed a Space Shuttle System, the main ingredient of which is called the Orbiter. This vehicle resembles an aeroplane; it has a gliding action, an external fuel tank and two booster rockets. The Orbiter can carry a crew of seven; it can remain in outer space for seven days and deliver a payload of 29,000 kilogrammes to the earth. The Orbiter will undoubtedly come into increasing use in the 'eighties and 'nineties. Its external fuel tank is capable of becoming a permanent space platform maintaining men in space for long periods of time, and this will probably be feasible before 1985.

By the mid-'eighties the US plans to effect sixty launches of her Space Shuttle each year. The Shuttle will carry devices known as sensors which are designed to detect the movement of strategic aircraft and to track ballistic and cruise missiles; it will also be ideal for installing weapons such as lasers and ion beams in space. Also in prospect is what has been termed the Nav Star Global Positioning System composed of twenty-four satellites capable of delivering weapons on target and able to navigate aircraft, ships and submarines.

The Space Detecting and Tracking System (SPADATS) of the US Air Force is the main system in the Western world for satellite surveillance. SPADATS aims to identify hostile satellites and to assign priorities for their destruction. SPADATS has at its disposal a wide variety of sensors and radar devices. Important amongst these is the Baker Nun Camera which has a high degree of accuracy in tracking satellites. The camera is basically a 3-ton telescope which is said to be capable of photographing light reflected from an object 'the size of a football' at a height of over 4,000 kilometres. However, it has some rather obvious limitations; in particular its efficiency in dull weather is poor and its rate of data acquisition rather slow.

SPADATS is much involved in estimating the orbital decay of satellites and it is the principal source of information which the West has regarding the Soviet space programme. The organization acts as an early warning system against space-borne weapons and can provide important targeting information for anti-missile systems. Present evidence suggests that the importance of SPADATS is increasing and that in the 'eighties its funding will be substantially augmented.

Much less is known regarding Soviet surveillance of orbiting objects, this being an area over which the Kremlin maintains strict secrecy. However, it seems probable that Moscow possesses optical sensors similar to the Baker Nun Camera. Deep-space tracking sites have been identified at Yevpatoriya in the Crimea and near Vladivostok; the Soviets also have a fleet of space tracking ships which operate mainly in the Indian and Pacific Oceans. Instead of utilizing systems such as the Orbiter, the Russians have tended to favour the launching of 'quick look' Cosmos satellites. Their anti-satellite programme is said to depend on techniques whereby they can get close enough to an enemy satellite to destroy it completely. In one such system the hunter killer satellite enters an orbit much lower than the target and rapidly accelerates up towards it.

Almost thirty-five years ago *The New Yorker* devoted its entire 'Hiroshima Issue' to John Hersey's classic description of what happened on 6 August, 1945. It did so 'in the conviction that few of us have yet comprehended the all but incredible destructive power of this weapon, and that everyone might well take time to consider the terrible implications of its use'. But by now the passage of time has dulled the memories of Hiroshima and Nagasaki. We have become desensitized to nuclear dangers; society's perception of the peril has faded and attempts to rekindle the dread and fear of a generation ago have largely gone unheeded. This is all the more reason why we need to be constantly reminded of the possible consequences of a nuclear war, that in such a conflict there can be no winners or losers, that a second Promethean visit could tear apart the cultural fabric which we have built up over millennia.

In 1946 Bernard Baruch, President Truman's special representative, presented his Plan to a fledgling UN organization. It was designed to place global nuclear resources under the ownership and control of an effective international authority. The presentation was dramatic as well as prescient. 'We are here,' he said, 'to make a choice between the quick and the dead. . . . We must elect world peace or world destruction.' Baruch certainly had no illusions about the change in the world which had been wrought by Hiroshima and Nagasaki. But his Plan foundered on the rock of Soviet intransigence, and since then we have lived through thirty-three years during which the 'balance of terror' between the Superpowers has been the major factor in preventing an atomic war and during which national governments, assiduously abetted by the Praetorian guard of the nuclear industry, have continuously peddled the ambrosia that the weapons aspect of fission power is under satisfactory control.

The two small bombs which were detonated over Hiroshima and Nagasaki produced awesome carnage and devastation. But they give little or no hint of the chain of events likely to ensue if a Third World War erupts and a nuclear exchange takes place.

A thermonuclear bomb of approximately 1 megaton capacity would blast out a crater with a surface area of about 12 hectares. All exposed plants, animals and humans over a huge area embracing thousands of hectares would be destroyed. A great fireball with temperatures equal to those in the sun's interior would pour forth heat, radiation and blast like a tidal wave from hell: soon it would develop into an enormous cloud of black smoke which would cast its ghoulish shadow over a tract of extraordinary devastation. Foliage in the countryside would be crisped as with the advent of autumn; terrible firestorms would rage over vast land masses causing incredible chaos and terror.

Descriptions of the likely effects of a nuclear exchange involving 10,000 megatons of combined fission and fusion power are now available.[8] The statistical bones of the exchange would, of course, be millions of immediate fatalities and hundreds of thousands of individuals condemned to a slower and exceedingly painful death from lung or bone cancer. There would be social disruption on a gargantuan scale and existing medical services would be totally incapable of coping with the hordes of wounded and victims of fallout. A plenitude of radioactive nuclides with half lives ranging from a few seconds to thousands of years would be spewed out over a vast area of the earth. Each global citizen would be likely to be exposed to a dose of between 5 and 10 rads. A large increase in the burden of debilitating and lethal genetic mutations would be produced and would be passed on to future generations.

Major climatological changes at the global level would be amongst the most spectacular results of such a nuclear exchange. The average temperature worldwide would be reduced by a few tenths of a degree for one to three years, due mainly to the dispersion of particulate matter in the upper atmosphere. The delicate web of meteorological equilibrium, with its intricate system of balance and counterbalance, would be torn asunder. A new ice age could be ushered in; alterations in global rainfall patterns would take place; there could be redistribution of deserts and profound effects on world agriculture.

The stratospheric content of nitrogen oxide would rise acutely after the exchange. The atmospheric ozone layer would be ruptured and the ozone content would fall precipitously – by 30 to 70 per cent in northern latitudes and by 20 to 40 per cent in the southern hemisphere. The time required for the restoration of ozone to its normal atmospheric level would be between two and four years. During this period the intensity of ultra-violet radiation penetrating to the earth from the sun would rise greatly. The heightened UV radiation would produce a pandemic of skin cancers and melanomata, not to mention a high incidence of snow blindness in northern latitudes and intractable cases of sunburn in more temperate parts of the world.

If instead of 10,000 the exchange involved 100,000 megatons – a figure by no means fanciful considering the likely extent of present and future nuclear arsenals – the effects would be qualitatively and quantitatively different. The atmospheric ozone layer would be depleted irreparably and the climatic changes would be permanent. Every global citizen, irrespective of his distance from the site of the holocaust, would receive a cumulative dose of radiation of between 25 and 100 rads. The survival of *homo sapiens* and of many other species would be jeopardized for all time. The nuclear *'Götterdämmerung'* so often prophesied since the uranium bomb eclipsed the sun over Hiroshima would have become an accomplished fact. Arthur Koestler's description of Spaceship Earth having been transformed into a 'Flying Dutchman drifting among the stars with its dead crew,' would have been vindicated.

From the beginning of the atomic age the connection between the peaceful and military uses of atomic energy has been glaringly obvious. Robert Oppenheimer touched the heart of the problem when he referred to the 'close technical parallelism' between the two aspects. Nations have always wished to promote the civilian atom and to derive advantages therefrom; but they have cowered under the threat of its military potential. The dual nature of atomic energy is mirrored in all the equivocations, obfuscations and misrepresentations which have characterized the international dialogue over the past thirty years. Still no success can be claimed in divorcing the two. Instead, both peaceful and warlike atoms have proliferated as an increasing number of nations have renounced their nuclear innocence. Our technical knowledge, far from providing reassurance, has merely increased fear and feelings of insecurity; our expertise is perceived by many as presaging dire adversity for the whole human race.

It is essential to recognize that nuclear weapons proliferation is a deep seated malady whose genesis is exceedingly complex. The palliation of the disease, much less its cure, will be enormously difficult and could well be impossible. The medicine would have to be strong, the surgery extremely radical. A favourite phrase of the economist J. M. Keynes was that we are ruled by our ideas and by very little else. What proposals have been made, therefore, to manage atomic proliferation and rebottle the nuclear genie?

So far proliferation has not been slowed by pious resolutions passed at the UN, by a plenitude of disarmament conferences including that of 1978, and by continuous appeals to logic and sweet reasonableness. Indeed, so completely barren have these approaches been that the view is now being openly canvassed that only 'punishing stimuli' in the form of a mini-Hiroshima – isolated nuclear detonations short of an actual holocaust – will galvanize mankind into activity and bring him back to his senses.

Bruce Stewart, Professor of Natural Sciences at Michigan State University, is one who argues cogently that 'atomic shock treatment' is the sole means of preventing the steady drift to Armageddon.[9] He lists methods short of actual nuclear war which might have the desired effect. These are, of course, very numerous and include the accidental launching of a missile due to malfunction or human fallibility, accidental explosions during the transport and storage of atomic materials and – increasingly in a world in which hijackings, kidnappings, bombings and wanton slayings come within the purlieu of the political terrorist and saboteur – the explosion or the threat of an explosion for purposes of radioactive blackmail. Yet many would aver that to advocate such a course can only be the counsel of despair. The stakes for mankind would be intolerably high; the roulette wheel would have to spin with dizzying speed. Also the risks and consequences of such an act are quite impossible to predict. Far from attenuating nuclear proliferation the reverse effect might be produced and the whole process could become a spark initiating a chain reaction which would spread like a bushfire around the world.

At the other end of the spectrum are those who insist that nuclear power be phased out as quickly as possible, that no more reactors be built and that the world move with maximum rapidity to the use of alternative energy sources. Some environmentalists adhere to this view and the Pugwash Conference of 1973 endorsed it. We are all entitled to our visions and our dreams, and there is no question that such a policy would have a salutary effect on nuclear proliferation. But in the real world of the final two decades of this century and beyond such a suggestion is patently ridiculous, so hopelessly utopian as scarcely to merit serious consideration.

The world is already a long way down the plutonium road and any pathway back will be long and arduous. Immense capital investment has already gone into existing reactor programmes; large numbers of plants are under construction and many more are in the process of being commissioned. Schemes for the reprocessing of spent fuels internationally as opposed to nationally seem to be foundering, and the Report of the Windscale Inquiry in Britain in early 1978 is a notable pointer in this direction. Some countries, particularly France, Federal Germany and the Soviet Union, are already committed to far-reaching programmes involving fast breeder reactors; others – the UK, India, Italy and Japan to name but a few – are evincing mounting interest in this area of high technology. The recycling of plutonium as a means of fuelling commercial reactors is being stridently advocated in many quarters. Although it is generally conceded that alternative energy sources hold considerable promise for the future, in no country are they regarded in official circles as a surrogate for nuclear power. The nuclear juggernaut, therefore, is very much on the road and there would seem to be no immediate prospect of slamming on the brakes, bringing the vehicle to a halt and putting the whole process into reverse.

In the minds of many people internationalism and above all supranationalism hold the key to the management of nuclear proliferation.[10] This view echoes the dictum originally enunciated in 1946 by

Dean Acheson, then US Under Secretary of State, and David Lillien-thal, Chairman of the Tennessee Valley Authority. The Acheson-Lillienthal Report – and also the Baruch Plan of 1946 – recognized that 'the development of atomic energy for peaceful purposes . . . and for bombs are . . . interchangeable and interdependent. . . .' Regarding systems of inspection the Report and the Plan were unyielding: 'There is no prospect of security against atomic warfare in a system which relies on inspections and similar police-like methods. . . . National rivalries . . . are the heart of the difficulty. . . . If the pro-duction of fissionable materials by national Governments, (or by private organizations under their control) is permitted, systems of inspection cannot by themselves be made effective safeguards. . . .' The Baruch Plan went on to recommend the immediate establish-ment of an International Atomic Development Authority which would place all strategic nuclear materials and facilities under 'effect-ive international control', would stop the manufacture of atomic bombs and dispose of all existing stocks, would take punitive sanctions against nations violating the rules laid down by the Authority and would not be subject to a Security Council Veto.

Would a modified version of the Acheson-Lillienthal Report have a greater chance of acceptance in the 'eighties than in the 'forties? The likelihood is slim. The Soviet Union vetoed the initial plan and proceeded to develop and manufacture its own bombs. Although Moscow has up till now shown great restraint apropos of nuclear pro-liferation, would she not be almost certain to resurrect her intransi-gence if such a proposal was mooted, bearing in mind that the creation of any supranational authority involving the capitalist world runs directly counter to the whole doctrine of Marxism-Leninism? And could co-operation be expected from aggressive nuclear vendors such as France and Federal Germany – or indeed from India, the newest member of the nuclear club? The Chinese Government would undoubtedly treat the proposal with a degree of disapprobation amounting to derision. China's diplomacy and propaganda are deeply rooted in the concept that the USA and the USSR are striving to be 'overlords of the world' and that in order to achieve this aim they will use any means at their disposal including nuclear threats and blackmail. Although in recent years, particularly under the new Chairmanship of Hua Kuo-feng, the voice of Peking's propaganda machine has become less strident towards the West, China, as the putative leader of the Third World, continues to advise developing countries to enter the nuclear arena in order to defend themselves against 'enslavement' by the Superpowers.

It is frequently stated that the virulence of the nuclear bacillus could be satisfactorily attenuated if the Non-Proliferation Treaty were improved and strengthened. The NPT, drawn up in 1968, coming into effect in 1970 and by 1979 ratified by 103 nations, was in essence a compact between the nuclear and non-nuclear powers. The former pledged themselves to end the arms race and to work towards nuclear disarmament; the latter, having foregone the option of developing their own nuclear weapons, were entitled to derive maximal benefit from the peaceful use of the atom. Inspections under the control of the Vienna-based International Atomic Energy Agency were to take place, but they were to be confined to the non-weapons states.

From its inception the flaws in the NPT were glaringly obvious. Two of the original nuclear powers – France and China – did not sign the treaty; nor did several other states with ambitious nuclear plans – India, Argentina, Brazil, Israel, Pakistan and South Africa, to name but a few. During the 'seventies a vast literature has accumulated on the manifold defects of the NPT – the ability of a signatory to withdraw giving only the most perfunctory of notice, the 'immense and dreary task' of the Nuclear Inspectorate, the total inadequacy of the safeguards and their relegation to an appendix rather than an integral part of nuclear energy planning, a security system as porous as an unglazed potter's jar, lack of sanctions possessing any semblance of teeth and, above all, the duplicity of the Superpowers who, in spite of the NPT, have permitted the arms race to continue at an even more frenetic pace than before.

The NPT Review Conference of 1975 spelled out clearly some of the means whereby this anaemic international instrument could be given a much needed blood transfusion. Safeguards should be made very much more stringent; indeed they should constitute the essence of the Treaty and should be brought into the negotiations *ab initio*. Plutonium recycling should be postponed indefinitely thus obviating any final commitment to the fast breeder reactor; plutonium in spent fuel rods should remain unprocessed. The accounting of nuclear materials should be greatly improved as should their control during transit.

The view of the Conference was that the Superpowers must demonstrate their 'good faith' in relation to the Treaty. This could be done in a number of ways. They could agree to to an underground test ban; they could stop the production of fissionable material for the manufacture of weapons; they could begin immediate negotiations within the framework of SALT to reduce and eventually to phase out their ICBMs, SLBMs and other strategic weapons; they could impose a surcease on the awesome qualitative developments in offensive and defensive weaponry previously described. The exemplar of the Super-powers would be decisive for only they have the capacity to steer the world away from the path of proliferation and towards any form of arms control.

In the late 'seventies, in the wake of growing international concern and anxiety about nuclear safeguards, the politics of proliferation took a further twist. The USA was the instigator; the flavour was definitely that of *déjà vu*. In October 1976 Gerald Ford announced his opposition to the reprocessing of spent fuel at the national level. In so doing he resuscitated the principal recommendation of the Acheson-Lillienthal thesis, namely that nothing short of international collaboration can halt the nuclear arms race. The steps taken by Jimmy Carter to follow up his predecessor's initiative have already been outlined in Chapter 1. They include the deferment of the repro-cessing of spent fuel from domestic plants while alternative options are being sought, attempts to persuade other nations to follow the US lead, and the establishment of an International Fuel Cycle Evalua-tion Programme to make a detailed study of the whole proliferation issue and to report back to him during 1979.

The USA is in an uniquely favourable position to act on prolifer-ation, largely because many countries with expanding nuclear pro-grammes depend on her for supplies of enriched uranium. Nations desirous of transferring batches of their spent fuel outside their terri-torial confines for storage and reprocessing elsewhere will now have to obtain American permission before doing so; and Washington has indicated that transfers of fuel which had originated in the USA will not be easy and will only be countenanced where a 'clear need' is seen to have been demonstrated. The US has already put on record that it looks with disfavour on the activities of countries such as Sweden, Switzerland and particularly Japan, which are currently negotiating to have their spent fuel reprocessed in other parts of the world – for example at Windscale in Britain and at Cap la Hague in France. Even before the result of the Windscale Inquiry was made public, press reports suggested that the US administration was unhappy with its likely outcome and through her Deputy Under-Secretary of State,

Joseph Nye, had sent a private warning to the British Government regarding the latter's long-term nuclear policy with special reference to
reprocessing.

The fostering of an international climate for a denuclearization is
an indispensable prerequisite for slowing the arms race and preventing the slide of humanity into nuclear war. For almost thirty-five
years statesmen have struggled to have nuclear power without proliferation. They have egregiously failed in their efforts and the result
is that the world is still faced with an unprecedented problem. Does
the recent US initiative provide a sufficient blend of realism and
idealism to enable *homo sapiens* to draw back from the abyss? Will it
leave a notable mark on the grand perspective of history? Or (as I
feel is more likely) will its seeds fall on ground already rendered arid
and infertile by distrust, bitterness, suspicion, hate, and above all, by
national rivalry?

Those worried about the menace of nuclear proliferation, but
nevertheless of an optimistic disposition, sometimes say that the world
can derive a small grain of comfort from the analogy of the slave
trade. The monstrous evil of slavery dominated history for almost two
hundred years and by the end of the seventeenth century it had
assumed colossal proportions. Apologists for the trade proclaimed
that it was an economic necessity and that if one country renounced
it others would inevitably reap the commercial benefits. Nevertheless
this morally indefensible doctrine – highly reminiscent of current
statements made by the pro-nuclear lobby – did not prevail in the
long term. Britain, the Superpower of that era, had been greatly enriched by slavery. Nevertheless she took the initiative in calling for its
international abolition. In 1833 the British Anti-Slavery Society
succeeded in forcing through Parliament a law which freed slaves in
British colonies, and in 1862 the USA, bowing to pressure from White-
hall, signed a treaty conceding the right of search by naval patrols.
Thereafter the international slave trade was reduced to a mere trickle
and the Brussels Act of 1890 for the Repression of the African Slave
Trade set the formal seal on abolition. A three-hundred-year saga of
infamy had come to an end. If the forces of idealism could triumph in
the case of slavery, so argue this school, then a similar outcome is
possible for the atom.

To me, however, a much more appropriate analogy seems to be
with international drug trafficking. Addiction to weapons is like drug
addiction. The Shah of Iran, with his fixation with the 'toys of death',

was in his own way just as much of a junkie as are the inhabitants of Skid Row dependent on heroin or cocaine. Increasingly severe penal sanctions in many countries for several decades have not stopped drug trafficking. Nor are they likely to prevent the selling of nuclear plants and fissionable materials.

As Arthur Koestler points out in *Janus,* one of mankind's outstanding characteristics is the contrast between his technological genius and his crass incompetence in managing social affairs. Satellites orbit the earth; astronauts land on the moon; computers and microprocessors reign supreme. Yet the Middle East is in chaos; Northern Ireland is a shambles; Southern Africa is about to explode; the Iron Curtain in Europe still stands. The contrast is especially vivid in relation to nuclear proliferation where the dissemination of the 'peaceful atom' to all corners of the earth has been highly deleterious for humanity and has merely produced what nuclear physicist Albert Wohlstetter once picturesquely described as the 'Damoclean overhang of countries increasingly on the edge of making bombs'.

Is there any possibility of turning the tide of nuclear proliferation? I share the doubts of many that such a course of action will be feasible. Probably the best that we can hope for – and it must be admitted that there is little sign of this at present – is an improvement in the calibre and inspirational quality of national leadership. Woodrow Wilson, who fought the greatest battles of his life on a stage of heroic dimensions, once wrote that the US President was at liberty 'in law and in conscience to be as big a man as he can'. If the proliferation dilemma is ever to be solved it will be mandatory for 'big men' to hold sway in the world's capitals for the foreseeable future.

NOTES AND REFERENCES

[1] See SIPRI Yearbook (1978).

[2] See William Epstein (1976) for a seminal and detailed description of this issue.

[3] Re-entry vehicles for new US ICBMs may compromise the MR 12A (300 kilotons yield) and/or the ABRV (500 kilotons yield) (J. Erickson, personal communication, 1979).

[4] There have been many reviews of this area recently. I recommend especially Fred M. Kaplan (1978).

[5] A leading article in *The Times* (1978), February 23, covered this point well; see also J. P. P. Robinson (1978), 'Neutron Bomb and Conventional Weapons of Mass Destruction', *Bulletin of the Atomic Scientists*, Vol. 34, No. 3, p. 42, and George B. Kistiakowsky (1978).

[6] See, for example, Farooq Hussain (1978).

[7] See SIPRI Yearbook (1978) for the best description I have read on the militarization of space.

[8] See the very authoritative report of the US National Research Council (1975), National Academy of Sciences, Washington DC; also Bernard T. Feld (1976).

Another major and influential study is Carl Friedrich v. Weizsäcker (ed.) (1971), *Kriegsfolgen und Kriegsverhüntung*, Carl Hanser Verlag, Munich.

[9] Bruce Stewart (1977), 'Some Nuclear Explosions Will Be Necessary', *Bulletin of the Atomic Scientists*, Vol. 33, No. 8, p. 51.

[10] This theme is well covered in Johan Jorgen Holst (ed.) (1972), *Security, Order and the Bomb*, Universitets Forlaget, Oslo, p. 208.

Chapter 3

OPEC in the Saddle

In *Syndromes of the Seventies* I dubbed energy the new hinge of history. Between now and 2000 AD energy will have an increasing effect on global *realpolitik* and will be a key factor in moulding the complex fate of nations. Energy shortages pose a major threat to the material living standards of the densely populated countries of the West; as such they are bitterly resented. Energy shortages have the propensity to provoke passions within the individual and between nation states; sooner or later they are likely to lead to episodes of conflict and military adventurism.

As I noted in Chapter 1, we lived for far too long in a fool's paradise. We had been warned by geologists years ago that oil and gas were finite resources. Geologists frowned upon our profligacy with our patrimony, but by then we had become increasingly hooked on cheap energy just like junkies on heroin or cocaine. Cheap energy had become central to our consumerist ethos; it was powering the juggernaut of economic growth along the highway of 'progress'. The traditional theologians of the past had promised affluence in heaven: the economic theologians of the mid-twentieth century seemed to be procuring it for us here and now.

The Yom Kippur War should have shattered our illusions forever. OPEC, of course, was not new, having been in existence since 1960. In its early years OPEC had been nervous, tentative and pusillanimous. But during the 'sixties it began to thread its way through the jungle of international diplomacy and as it did so it progressively gained in strength. OPEC's ultimate intentions were clear from its inception – to confront and eventually to emasculate the international oil consortia, and to banish forever the era in which the Western world regarded these countries' oil reserves as mere extensions of their own energy resources. By the early 'seventies, OPEC was poised for action and the eruption of hostilities between Arabs and Israelis in the autumn of 1973 provided an ideal opportunity. The playing of

the oil weapon against nations like the Netherlands deemed to be unduly sympathetic to the Israeli cause, the Arab embargo itself, the
quadrupling of oil prices, the rapid accretion of petrodollars – all
these form part of the history of the 'seventies. And with them the
world has changed irrevocably. The industrialized countries have lost
the secure anchorage of cheap energy. They are drifting in un-
charted waters, the hands of their pilots trembling with the palsy of
apprehension, their grip on the levers of state fumbling and indecis-
ive.

In 1979 OPEC is a powerful global force casting long shadows over
contemporary events. Most of its member states have or had explicit
energy policies. Whether such policies will represent the dream or the
reality, the quest or the conquest can only be determined by global
factors of supreme complexity and unpredictability.But what can be
stated with assurance is that such policies, because they will have repercussions extending far beyond the territorial confines of the nation
states in which they were promulgated, will constitute a dominant
strand of late-twentieth-century history. This chapter attempts to
review the ingredients of these policies in some of the key members of
OPEC.

Half the world's reserves of petroleum are located in the Arab states
which ring the Persian Gulf. Half the world's export trade in the
'black gold' is under Arab suzerainty; Saudi Arabia alone has one
quarter of the earth's oil reserves. The annual oil output of the Gulf
States was about double that of the USA in the mid-'seventies; before
balance of payments problems hit some of its members, the income
accruing to OPEC as oil revenues ran into billions of dollars.

The seven Arab oil producers of the Gulf have a combined popula-
tion of about 22 million – less than 0.6 per cent of the world total.
Iraq (11.8 million) is the most populous, Saudi Arabia has 7.6 million,
Kuwait 1.1: The remainder – Bahrain, Qatar, Oman and the United
Arab Emirates – each have less than half a million people.

The Gulf States continue to show the demographic stigmata
associated with under-development. Birth rates remain high, in the
range 40 to 50 per 1,000 population; the average infantile mortality
rate is 112 deaths under 1 year per 1,000 live births and this is sixteen
times greater than the corresponding figure for the countries of the
EEC. Population growth rates in the Gulf are among the highest in

the world – over 3 per cent per annum in all countries other than Saudi Arabia – suggesting that if present tendencies continue unchecked, numbers could double by 2010.

Drilling for oil in the Persian Gulf is, of course, much easier than in most other parts of the world. It is a shallow sea, with a depth not exceeding 200 metres throughout; weather conditions are favourable, particularly the absence of wind. The Gulf has by far the biggest aggregation of offshore fields anywhere on earth. There are over twenty of them and these include the world's largest, the Safaniyah-Khafji field.

Huge quantities of natural gas – about 3 trillion cubic feet – are produced by the Gulf States each year. Total reserves have been put at over 50 trillion cubic feet – twice those of the USA. Most of it comes under the heading of 'associated gas' because it is dissolved in oil at the temperatures and pressures of the oil reservoirs and is liberated only when the oil is brought to the surface. Demand for natural gas in the Gulf States has traditionally been low because economic incentives to develop it have been lacking. Most of the gas has simply been 'flared' and wasted, and only a very small part of it has been utilized to generate power, distil water or manufacture fertilizers.

In the energy-hungry world of the late 'seventies demands for natural gas are becoming clamant and exports of this fuel from the Gulf States to the industrialized countries are mounting rapidly. Large tankers are being built to convey it; new plants are being constructed for the liquification of natural gas and its conversion into methanol. Associated gas is now a favourable economic proposition; the search for gas unassociated with oil is being stimulated and substantial new reserves are likely to be discovered.

The state of fossil fuel reserves is of course crucial in the formulation of any energy policy in an oil-producing country. Consideration has to be given to factors such as size, quality, depletion and the possibilities for accretions to them. Proved oil reserves in Saudi Arabia in the mid-'seventies were put at 104 billion barrels, in Kuwait at 73 billion, in Iraq at 35 billion, in Abu Dhabi at 30 billion; other Gulf States – Bahrain, Qatar and Oman – had much lower figures. In 1975 production was ranging from 8.5 million barrels per day in Saudi Arabia to 70,000 barrels per day in Bahrain. These estimates of reserves were based on the amount of oil which could be produced by the methods available at that particular time, and they took no account of factors such as improvements in technology, fluctuations in price and the discovery of new fields. Of the seven Gulf States, Saudi Arabia and Iraq are by far the most likely to yield new discoveries and, given the more sophisticated technology likely to become available in the 'eighties, new finds in these countries could be quite sizeable.

The level of income to be derived from oil is another obvious parameter in framing an energy policy. It is a matter of fiendish complexity. It depends directly on the level of oil production and on the price attainable per barrel in world markets. But in such calculations broader and much less predictable issues must also feature. They include the size, aspirations and projected living standards of the indigenous population, the future role of oil in global commerce and the effects which could accrue through competition with other forms of energy.

In all the oil-producing states social and political considerations must of necessity weigh heavily in determining how the income derived from the reserves should be spent. The Gulf States, with their small populations and relatively massive reserves, have in theory a plethora of options at their disposal. They can put surplus money into overseas investment; they can use it to operate training programmes for their own nationals in other parts of the world; they can channel it into domestic industrialization and bring into their countries from overseas battalions of expert technicians, artisans and craftsmen together with an adequate labour force. They can and have played the 'arms for oil' game.[1] Saudi Arabia has been particularly active in this respect but other Gulf States too have become the new military laboratories of the world.

Until balance of payment difficulties associated with the falling dollar hit some of these countries in the late 'seventies, the process of development proceeded at a pace which could only be described as frenetic. Vast programmes for public works were embarked upon – for schools and hospitals, road building, agriculture development, factories, power plants, electrification, water and sewerage systems.[2] But rapid industrialization was not long in bringing a surfeit of problems to the Gulf States and gradually the extreme euphoria generated by the Yom Kippur War evaporated. The nigger in the woodpile has been the post-1973 inflationary spiral together with the weakness of the US dollar, the currency on which all oil transactions continue to be based. The cost of machinery and heavy constructional equipment has soared; there have been massive congestion at ports, intractable bottlenecks, mounting administrative difficulties and readily discernible flaws in national infrastructures designed to cope with the development process. Doubts now exist in many quarters in the Gulf States as to whether the ambitious goals Governments set themselves in the heady days of 1973 will be attained or will forever remain a mirage. Certainly industrialization programmes will pose increasingly important social problems for the Gulf States. Local culture could well be destroyed as attempts are made to assimilate labour forces emanating from all corners of the world. Traditional religious practice is likely to come under strain; Islam, although seemingly resurgent at present, may well become embattled. The ideological cleavage between young and old will be sharpened; the issue of women's rights will flare increasingly in the public consciousness; domestic inflationary pressures will continue to exert their malign effects.

Central to the energy policies of all the Gulf States is the conservation of a finite resource.[3] The threat posed by the ultimate exhaustion of oil reserves is omnipresent; therefore wealth from oil should not be squandered indiscriminately. Since the oil boom is ephemeral – the merest ripple on the broad pool of history – time must be gained to find energy sources which can be substituted for it and which at the same time will be able to maintain their peoples at a desired level of affluence.

Individual Gulf States vary to some extent in the ingredients of their new energy policies. At current rates of production, *Iraq* has sufficient oil to serve her needs well into the twenty-first century. The yield from existing fields is likely to be raised by technological advances and substantial new reserves could well be discovered. Development projects in Iraq are noteworthy not only for their diversity but also for the great number of nationalities involved. Iraq, like her neighbours, has been busily transmuting her oil reserves into arms.

After Saudi Arabia and the Soviet Union, *Kuwait* has the largest oil reserves on earth. Measured by per capita GNP – currently estimated at $11,510 – she is also the world's richest country. Kuwait's oil reserves are so much greater than the needs of her indigenous population that industrialization and development have been able to proceed at the gallop. Kuwait's weaponry is awesome for a country of its size and she is continuing to buy weapons with unabated zeal – Sky-hawk planes from the USA, Mirage fighters from France, Chieftain tanks from Britain, to name only a few.

Officially the Kuwaiti Government is committed to a rigorous policy of oil conservation. The terrain is small; most of the oil likely to be found is already being used; the possibility of new discoveries is remote. However official policy has often been disregarded. Instead purses have clinked and Kuwait's oil reserves are being depleted at a dangerously rapid rate.

The energy policy of *Saudi Arabia* is by far the most important of that of any of the Gulf States. Moreover the country is pre-eminent in the Moslem world through the holy cities of Mecca and Medina. Islam finds a ready focus in Saudi Arabia; Moslem leaders – in Libya, Pakistan and now in Iran – turn to it increasingly for inspiration. Saudi policy with regard to oil pricing and production has been characteristically cautious and conservative; it remains so in 1979. From 1973 onwards Saudi officials, usually epitomized by the re-doubtable Sheikh Yamani, have consistently opposed the large price rises demanded by other OPEC members on the grounds that they would effectively wreck the world economy and would in the long term be inimical to Arab interests. However, in the face of continuing global inflation, US financial weakness and the recently concluded Israeli-Egyptian treaty, Saudi policy in the 'eighties could well be modified, and the Government could find itself much more sympa-thetic to other OPEC nations like Iraq, Nigeria and Venezuela who have been consistently demanding a rapid escalation in the price which consumer nations must pay for oil.

Saudi Arabia launched her second five-year development plan in 1975. Its size was massive, the expectations raised almost immeasur-able. 1,600 million cubic feet of liquid natural gas were to be tapped and distributed every day; the construction of two new industrial cities on the east and west coasts at Jubail and Yenbo was to proceed at a frenetic pace; five petrochemical complexes were to be built, not to mention steel plants and an aluminium smelter. The lack of public debate on the success or otherwise of the plan has been notable; one can only conclude that its dynamic has not been maintained.

After Iran under the Shah, Saudi Arabia has been the most pro-lific arms buyer amongst the oil-producing countries. The Govern-ment is, of course, violently anti-communist by nature and has turned to the West rather than to the Eastern bloc for supplies. In 1976 alone

US arms sales to Saudi Arabia, mediated mainly through the Lockheed and Northrop Corporations, exceeded $2 billion; in the UK in that year the British Aircraft Corporation and Rolls-Royce began to purr contentedly. To the arms peddlers it seemed that as regards their merchandise the walk in the Gulf States was rapidly quickening into a gallop. It would, of course, not be in the nature of such assiduous vendors to question the global effects that their activities might have in ensuing decades.

The policy of the *Bahraini* Government was and remains the extraction of the maximum immediate benefit accruing from the country's fossil fuel reserves. Bahrain has only one major oil field – at Awali; production from there has now reached its peak and is likely to decrease quite rapidly. No major offshore oil has so far been discovered in Bahrain and the tempo of the industrial development in the country has up till now been slower than in most of its neighbours.

Qatar has quite small oil reserves as compared with other OPEC members. In 1976 she produced 23 million tons and exported most of it. Her revenue during that year amounted to $202 million, 97 per cent being derived from oil. There seems little prospect of further major oil discoveries in Qatar during the 'eighties, in the course of which production will almost certainly plummet. In the long term natural gas, heavy industrial development and refining might shore up Qatar's economy. But for the immediate future the high material living standard of people in the country – exemplified by a *per capita* GNP in excess of $8,000 – is crucially dependent on oil supplies. The Qatari Government has frequently affirmed that it is vitally concerned with oil conservation. Yet up till now, and even in an era of manifest world overcapacity for oil resulting from the economic recession of the late 'seventies, Qatar has not cut her production significantly. However, if, as is to be expected, oil prices continue to escalate in the early 'eighties and beyond, a reduction in output could well become mandatory.

Abu Dhabi and *Dubai* are the dominant members of the United Arab Emirates. Of the two, the oil production of the former is much the larger and its officials the most experienced. On the other hand, Dubai is the most populous of the Emirates; it is an advanced financial, commercial and trading centre with a reputation for gold smuggling. The Emirates do not yet seem to have explicit energy policies. Abu Dhabi will undoubtedly be much influenced by events in Saudi Arabia while Dubai still seems reluctant to take over full control of her offshore oil production facilities, and in 1974 she concluded a new concessionary agreement with a US oil company spanning a period of thirty-five years.

The Emirates are also very much in the weapons business. Like some reckless croupier, they seem determined to raise the arms stakes throughout the whole area. Their impressive array of military hardware includes Mirage fighters and a plethora of missiles and armoured vehicles. Official pronouncements from the Emirates pledge continuing support for the Palestinian cause, call stridently for Arab solidarity in face of the 'Israeli menace' and denounce the recent Israeli-Egyptian treaty.

In 1978 Iran had a population of 36 million; it was growing at 2.8 per cent per annum which meant that numbers could exceed 70 million by 2000 AD. The Iranian birth rate remained obstinately high; family planning programmes, although given fitful approval support by the Shah and his entourage, were having little or no impact, particularly in the rural areas. The flight of people from the countryside to cities was continuing apace; already about 50 per cent of the population was urbanized and Tehran was becoming a monster. Soaring oil revenues in the wake of the Yom Kippur War were being used to some extent to lay the foundations of a modern industrial state. But the transcendent feature of Iran under the Pahlevi dynasty was the truly formidable build-up of military hardware. Iran had become the dream of the arms salesman. The Shah – confident, patronising, rich himself beyond the dreams of avarice – came to survey his fief like some medieval warlord. He seemed set to tread a path of solipsistic phantasy; he had become fascinated with the gadgetry of the toys of death and his craving for arms before his fall early in 1979 seemed insatiable.

Iran has proved oil reserves of over 65 billion barrels; at the global level these are exceeded only by Saudi Arabia and Kuwait. In 1975 the National Iranian Oil Company stated that the country was producing 5 million barrels of oil per day; 90 per cent of the production was being exported, the remainder was being used domestically. Big increases in production were projected for the late 'seventies and early 'eighties.

Iran has modest coal deposits and considerable hydroelectric potential. She is exceedingly rich in natural gas; unofficial estimates put reserves at between 270 and 400 trillion cubic feet, but they could be as high as 600 trillion cubic feet. Reserves of natural gas in Iran constitute one-seventh of the global total and are second only to those of the Soviet Union. Until very recently, as in the Gulf States, Iranian natural gas was 'flared' at the site of production and completely wasted. The potential of the resource has now been recognized, and the Shah saw it as a major domestic energy source and a lucrative item for export.

The Shah was in fact one of the first OPEC leaders to spell out an explicit energy policy for his country.[4] That it would be a major factor in his expulsion from the country could not, of course, have occurred to him at that time. The policy was claimed to rest on the twin pillars of prudent conservation and efficient exploitation (the former was particularly ironic as the Shah would sell oil to anyone for profit and seemed determined to deplete the country's reserves at breakneck speed). Hard technology involving oil, gas, coal and very soon nuclear fission in large amounts, were the lynchpins of the programme. Soft energy technologies – from the sun and its variants, including biomass – were not taken seriously; the twenty-first century would be time enough to look at them. A 'rational' separation was to be effected between the energy source and its utilization, and a mismatch must not be seen to exist between energy quality and need. Nuclear fission and coal were to be used for electricity generation for industry, for lighting and for certain forms of transportation. At production rates current in the late 'seventies it was freely recognized that oil was unlikely to last for more than thirty years. Therefore, the use of petroleum as an energy source must be restricted. In 1977 petroleum accounted for 65 per cent of the country's energy budget; by 1987 its contribution was scheduled to have shrunk to 57 per cent, by 1992 to 42 per cent. The future for petroleum was not as a fuel but rather as a raw material base essential for the manufacture of foods, medicines and petrochemicals.

In the immediate future the Shah was determined that natural gas would replace oil as the major source of Iran's primary energy. However, the hegemony of gas would be relatively short and by the early years of the twenty-first century nuclear fission power would be firmly in the saddle as the main energy source. By this time, gas, like oil, would be relegated to the status of a raw material mainly for use in the manufacture of petrochemicals. In 1972 Iran derived 17 per cent of her energy needs from natural gas; by 1982 this should have risen to 32 per cent, and for the next twenty years it would remain at or about this figure.

Coal will never be a major energy source in Iran, and what was present had been earmarked by the Shah for the emergent steel industry. However a significant increase in hydropower was projected. In 1972 installed hydropower amounted to only 800 megawatts; by 1992 this should have risen to 10,000 MW, by which time it should be contributing some 6 per cent of the country's total energy budget.

The Shah and the janissaries of his bodyguard took a definite decision that an increasing proportion of Iran's energy needs must be met from nuclear fission power. Iran under the Shah had no anti-nuclear lobby (the secret police, Savak, took care of that) and Iran began to train large numbers of atomic scientists both at home and overseas. She started to construct several nuclear reactors during the 'seventies and negotiated deals for their installation with countries such as France, Federal Germany and the USA. The Shah projected that by 1982 8.5 per cent of the country's generating capacity would be derived from fission; by 1992 this would have risen to 20 per cent and by then the installed capacity would exceed 20,000 MW.

All the energy sources already mentioned were scheduled to contribute to electricity generation in Iran. And the annual growth of electrical consumption was to be massive. In 1900 Iran possessed only one electricity plant and it supplied power for the capital, Tehran. By 1972 installed capacity was still a paltry 3,000 MW. But by 1990 electricity generation was projected to have risen more than twenty-fold and to be well in excess of 65,000 MW.

The Shah's Government did not attempt to hide the fact that by the mid-'eighties the country's petroleum reserves would be dwindling. It attempted to push Western-style industrial development *à toute outrance*. Between 1973 and 1978 it planned to spend $112 billion on a bewildering variety of projects, most of them highly capital intensive. But very soon the Shah faced a balance of payments problem and was having to run fiscal deficits. The programme would now cost 50 per cent more than originally envisaged; prices of imported goods were soaring, domestic inflation running rampant. And, even in a dictatorship as tight as that of the Pahlevi dynasty, a tide of rising expectations could not be resisted. Material living standards would have to be seen to be increasing if internal political stability was to be maintained. At every OPEC meeting from 1975 onwards

Iran's representatives stridently demanded a steep rise in global oil prices. But Nemesis eventually overtook the Shah. His oil profligacy was deeply resented, his nuclear policy suspect; above all his fixation with military hardware could no longer be tolerated by the populace.

For any country suddenly faced with a cataclysm of wealth, arms provide the easiest and quickest way to spend money. They bring prestige to rulers; they invest the country with the magic aura of high technology; they avoid the huge administrative problems associated with programmes of public works. The Shah epitomized these reactions. He armed his country to the teeth, and by the late 'seventies Iran possessed the most extensive armoury in the world outside the USA, the Soviet Union and Western Europe.

The military build-up which had started in the 'sixties gained appreciable momentum after the Yom Kippur War. The US was the main supplier. In 1973 the Pentagon announced that it had concluded the biggest arms deal ever with Iran and by the end of 1974 half of the exports from the Pentagon were being directed to the Shah. The Shah had by this time become fascinated with sophisticated weaponry. He had to, for example, have the Tomcat, a swing-wing fighter aircraft, highly innovative in design, packed with electronic gadgetry, manufactured by the US Grumman Corporation and designed to ensure US air supremacy in the 'eighties. Early in 1976 the first Tomcat was delivered to the Shah; many more have followed, and by 1978 it was estimated that the country was spending nearly one third of its Gross National Product on defence.

The energy policy of Iran's new revolutionary government is not yet clear. But oil conservation is likely to be a more prominent feature than in the past and hopefully the massive nuclear expansion projected will not now take place.

Few countries on earth possess such a plenitude of natural resources as Venezuela.[5] She has oil, natural gas, coal, oil shales, tar sands, uranium, thorium, geothermal energy, winds, oodles of sunshine, tides and massive hydroelectric potential. Venezuela, unlike Iran under the Shah and some of the Gulf States, has never produced an explicit energy policy. The options open to her are manifold, but traditionally Venezuela has followed a 'hard' path and no immediate change seems likely. Yet Venezuela has the capacity to become the pacesetter of the world in 'soft' technologies and in so doing she could make her own distinctive imprimatur on the pages of twenty-first-century history.

The surge of petroleum production in Venezuela over the past fifty years has been spectacular. In the 1920s the country was producing about 500,000 barrels per year; by 1940 the figure was 186,000,000; by the 'seventies it was over one billion. Venezuela is the second largest oil exporter in the world – after Saudi Arabia. She was a founder member of OPEC in 1960 and has played a notable role in framing the policies of the cartel.

The traditional sources of Venezuela's oil are her inland geological basins. Three-quarters of her production comes from the Maraçaibo. This has 80 per cent of present reserves, will most probably house the major share of reserves yet to be discovered and contains within it the Bolivar Coastal Field which is the third largest in the world. The Maturín Basin is the second largest supplier, while the two other traditional basins, Falcon and Barinas, make a relatively minor contribution. All the traditional basins also contain deposits of oil shales and tar sands, the richest being in the Maturín in the eastern part of the country.

By 1973 the cumulative production of natural gas in Venezuela was estimated at 34 trillion cubic feet. Proved reserves amounted to 38 trillion cubic feet while undiscovered reserves of 'associated gas' were put at 13.2 trillion cubic feet. It has been estimated that Venezuela's total gas reserves could well exceed 100 trillion cubic feet. The main gas sources are also the Maraçaibo and Maturín Basins, the latter containing a relative abundance of gas unassociated with oil.

Coal is widely distributed in Venezuela but so far it has been exploited to a very lmited extent. The main deposits are at Naricual near Barcelona, the Perija foothills in Zulia and the Lobatera area north of San Cristobal. Coal resources have been put at 12,800 million tons.

Venezuela is particularly well endowed with renewable energy resources. On average the sun shines for eleven hours per day on the country, depositing upon it 1.2×10^{12} megawatts of solar power. Trade winds blow seasonally from the north-east; hot springs are almost ubiquitous; tidal power has great potential particularly at the mouth of the Orinoco River and in Lake Maraçaibo. Up till now, however, accurate evaluations of geothermal and tidal resources do not seem to have been carried out; the need to do so is obvious. Hydroelectric reserves in Venezuela are formidable; they could be tapped at many sites, particularly in the tributaries of the Orinoco River and in rivers draining into Lake Maraçaibo. The production of hydroelectricity is reputed to have doubled between 1962 and 1974 and a recent estimate put it at about 30,000 MW.

A. R. Martinez, a prestigious authority and a contributor to *Energy Policies of the World* (1976), has spelled out *his* ingredients for a Venezuelan energy policy. During the 'eighties oil production should be reduced for reasons of conservation, and exports of this fuel should be strictly limited. Wherever possible heavy oils should be substituted for medium and light crudes and the total refining capacity of the country should be stabilized at a figure of about 1 million barrels per day. Attention should be given to the synthetic production of oil from tar sands and oil shales. Although such procedures are very expensive at present, they are likely to become much more economically attractive in the future.

Martinez regards previous Governmental policies in relation to natural gas as singularly inappropriate. The country has been much too profligate with this precious resource. Even now far too much gas is being 'flared', and Venezuela has become too dependent on gas as a source of primary energy. Gas should be increasingly conserved; its production should be strictly regulated; it should be priced realistically. At the same time major geological surveys should be undertaken in the traditional basins to determine gas reserves with a greater degree of accuracy.

The use of coal as an alternative to gas and oil for the generation of electricity should be encouraged. But in Martinez's view the keystone in the country's future energy policy should be the utilization of hydroelectric power. Current projects in this field should assume an air of urgency; others should be initiated and rapidly developed. For instance the hydraulic resources of the Caroní River are almost certainly dazzling as are those of the Caura River and of others draining from the Andes. By the early 'eighties 80 per cent of the country's electricity demand could readily be met from hydraulic sources; by the end of the century, all the need could be met in this way.

It is ironic that, in spite of her oil bonanza, Venezuela retains many of the characteristics of an underdeveloped country. Her rate of population growth remains rapid – close to 3 per cent per annum in 1978 – and by 2010 numbers could have doubled. The Venezuelan birth rate is still high, her infantile mortality rate nothing short of disgraceful. *Per capita* GNP in Venezuela is low compared with many of her OPEC partners and the shanty towns that have proliferated in and around her major cities, particularly Caracas, are an affront to humanity, a dereliction of social justice, a festering sore on the face of the country. Given enlightened leadership in the next two decades the situation could, of course, alter dramatically. But the political will must exist to effect a massive redistribution of wealth and resources and if this is not done rapidly social disruption and upheaval are certain.

What are OPEC's prospects for the rest of the century? The question is almost impossible to answer. Nevertheless, various bodies including the Organization for Economic Co-operation and Development (OECD) and the British Department of Energy have attempted to do so. One of the best descriptions I have read is by Andrew R. Flower in *Scientific American* (1978).

The OECD report[6] forecasts a considerable rise in the global demand for OPEC oil and natural gas liquids – from 33 to 40 million barrels per day – between 1980 and 1985. The demand will only be less if the industrialized countries adopt meaningful policies of energy conservation, and at the time of writing, this seems most unlikely. By 1980, the report avers, OPEC will have the potential to expand its oil production to 45 million barrels per day, and allowing for domestic demand and world 'needs', this would still leave about a quarter of its productive capacity underutilized.

The British Department of Energy[7] is exceedingly cautious in forecasting OPEC intentions. It concludes that the demand for OPEC oil in 1985 is most likely to be in the range 1,500 to 2,050 million tonnes per year* and that within the cartel itself 'substantial spare capacity' exists 'even at the top end of the demand range'. The Department expects that more than half of the expected increase in capacity will emanate from Saudi Arabia. Iran is not mentioned in the report and political repercussions in that country following the deposition of the Shah will undoubtedly exert a major effect.

Andrew Flower described his participation in a Workshop on Alternative Energy Sources held under the auspices of the Massachusetts Institute of Technology[8] in order to study world energy supply and demand with particular reference to the non-Communist world. The Workshop formulated two basic scenarios for the future –

* There are approximately 7.5 barrels in each metric tonne.

one assuming high economic growth rates and energy prices, the other low growth rates and constant prices.

The unpredictability of OPEC production was stressed throughout the Workshop. It was concluded that to achieve the most 'optimistic' profile OPEC output would have to reach 50 million barrels per day by 1995. This was considered unlikely for technical and particularly for political reasons, and it seemed likely that some OPEC members would deliberately restrict production in order to prolong the life of their reserves. Venezuela and Eucador could well set a ceiling on production during the 'eighties; Saudi Arabia, Libya and Kuwait are earning more revenues from oil than they can currently absorb; at the time of writing the situation in Iran is completely unpredictable.

Saudi Arabia, as the major oil producer, holds the key to much of the future. She was producing 9 million barrels per day in 1977; obviously much pressure will be exerted upon her by Western countries to increase this figure. But the political situation in Saudi Arabia is far from monolithic, and current events in neighbouring countries could well make her Government more rather than less intransigent *vis-à-vis* oil supplies in the future.

The Workshop's first scenario of high growth and high prices with continuous addition to reserves, envisaged a peak OPEC production in 1989 of some 71 million barrels per day. Supply could be maintained at about this level for some time into the twenty-first century but by 2025 would have dropped to 33 million barrels per day. If the low growth-constant price scenario dominated the future, OPEC production would be constrained to 55 million barrels per day in 1983 and thereafter would fall gradually to below 33 million barrels per day after 2013.

One of the major difficulties about all such forecasts is the inability of most Western-dominated organizations to fathom, foresee and react to the twists and turns of OPEC policy. To Western political leaders OPEC is an *avis rarissima* of which they are profoundly distrustful and suspicious. OPEC sings an unfamiliar tune, a siren song fraught with peril; its policies are arcane and redolent of Machiavelli. OPEC has already cut the jugular vein of cheap energy; now it could sever the carotid artery of economic growth. The very existence of the organization is challenging and provocative, not unlike a red rag to an infuriated bull.

OPEC governments naturally perceive the world in a totally different light from Western politicians fixated with economic growth.

As mentioned above, OPEC (the Shah was exceptional here) is basically concerned with conserving a finite resource but yet at the same time maintaining a rapid tempo of domestic industrialization. Herein lies the fundamental conflict between producers and consumers of oil, a conflict that shows no signs of being resolved and can only deepen over the next two decades. OPEC asserts as a bedrock article of faith that, in the absence of the cartel, its members would be greatly disadvantaged in world terms and one by one would be progressively emasculated. This credo seems rational and pragmatic and there is no question that within the organization it is deeply felt. Accordingly, in spite of serious policy differences which continue to exist amongst the various oil-producing nations and which are particularly concerned with pricing in world markets, the likelihood that the cartel will collapse and disintegrate is slim. Instead, I suspect that the shadows which OPEC will cast over history will be long, that its authority will be strengthened rather than weakened and that its ability to exert significant leverage on international diplomacy will increase during the next two decades.

NOTES AND REFERENCES

[1] See Anthony Sampson (1977), *The Arms Bazaar*, Hodder & Stoughton, London, for a detailed description of this facet.

[2] A good description of this phase is given in Jean Paul Cleron (1978).

[3] A fine review is provided in Gerard J. Mangone (ed.) (1976). The chapter by Thomas C. Barger (pp. 121-204) is devoted specifically to the Arab States.

[4] See Jahangir Amuzegar's chapter on Iran, ibid., pp. 295-374.

[5] See Ambil R. Martinez's chapter concerning Venezuela, ibid., pp. 205-86.

[6] *World Energy Outlook* (1977).

[7] *Energy Policy* (1978), p. 8.

[8] William F. Martin (ed.) (1977), *Energy Supply to the Year 2000*, World Atomic Energy Society, Massachusetts Institute of Technology. The Project Director was Carroll L. Wilson.

Chapter 4

North America at the Crossroads

The role of the USA in world energy markets is crucial. The country houses 6 per cent of the planet's population; yet she consumes about 40 per cent of the available energy. The USA is the energy junkie of the earth; she is caught in the iron grip of rising demand. Her addiction to energy is relentless and shows no signs of slackening. Energy is inexorably linked in the public mind with the realization of the American dream. It has been a major factor in the prodigious economic growth which the country has enjoyed since the end of the Second World War; it has been the lynchpin of prosperity, the ticket to the rich gadgetry and manifold appurtenances of a consumerist society unique in the world's history. But now, for the first time since the establishment of the Union, future expectations are unlikely to be matched. Harsh geological imperatives will have to be obeyed. Barring coal, of which there is an abundance, and proven and possible oil shales, which are plentiful, US fuel reserves are now quite modest. For example, the rest of the world has twelve times as much petroleum as does the US and six times her quantity of natural gas.

In the 1950s the then Secretary of State John Foster Dulles, that apostle of brinkmanship, talked on various occasions of the US making an 'agonizing reappraisal' of her foreign policy. Now an even more agonizing reappraisal is at hand: it concerns the country's energy policy for the rest of the century and beyond. Like other industrialized nations the US will have to choose between two energy paths. She can opt for the traditional 'hard' path based mainly on oil, gas and nuclear fission. Or she can go for the 'soft' path which has the sun as its basis and which slowly, yet ineluctably, will move the country away from growthmanship and towards a more sustainable energy situation. No optimism can be expressed that the soft path will be favoured until a cataclismic situation develops and makes it mandatory. All the evidence available at present suggests a philosophy of 'goodies today and to hell with tomorrow'.

Were the US eventually to opt for a soft energy pathway the decision would be as momentous and fundamental as any in her history. It would rank with Lincoln's decision not to condone slavery and to preserve the Union at all costs. It would be important as Woodrow Wilson's resolve, albeit reluctant, to enter the First World War on the Allied side; it would rank in importance with the events which flowed from the Japanese attack on Peal Harbour, with Hiroshima and Nagasaki, with the Marshall Plan, with the US involvement in the NATO alliance. Jimmy Carter spoke the truth when he dubbed his energy plan of 1977 'the moral equivalent of war'. Its subsequent emasculation by the Congress, the intense pressure by vested interests to block it, the emergence of a mouse where there should have been an elephant, the downgrading of the energy issue in the President's 'State of the Union' message of 1979 – all have now passed into history. The veteran left-wing Italian politician, Antonio Gramsci, once observed: 'The crisis consists precisely in the fact that the old is dying and the new cannot be born. In this interregnum a great variety of marked symptoms appear.' The analogy with President Carter's dilemma is apposite.

For the US to continue, as it is doing, with a hard energy path can be compared to the reaction of the captain of a great ship which set out on her maiden voyage across the Atlantic in 1912. A message came across the ether that there were icebergs on the course he was pursuing. But the captain did not heed the message; he looked neither right nor left but sailed straight on. This, of course, is what has come to be known as *Titanic* seamanship. But it is precisely what American technological hawks are currently recommending and it will inevitably drive the ship of State into increasingly perilous waters. When the history of these times comes to be written, it will no doubt be recorded that soft-energy proponents did their best to save the nation from its folly. But before the policies which they adduce are likely to be put into practice, reserves of fossil fuels in the USA must sink much lower and the whole concept of the finite planet will have to be much more deeply imprinted on her citizens. Only when this stage is reached will the credo of the soft-energy proponents permeate the hearts and minds of the people and be equated with the nation's eventual destiny.

Meanwhile the premises of official policy as enunciated by the conventional wisdom remain tailored to a Procrustean bed. 'Project Independence' was the US reaction to the Arab oil embargo of 1973 and was a major hallmark of the later days of the Nixon administration. Project Independence proclaimed that the US must become self-sufficient in energy with maximum speed and preferably by 1980. To achieve this hard technologies were to be expanded at breakneck speed. Yet the whole concept of Project Independence, looked at from 1979, had no overlap with reality; its logistics were mind-boggling, its economics totally fanciful. The dynamic behind Project Independence had already waned by the mid-'seventies. But although the details of the plan were quickly forgotten, its general guidelines were not; and they continue to be reiterated by prestigious bodies like the Energy and Research Development Administration (ERDA), the National Science Foundation and the US Department of Energy.[1]

Thousands of giant power stations are planned, many of them coal-fired. By 1980 coal production should have risen to 800 million tons per year, by 1988 to 1,000 million tons. By the mid-'eighties 170 new coal mines should have opened, by 2000 the number could rise to 1,200. By the end of the century strip mining will cover vast areas of land, particularly in the western states. The conversion of coal to gas and oil is a centrepiece of the policy and new technical processes currently under development are expected to lead to the emergence of a new industry of mammoth proportions. During the next twenty years the handling of materials will be prodigious and this will be associated with an orgy of pulverizing, crushing, condensing, scrubbing, separating and disposing of residues. Mined coal, along with gas and oil derived from coal, is expected to generate electricity on a scale never before envisaged, in order to satisfy a demand for this commodity which could have trebled by the first decade of the twenty-first century.

Massive electrification is at the kernel of the US hard energy policy. Indeed, one academic enthusiast espousing this view – Professor Bupp of Harvard University – has described it as 'the most important attempt to modify the infrastructure of industrial society since the introduction of the railroad'. Virtually all energy futures for the USA predicate that demand for electricity will grow more rapidly than any other segment of the energy industry.

Recognized authorities state that electrical generating capacity must double every ten years. Electricity, they aver, will be mandatory for the expansion of the electric car industry, for forms of mass transport such as trains and buses, for all-electric houses, for a myriad of industrial purposes. In 1970 the US generated 341,000 megawatts of electricity; by 1980 this figure is expected to have doubled. By the late 'eighties a further 650 electricity generating plants should have been added. By the early years of the twenty-first century there should be 2,400 plants each of 1,000 megawatts, this being equivalent to the addition of fifty plants to each of the fifty States of the Union. Certainly the concepts of the hard technological school are breathtaking and one cannot but admire their magnificence. The fact that they have no conceivable overlap with reality and are incapable of achievement seems almost of secondary importance.

The conventional wisdom is now prepared to accept that the US oil situation is precarious. Production has already reached its peak; proven oil reserves are estimated at about twenty times the amount currently being consumed in one year. Even at its peak output during the 1980s the amount of oil recoverable from the Prudhoe Bay field in Alaska will be equivalent only to about two years' supply at the high rate of economic growth still being confidently predicted in official circles. Oil imports, particularly from the Middle East, are increasing year by year and currently amount to about 80 per cent of total consumption. Their cost is prodigious. In 1971 the United States spent $45 billion on imported oil; by 1985, if present tendencies remain unchecked, the import bill for oil could have soared to an astronomical $500 billion. Dependence on overseas sources for a commodity as vital as oil is feared and resented by the US Government. It is an affront to the American sense of rugged independence, to the 'frontier spirit' which has featured so much in American history. The era of US self-sufficiency in mineral resources has passed, never to return; both Government and people find this very difficult to accept.

The situation in respect of natural gas is even more perilous than for oil. Known gas resources in the US are very limited and during recent winters domestic and industrial gas shortages, particularly in the Middle West, have served to remind the populace that the energy crisis, far from being an ephemeral phenomenon which could be conveniently forgotten in an atmosphere of 'business as usual', was instead a dominant historical force. In the past Federal regulations had kept the price of natural gas unduly low, and large numbers of consumers switched to it early in the 'seventies. Because of this the industry was unable to attract new capital to it and much-needed prospecting was postponed. Increasingly severe gas shortages in the US in the 'eighties and 'nineties now seem inevitable.

Pressures on indigenous oil and gas supplies will mount relentlessly. Arctic and offshore oil wells will be sucked dry. A multitude of pipelines will be constructed: they include the Alcan, 5,500 miles long, scheduled to go into operation in 1983 at the highly optimistic cost of $8 billion and intended to transport natural gas from Alaska across Canadian territory to markets in the Middle West and Western USA. More refineries are planned, more compressor stations, more transmission towers, more distribution and monitoring systems, more and more obtrusive evidence of the paraphernalia which follow in the wake of hard technology.

The production of synthetic fuel from coal and oil has a long history dating back to the nineteenth century, and as already mentioned, hard-energy proponents in the USA see increasing production of synthetic fuels as an essential ingredient of their policy. By the late 'seventies, organizations such as the US Office of Coal Research, the Bureau of Mines and several oil companies were heavily involved in this general area. Five western states – North Dakota, Montana, Wyoming, Utah and Colorado – account for more than half of the massive coal reserves of the US (currently believed to exceed 500 billion tons) and they have been selected as the site for the large scale production of synthetic fuels. Initially twenty-five new plants are planned and if, as is hoped, the programme proceeds with great speed, about 10 per cent of the nation's natural gas requirements and as much of its oil might be produced in this way by the late 'eighties. It is salutary to recall that if the Moloch of hard technology has to be fed by a project of this kind, more coal will have to be mined in the US in the next twenty-five years than in the whole of the country's past history.

Oil shales and tar sands, particularly the former, are also being heavily backed as major contributors to the energy pool. Colorado, Utah and Wyoming are the states which house the shales; the richest deposits of tar sands are in Canada in Alberta at Athabasca and Peace River. Reserves of shales and tar sands are vast, as is their potential as an energy source. Up till now the costs of oil production from shales and sands have been quite staggering, although it now seems possible that in the longer term they may come within the range of economic competition. However, the overall contribution to US energy needs provided by oil shales and tar sands will remain small for the foreeable future and is unlikely to exceed 5 per cent before the end of the century.

The assertion is frequently made that by 2000 AD nuclear stations will carry half of America's electricity load. Fission is much favoured by hard-technology proponents, and it is promulgated that by 1985 100 new uranium mines will have opened, numerous new enrichment and reprocessing plants will have been built and more than 150 1,000 MW reactors will have been constructed.[2] By 2000 the reactor score is forecast to have risen to 800, including by this time a sizeable number of fast breeder reactors.

The Carter plan of 1977 was the first realistic attempt by any US Administration to grapple with the country's energy dilemma. The plan stated that for the next twenty years the US would have to rely for the bulk of its energy supply on conventional sources now available – oil, natural gas, coal, nuclear fission and hydroelectric power. Federal policies should be designed to stimulate the expanded use of coal supplemented by nuclear power to fill the growing gap created by recent energy demand and relatively stable production of oil and gas. The Carter plan envisaged that by 1985 the rate of energy increase should be less than 2 per cent per annum and that petrol consumption should have been cut by 10 per cent. Large 'gas-guzzling' cars were inefficient, anachronistic and inappropriate; they should be replaced as rapidly as possible by smaller models less profligate in energy use. By 1985 imported oil should have been reduced from 16 to 6 million barrels per day. By this time coal production should have risen by 400 million tons a year; 90 per cent of the nation's homes should be properly insulated and solar energy should be in use in at least $2\frac{1}{2}$ million of them. The plan stressed the pivotal role which energy conservation must play in the future. In the absence of a realistic national commitment to save fuel, all the other proposals would be rendered nugatory.

The Carter plan and similar projections issued by bodies like the Federal Energy Administration and the Institute for Energy Analysis at Oakridge are designed to 'buy time' through energy conservation so that the construction of nuclear and coal-fired electric power stations can be promoted and the production of synthetic fuels, mainly from coal, can be stimulated. However, there are other organizations whose projections are a good deal more radical. For instance, a scenario outlined by the Ford Foundation has stated that by making major changes in industrial practice and in the transportation sector in the direction of fuel conservation, the consumption of conventional energy in the USA need only rise from 74 quadrillion Btu (Quads) in 1976 to 80 Quads* by 2000. A Committee on Nuclear and Alternative Energy Sources sponsored by the National Academy of Sciences went even further. It postulated that, given the national will to conserve energy, reduce economic growth and modify life-styles in tune with a more sustainable type of society, energy consumption in the USA could readily be reduced from 74 to 54 Quads by 2010.

The official commitment to hard technology bristles with problems, and many of these are highly intractable. In the first place the economics are mind-boggling. The massive electrification programme envisioned through the use of coal and nuclear fission is enormously capital-demanding, and there is no immediate likelihood that its overall cost could be borne. Oil and gas from offshore wells, Prudhoe Bay and the Arctic regions will be prodigiously expensive to extract and handle. It need hardly be stated here that synthetic fuels are many times more capital-intensive than are the direct fuel technologies currently in use. In the next twenty years, the US energy industry, propelled along its hard path, could take on a guise of a huge national parasite with an insatiable appetite for investment. Other sectors of the economy would have to be starved; the inflationary spiral would be given a further decisive twist. Far from palliating unemployment, the investment would be likely to reduce jobs and swell dole queues throughout the country.

Ecological stresses associated with hard technology will inevitably mount rapidly. Drilling for oil in fragile areas like the Arctic and offshore could fracture ecosystems irreversibly. Huge tracts of land, especially in the western states, are destined to be despoiled through coal, shale and uranium mining and there is almost no likelihood of eventual restoration. Groundwater would be polluted and aquatic life placed in peril. The long-term commitment to coal as a major source of energy would be likely to cause air pollution to a degree not yet experienced in any industrial country. The carbon dioxide content of the atmosphere could have doubled by the early years of the twenty-first century, the well-recognized 'greenhouse effect' would be increasingly prominent and there could even be irreversible climatic changes.

Hard technology could also prove a catalyst to social and political disturbance. Centralized energy systems, particularly those powered by nuclear fission, are already a potent attraction for terrorists and

* One Quad (10^{22} Btu) is equivalent to the energy stored in 390 million tons of high-grade coal or 170 million barrels of crude oil.

saboteurs. Armed guards and paramilitary personnel would have to be used increasingly to maintain such systems. Democracy could be placed in peril and the trappings of totalitarianism might be difficult to resist.

Probably the most malign implication of the current US fixation with the hard energy path is its eventual effect on the rest of the world. Increasing American reliance on atomic power as a major energy source can only stimulate nuclear proliferation at the global level and further undermine the effectiveness of the Non-Proliferation Treaty. The emergence of more nuclear weapons states will become a virtual certainty; the chances of an atomic holocaust will loom even larger.

Excessive dependence by the USA on oil imports is also likely to have grave international repercussions. A real threat to the country's materialistic and highly industrialized life-style would arise if, for example, OPEC oil supplies were inadequate or if a further oil embargo were imposed for political reasons by the oil-producing states.* Under such circumstances the possibility of US military forces occupying foreign oil fields could well be considered, and indeed as early as 1975 in a Report by the Committee on International Relations to the Congress, this matter was debated. The document stressed the difficulties of such an operation. The installations, having been seized, might have to be garrisoned for months or years; in order to supply the demands both of the US and of her allies, safe overseas passage of petroleum products would have to be guaranteed; damage to key installations by saboteurs and terrorists was possible; so also was intervention by the Soviet Union. However, the very fact that such a plan was being scrutinized sent a *frisson* of fear round the world. Can one be sure that such a strategy will not appear more attractive in the 'eighties as global oil supplies progressively dwindle?

It has already been stressed that the energy policies adopted in the next two decades are likely to mould the future of the USA and other industrialized countries for generations.[3] There is still a chance to alter course to a more sustainable energy profile. But there is currently no sign that these countries will do so and the longer the choice is post-

---

* The current situation in Iran is only one example of possible scenarios for the future.

poned the more difficult will it become. Yet the lesson of history is that society has great powers of adaptation. It took in its stride the technological revolutions which brought the railways, the motor car and the computer. It presided over the transition from wood to coke and coal, and during the twentieth century from coal to oil and natural gas. The scene has now been set for mankind to turn to the sun and its variants for its salvation.

Soft technologies emanate from sources which are eternal and they utilize energy income rather than depletable capital. Usually the methods employed are relatively simple and the quality of the energy is finely tuned to the need to which it is put. Above all, soft energy paths have infinite variety and versatility, presenting the human race with a uniquely rich *smörgasbord*. The best approach to them is undoubtedly to adopt the Maoist doctrine of letting a thousand flowers bloom and cultivating the best varieties.

Solar energy is ubiquitous. But it is also intermittent and highly diverse in its manifestations. Some solar systems, particularly those used for industrial purposes, may require equipment even larger than that needed for conventional forms of energy. Because of their diffuse nature, solar systems will also require extensive collection areas, larger than those required for comparable amounts of energy derived from fossil fuels or nuclear fission. Another basic problem in relation to solar energy has always been that of storage. But there have been considerable technical improvements in this field in recent years, especially those involving the use of insulated storage tanks for water.

The USA is already well on the road to developing reliable solar collectors, and a considerable amount of the solar budget of ERDA and similar bodies is being devoted to this end. 'Flat plate' collectors of increasing sophistication are being constructed and are being utilized on a mounting scale in homes and buildings. They concentrate the radiation and transfer the heat to air or water; they can be combined with double glazing and with special chemical coatings on the surfaces of buildings so that heat absorption and emission are improved. The collectors can also incorporate mirrors which have specially designed lenses and curved surfaces. In addition to concentrating the radiation they can be adjusted to 'track' the sun's movement and so obtain maximal efficiency. Photovoltaic devices employ specific materials such as silicon, gallium and cadmium and have been used extensively in space research and in the satellite programme. At present such devices remain spectacularly expensive; to make them economically attractive their cost would have to be reduced by a factor of about 500. However, one does not have to be clairvoyant to predict that the technology of photovoltaic devices will rapidly improve and that the production of these devices *en masse* is only a matter of time.

Solar energy for heating buildings is already becoming economically attractive in the USA; very soon solar cooling will be in the same category. Such systems can either be active, involving collectors, pumps and pipes, or passive in south-facing buildings. Combinations of both are also feasible. The heating of water by solar energy does not require complicated equipment; storage is not a major difficulty and because hot water is required throughout the year, relatively little of the solar energy which has been collected need be wasted.

Solar energy for space heating presents more complex problems. Costs are forced up because the collectors tend not to be used during the warmer parts of the year. However, ways are being sought to store the heat collected during the summer months; alternatively the excess heat could be used to drive air-conditioning systems. In American houses with southern exposures it is already quite feasible to generate most of the winter space-heating requirements from the sun. Large south-facing windows are required; heavy interior wall and concrete floors act as thermal 'shock absorbers' which store the heat at peak times and release it at night and during cloudy weather.

The possible use of solar energy to generate electricity for industrial and domestic purposes is crucial in a country in which the demand for electricity has been soaring in recent years. Much of ERDA's solar budget is currently being used to determine which type of solar power could be utilized for centralized electricity production, and a number of pilot plants using concentrating collectors are scheduled to be built in the western part of the country in the early 1980s. However, many authorities believe that the USA would be much better served by a decentralized system for electricity distribution like that proposed for Sweden. Such a system would be likely to effect large savings in transmission and distribution which currently account for about half of the cost of electricity supply to the average consumer.

District heating delivers heat to a building in the form of hot water or steam from a central generator. District heating is already quite common in Europe, especially in Sweden, France, Federal Germany and Eastern bloc countries. At present this system is rare in the USA, but as the thrust towards solar power becomes stronger, district heating is likely to gain greatly in popularity. It has, of course, numerous advantages. It favours cogeneration – the recapture of waste heat from generators and other industrial heat processes; it reduces fuel costs because furnaces installed in individual buildings are capable of burning fuel of poorer quality than can large centralized plants. It also tends to reduce air pollution because specialized filtering techniques, not available in large units, can be utilized.

Everywhere on earth, and not least in the USA, solar power has a tremendous potential for the conversion of organic materials into useful forms of energy. Chemical fuels like methanol and alcohol are likely to become essential features of the global solar economy of the twenty-first century and beyond.[4] Even now numerous techniques for bioconversion are available and are being utilized in various parts of the world. For instance, China is reputed to have 2 million and South Korea 30,000 'biogas' plants which rely on anaerobic digestion of wastes. Bioconversion techniques must, of necessity, be closely interwoven with agricultural practice and forestry so that ecological stability is maintained. Through their ability to convert agricultural, factory and cooking wastes into liquid fuels, particularly methanol, they open up exciting possibilities for a viable transportation system in the early twenty-first century, by which time the internal combustion engine powered by oil will have passed into history. Chemical fuels may also be desirable for the provision of high temperature heat for industrial processes. This might be done through the 'cracking' of water to produce hydrogen or – perhaps more realistically because of the enormous current costs and technical problems associated with the electrolysis of water – through the conversion of organic wastes derived from the process of photosynthesis.

Even more ambitious schemes are now under consideration in the USA. They include the possibility of growing 'energy crops' for direct conversion into gas and liquid fuels. Energy plantations utilizing fast-growing trees are being considered. Algae which today clog American rivers, lakes, ditches and canals could be recovered as an energy resource during sewage treatment, and according to a recent estimate by the National Aeronautics and Space Administration, the conversion of their energy from solar to chemical could be as high as 5 per cent.

Possibilities for the production of fuels derived from solar bioconversion are full of challenge and hope, but they constitute no panacea for the energy crisis. Economically such methods remain unattractive; major technical problems have to be resolved and violent opposition from hard-energy proponents is assured. However, advocates of such techniques should not be deterred by being branded as mavericks. After all, did not Bertrand Russell in his *Liberal Decalogue* of 1950 proclaim that every opinion now accepted was once considered eccentric? Zealots for bioconversion could well take solace from this most sagacious and prescient of men.

Another manifestation of solar power, wind energy, is receiving increasing attention in the USA. When viewed globally the potential for wind power is enormous and according to the World Meteorological Organization 20 million megawatts of wind energy could be harnessed at selected sites throughout the planet. Wind power, unlike some of the other variants of solar energy, could be utilized in a centralized manner and fed directly into the electricity grid, and it has been estimated that 100,000 wind power generators, each of 1,000 kilowatts and operating at about 40 per cent capacity, could supply more than 300 megawatt hours of electricity per year. This figure is equivalent to 15 per cent of current US electricity consumption.

Research and development designed to generate electricity by wind power seems at last to be receiving due attention in America. Organizations like ERDA and NASA are heavily involved, with commitments running to millions of dollars. The blade design of windmills is being appraised. Such designs range from traditional horizontal axis rotors by means of which the wind is intercepted head on, to more exotic vertical type rotors in which the blades are at right angles to the earth's surface and to the direction of the wind. Storage of electricity derived from wind power remains a formidable and intractable problem. It could, of course, be accomplished by equipping individual wind stations with batteries, but this would add enormously to the cost of the operation. We often tend to forget that wind power is not restricted to the manufacture of electricity. Wind energy can also pump and compress air, and even now in the West and Middle West of the USA a substantial market exists for water-pumping windmills.

Within the USA, solar power and its derivatives could undoubtedly provide a rich admixture of energy resources. In the sunny South-West of the country direct collection of solar energy would be the procedure of choice. In the Great Plains and in the New England states wind hydraulic power would play a pivotal role. Off the coasts of Florida, Louisiana and Texas, and in the Gulf of Mexico, the siting of ocean thermal gradient electricity generators would be appropriate, while in the Middle West attention would centre on the production of fuels from agricultural wastes.

The USA and the rest of the industrialized world badly need a transitional period spanning several decades during which they can adjust to a more sustainable type of energy economy. Although at present there seems little likelihood of such a development, the bricks and mortar out of which such a bridge could be fashioned are rather familiar. Had they been utilized immediately after the Yom Kippur War, and had an atmosphere of *carpe diem* nonchalance and Micawberism not prevailed in political circles in the Western world during the past six years, the history of the final quarter of the twentieth century could undoubtedly have been vastly different.

The first step towards a sustainable future in the USA and other industrialized countries is quite clear. It is to institute as a matter of prime urgency a massive and sustained programme of energy conservation. The main *desideratum* must be an immediate end to the era of energy profligacy which has already lasted for far too long; matching the quality of the energy to the purpose for which it is being used must become a *sine qua non*; the laws of thermodynamics must no longer be flouted with casual abandon. Methods of energy conservation are, of course, legion and some of them are discussed elsewhere in this book. Adequate insulation of buildings is mandatory – the US Institute of Aeronautics states that by this means the country could save the equivalent of 12 million barrels of oil a day by 1990; the transportation sector badly needs attention and some of the changes proposed in Chapter 6 in this area for the UK would be equally applicable to the USA.

Cogeneration is a vital piece in the jigsaw of energy conservation. The Dow Chemical Company, reporting to the US National Science Foundation as early as 1975, emphasized its potential. By 1985 the US could meet half of its energy needs by cogeneration; the method would save the country between $20 and $50 million in investment in hard technology; fuel equivalent to 3 million barrels of oil per day would be saved; 50 atomic power plants would not have to be constructed. If combined with district heating on a realistic scale the savings made by cogeneration would be even greater.

Another advantage which would flow from a positive commitment to energy conservation would be in respect of jobs; this is because the techniques that would be employed are relatively labour intensive. For example one estimate states that for every Quad resulting from switching intercity plane transport to the railroad 930,000 jobs would be produced. A full-blooded energy conservation drive might also tend to damp down inflationary pressures in the economy, would have few deleterious effects on the environment and – of special importance in the short term – would greatly reduce US dependence on imported oil. Energy conservation could and most certainly should be encouraged by operation of the fiscal system. Subsidies for non-renewable fuels – gas and oil in particular – should be phased out as rapidly as possible and their prices raised to international levels. Another suggestion that has been made is that an energy royalty should be imposed on oil, gas, coal and uranium at the wellhead or mine.

During the period of energy transition, great selectivity would have to be employed with regard to gas and oil. They would have to be utilized sparingly and should be increasingly reserved for functions – the petrochemical industry is the most outstanding example – for which they are peculiarly suited. On the other hand coal might have a temporary renaissance. For many years now coal technologies have been the Cinderella of the energy industry. But not so now. Exciting new developments – flash pyrolysis, hydrogenation, solvent extraction, underground gasification – hold considerable promise. But probably the most important development for the coal industry during the transitional period would be the increasing use of fluidized beds.

Fluidized bed combustion entails the treatment of powdered coal by hot air jets. When the coal burns its heat is transferred to a boiler in which steam is raised. The technique has several advantages. It diminishes atmospheric pollution through the emission of sulphur dioxide. Its versatility is notable; it can power industrial complexes, especially those operating through cogeneration; it can be readily engrafted on to existing municipal power stations; the size of the boiler can be altered considerably without the system losing efficiency and the procedure is therefore well suited for domestic use.

Emergent technologies within the industry suggest that coal could readily substitute for oil and gas during the transitional energy period. Also the substitution could be effected by a relatively modest expansion of coal production in the USA lasting until the end of the century or possibly up to 2020. The enormous increase in coal mining and production predicted by Project Independence and later government-sponsored schemes would therefore become unnecessary.

The sea of history is full of famous wrecks. Throughout the ages mankind has tended to reject situations when they were manageable, to intervene only when they were out of hand, to apply too late remedies which had they been practised earlier, might have effected a cure. The USA and other developed countries are eschewing soft energy technologies at their peril. Unfortunately, however, in so doing they are acting according to well established precedents in the evolution and conduct of human affairs.

The crisis of 1973 affected Canada less than other major industrial powers. On paper at least, Canada was still an energy exporter. But because of an admixture of geography, traditional practice and bottlenecks in respect of transport and distribution, the totality of Canada's energy resources could not be made available to her population. While about half of the crude oil produced in western Canada was being exported, either through the Panama Canal or via the St Lawrence Seaway, eastern Canada was dependent on imported oil derived mainly from Venezuela.

In December 1973 Prime Minister Pierre Trudeau outlined the main ingredients of his country's energy policy. An overall authority should be established to allocate energy supplies in an equable manner and, if necessary, to ration them in times of emergency. Oil from western Canadian provinces should supply the east of the country, and in particular a pipeline should be constructed to serve Montreal and other areas of Quebec Province. Governmental pricing policies should be reviewed in order to provide incentives for the exploitation of domestic oil resources in frontier areas and in the Arctic; tar sand technology in the Athabasca region of Alberta should be given a considerable boost.

Since then much has happened. Traditional supplies of oil and natural gas from sedimentary basins in the western part of the country have been steadily declining. Drilling experience in Canada's frontier zone has been disappointing. Athabasca tar sands are believed to contain vast quantities of energy – about 1 billion barrels of recoverable synthetic crude oil – but since 1973 the problems associated with extraction of the material have been very much to the fore. They include: lack of sophistication of technology, burgeoning environmental depradation, unacceptable social impacts and, above all, the massive amount of capital investment which would be required to mount such a programme.

Canadians, like Americans, have not profited from the lesson of the Yom Kippur War and continue to use oil with extreme profligacy. By the late 'seventies they were consuming 4 million barrels per day and if the present increase in energy demand – estimated at 5.5 per cent per annum – is permitted to continue, the figure will have risen to an astronomical 14 million barrels per day by the late 1990s. Canada's energy growth is already pressing hard against her social and economic limits. And her dependence on imported oil is increasing – so much so that by 1985 OPEC might be expected to supply about 50 per cent of domestic demand.

Electricity consumption in Canada has been rising remorselessly since the end of the Second World War. By the mid-'seventies electricity was providing about 40 per cent of the country's primary energy demand. The Canadian Government has stated firmly that in the future the country must 'go electrical' to an even greater extent and has suggested that by 2050 90 per cent of the country's energy requirement should be met in this way. Canada is much more fortunate than the US in her situation *vis-à-vis* hydroelectric power. This is, of course, a renewable resource, has traditionally provided the lion's share (over 70 per cent) of the nation's electricity, and could do even better. But in spite of such good fortune, for more than twenty years Ottawa has been supporting the development of nuclear fission as the method *par excellence* of electricity generation. The Candu reactor is the result. By the end of 1976 Canada had seven such plants with a total nuclear power capacity of 2530 megawatts of electricity. She had also been an active vendor in international markets, having supplied her Candu reactors to India, Pakistan, Argentina and South Korea.

Canada is, of course, along with the USA, the Soviet Union, Australia and South Africa, one of the world's main producers of uranium. An estimate made by the Department of Energy, Mines and Resources in the mid-'seventies put the total quantity of Canadian uranium at 530,000 tons; prospects of increasing the yield by further exploration seemed good and a marked increase in the annual domestic consumption of uranium was forecast.

The Canadian situation in relation to natural gas is probably more worrisome than for any other conventional fuel. Most of the country's gas resources are in the West. At present rates of consumption, proved reserves could be exhausted by as early as 1990, and if the export of gas to the US continues at its present rate, the exhaustion date could be brought forward to 1985. Obviously the Canadian Government places high hopes on the discovery of new gas fields, particularly in frontier areas such as the Mackenzie River Delta and the Beaufort Sea. Otherwise Ottawa would presumably not have agreed to the construction of the Alcan pipeline mentioned earlier. Alcan will carry Alaskan natural gas to the USA and Canada, and it contains a 750 mile spur from White Horse in the Yukon territory of the Canadian gas fields near the Mackenzie River Delta.

The Canadian Government is currently in the throes of framing a new national energy policy.[5] Hard technology is in the saddle. Oil, gas and nuclear fission hold primacy; frontier and Arctic areas will be squeezed for fossil fuels. But, as elsewhere in the industrialized world, the promised El Dorado is unlikely to be achieved, and an embarrassed Government could be as powerless to enforce its policy as a surgeon who has all his instruments assembled for the operation and sees the operating table being wheeled slowly away from him. However, it should again be stressed that Canada has distinct advantages over her southern neighbour. She has many fewer consumers – 23.5 million as compared with 216 million – and her population density (2 persons per square kilometre) is amongst the lowest in the world. She is much better endowed with a renewable resource, hydropower. Furthermore, in Canada there could come to develop a more flexible outlook apropos of other renewable resources. In the maritime provinces bioconversion techniques are being looked upon with some favour and one of the few wind hydraulic systems under development in North America is located in Prince Edward Island.

Overall energy pricing in Canada requires urgent review. Domestic prices of oil and gas are kept artificially low by subsidy and must rise to international levels. Canadians must be forced to face up to the harsh realities of an energy-hungry world and discard the cosy carapace which has surrounded them for far too long. A meaningful energy conservation programme modelled on that projected for the USA is, of course, mandatory. By the mid-'eighties the average rate of energy growth in Canada should be reduced – the Government say by 2 per cent per annum from a current figure of 5.5 to 3.5. The new pricing policies envisaged are intended to promote energy conservation. But there must be other savings of a more specific kind throughout the economy and these will certainly affect personal life-styles. Large gas-guzzling cars are far too numerous in Canada; most Canadian homes, offices and industrial buildings are outrageously profligate of energy. Belatedly, a National Building Code is in the process of preparation; it should provide guidelines for cutting energy consumption in new buildings by 50 to 75 per cent and should lay down criteria for the insulation of existing properties.

Pari passu with conservation measures, the Canadian Government has announced its firm resolve to increase exploration and development of new energy sources. The target is to double such activities by 1980, and to attempt to do so 'under acceptable social and environmental conditions'! Ottawa freely admits that capital costs will be enormous. Measured in dollars valued at 1975 purchasing power the programme would need an investment of $40 billion, of which $10 billion would have to be spent between 1976 and 1980; and this estimate does not allow for continuing inflationary pressures within the Canadian economy. More detailed information than currently exists is required on fossil fuel resources ultimately recoverable from Canada's frontier areas, and detailed geological surveys are now underway, particularly in the Beaufort Sea offshore areas and in her Arctic islands. An accurate assessment of the country's uranium reserves with a yearly audit would seem long overdue. Drilling for coal, virtually discarded many years ago, should recommence. Novia Scotia and New Brunswick have already started mining on a small scale; other provinces such as Alberta and British Columbia might do likewise.

Substitution of one energy fuel for another will obviously become necessary in Canada. In the Government's view short-term reliance on imported oil will only be reduced if domestic coal and nuclear fission are substituted. New delivery systems for fossil fuels are scheduled to take pride of place. In addition to the Alcan a provincial pipeline system has now been extended to Montreal, and western Canadian oil is being pumped into that market. As of now the pipeline can deliver 250,000 barrels a day and official estimates state that the amount could be readily increased by a further 100,000 barrels a day.

Unfortunately, as in the USA, renewable energy resources feature to a very limited extent in the Canadian energy scenario. The Government has recorded its awareness that tidal, solar, wind and geothermal sources, together with bioconversion techniques and possibly nuclear fusion, have great potential for the future. But as the Canadian Department of Energy has stressed, energy is 'essential to the development of a high quality of life . . . indispensable to generate wealth . . . to produce the surplus of goods and services, improve the quality as well as the prosperity of our living.' The siren song of consumerism is sounding loud and clear. The seed corn for future economic growth must be planted now. The Canadian Government would seem to be in the process of preparing a Lucullan banquet of hard technology which, it appears, the populace will be proud to eat. Given such a situation the dice seems heavily loaded against renewable energy sources, at least for the foreseeable future.

NOTES AND REFERENCES

[1] A good account of the aims of hard-technology proponents in the USA is provided by Amory Lovins (1977).

[2] As of 1979, 70 plants are in operation, 90 under construction and 35 at the licence-seeking stage.

[3] *The Ecologist* (1977), 'The Future of America', August/September, makes this point clearly; see also George L. Tuve (1976).

[4] This has been well recognized in the document *Solar Sweden* referred to in Chapter 5.

[5] See *An Energy Strategy for Canada* (1976).

Chapter 5

Energy Futures in Scandinavia

The Nordic countries – Sweden, Norway, Denmark, Finland and Iceland – have a combined population of not much more than 20 million. Yet throughout most of this century these nations have been the pacesetters in many major areas of social change. They were amongst the first to introduce liberal abortion laws, to abolish capital punishment, to humanize their penal codes, to modernize their prisons, to provide adequate social benefits for all their citizens. In recent years their record in terms of Third World aid has been outstanding and the proportion of their Gross National Product which they devote to this end is amongst the highest of any region in the world.

The Arab oil embargo and energy crisis of 1973 were weathered better by the Nordic countries than by the rest of Europe. Fuel cuts were unnecessary, blackouts were avoided; petrol rationing was not contemplated. But, as elsewhere, the malady had only been palliated, not cured. Coherent energy policies would have to emerge; increasingly the governments of these countries would have to grapple with the tentacles of the energy hydra. Study of the region as a whole is fascinating, because it represents in microcosm a dilemma which faces the whole of the industrialized world and in which a plethora of factors – geological, social, political and economic – will undoubtedly play a role.

The Swedes are acutely aware of the previous historical transitions which have occurred in energy sources. In the early twentieth century Swedish coke and coal had come to replace wood as the dominant form of energy. For the next seventy-five years oil reigned supreme, the influence of hydropower grew slowly and from the 'sixties onwards nuclear fission began to carve out for itself a sizeable energy niche. During this period district heating schemes and cogeneration became increasingly popular, Sweden being a successful pioneer in both these areas.

It is now generally recognized in Sweden that a watershed has been reached and that the world stands delicately poised between two epochs. In the first energy was cheap and abundant and the demand for power rose spectacularly every year. Economic expansionism was taken for granted, world prosperity seemed assured; in Sweden itself material living standards became amongst the highest on earth, *per capita* GNP approaching $9,000 by the mid-'seventies.

The incoming epoch will be strikingly different and the pro-dromata are already in evidence. Policies of unfettered economic growth still receive ritual obeisance from politicians and entrepreneurs; yet most people recognize such statements for what they are – a theatrical smokescreen disguising an underlying malaise. The world recession, combined with astronomically high taxation, hit Swedish trade very hard during 1977. Manufacturing industry found life much less easy, exports were waning, the balance of payments became unfavourable, living standards tended to stagnate.

Energy supplies in the incoming epoch will be much less secure. Oil will perforce still have to be a dominant source, but necessity dictates that it will have to be derived from areas of the world which officials in Sweden view with apprehension because of their instability and political sensitivity.

At present about 75 per cent of Sweden's energy demand is met through the importation of crude oil and oil products. Sweden uses 1.1 per cent of global oil production; but she has no guarantee of receiving even this very modest share of the cake when world oil production stagnates and begins to fall well before 2000 AD. Dependence on imported oil will have baneful effects on the country. The economy will be thrown into disarray with a mounting balance of payments deficit; even more important, Sweden's freedom of diplomatic action could be eroded, with a tendency to render nugatory the position of neutrality which the country has traditionally followed in international affairs. The Swedish Government is on record as saying that it will diminish dependence on oil imports by at least 15 per cent by 1985. During this period the rate of growth of energy consumption will be reduced from 5 to 2 per cent per annum, and energy conservation – an area in which Sweden already has an outstanding record in the Western world – will be stimulated by generous subsidies designed to improve standards of insulation. Meanwhile the government is exhorting Swedish industry to be less profligate with energy, to tighten its belt and specifically to recover much of the waste heat it generates. The National Industrial Board in Sweden estimates that up to 1 million tons of oil could be saved between now and 1985 merely by 'recycling' waste heat; by 2000 about one-third of the country's total energy demand could be met in this way.

Coal is unlikely to feature significantly in any future Swedish energy scenario. Little is left in the way of indigenous deposits: transportation and stockpiling facilities are poor. Swedish natural gas is present in small amounts, the main sources of importation being the North Sea, the Middle East and Siberia. Shale oil in Sweden is somewhat more promising, and one estimate suggests that 1,000 million tons of oil equivalent could be extracted by technologies likely to become available quite soon. But, as everywhere else where this energy source is bruited around as a panacea, massive extraction of shales would cause severe economic and social dislocation, and for this reason it is unlikely to become a major source of power in Sweden in the foreseeable future.

About 12 per cent of Sweden's landscape is covered with peat, and the somewhat optimistic claim has been made that if the country maintained its fossil fuel consumption at the current level but substituted peat for oil, the former could last for as long as 150 years. Nevertheless, peat could well become an important energy source in Sweden as the twilight of the petroleum era deepens. Peat could also form an important adjunct during the period of transition to the renewable types of energy systems described later in this chapter.

Hydropower currently provides about four-fifths of Sweden's electricity consumption and 15 per cent of her total energy use. In the late 'seventies the annual production of hydropower was approximately 60 terawatt hours. There is still some potential for increasing hydropower production in Sweden; but in the future it is probable that ecological restraints will operate to an increasing extent and that fewer and fewer rivers will be able to be harnessed for this purpose.

Uranium is an abundant fuel source in Sweden. The country is thought to possess about 1 million tons, of which at least 30 per cent is considered to be ultimately recoverable. Enthusiasm for nuclear power waxed strongly in Sweden in the 'fifties and 'sixties, and successive Swedish Governments, all Social Democratic in hue, came to look on atomic fission as the energy panacea. Governmental decisions of twenty years ago seemed to have foreclosed Sweden's options and effectively forced the country into a nuclear straitjacket. By 1977 six light water reactors had been built with a generating capacity of 5,000 megawatts of electricity. A further five plants were in the process of construction, and by 1981 the total generating capacity of the country was expected to exceed 7,000 megawatts. But the anti-nuclear lobby burgeoned in Sweden and this was reflected in the result of the general election of September 1976 when the pro-nuclear Social Democrats suffered a *dégringolade* at the polls and a Centrist Government, led by Thorbjorn Fälldin, took office on an anti-nuclear ticket.

The new Government immediately made it clear that it had received a *damnosa hereditas* from its predecessor. For some time it held the anti-nuclear line: the atomic juggernaut in Sweden slowed; no new plants were commissioned and the Government pledged that the moratorium on construction would stay until the nuclear power industry could guarantee absolutely safe disposal of long-lived radioactive wastes. But pressures on the Government mounted; the business community was furious as entrepreneurial activity waned. Then in June 1978 Sweden's prestigious Energy Commission decided by a majority of ten to five that nuclear waste *could* be safely treated and stored, and that atomic power should continue to be a major energy source in Sweden. Mr Fälldin resigned in the autumn of that year in a storm of personal vilification; the Centrist coalition which he had led was in disarray. With the return of the Social Democrats likely in this year's general election, a nuclear future for Sweden now seems probable. Yet, even if such an electoral shift takes place, the lead time involved in the mining and enrichment of domestic uranium will be long and it could well be a *fin de siècle* activity.

Solar Sweden, produced in 1977 by the country's Secretariat for Future Studies, is one of the key energy documents of the decade. *Solar Sweden* represents the first serious attempt of any country – industrialized or non-industrialized, developed or developing – to provide a detailed, imaginative and substantive discussion about the feasibility of building an energy system based solely on domestic and renewable resources.

Solar Sweden is about the state of the nation in the year 2015. By then the production of energy from biomass – the fraction of solar energy stored as organic matter – will have become crucial. Biomass will be derived from numerous sources – from energy plantations including bogs and forest land, through aquaculture by growing algae in dams, lakes and coastal areas, from straw and reeds, from wastes associated with the logging industry and from barks and lyes. Within the industrial sector biomass of high energy content will be the major power source.

The scenario postulates a bright future for solar heating in the Sweden of 2015. Space and district heating will be based on plants designed to generate both electricity and heat with biomass as the basic fuel. The electricity sector in Sweden is expected to expand considerably and to become increasingly efficient; hydropower, wind power, solar cells and fuel cells of various types will be making a sizeable contribution to it.

Within the transport sector oil will, of course, be no longer generally available in Sweden in 2015. Of the alternatives to oil, methanol is perceived as the best, being preferable to hydrogen. Methanol needs no large-scale network for its distribution. It can be readily stored and, unlike hydrogen which requires an abrupt change to a completely new technology, methanol can be introduced smoothly and gradually as a new energy carrier. Also, methanol can be readily mixed with petrol and up to 20 per cent of it can be added to the mixture without making substantial alterations to car engines in use today. Fuel cells containing methanol can also be utilized in the transport sector, and a cell has recently been developed which can run continuously for over 30,000 hours on a mixture of methanol and air. Methanol can be produced from natural gas and coal, and there is every likelihood that wood, wastes and other forms of biomass could also act as sources for it.

There will undoubtedly be many vociferous criticisms of *Solar Sweden*. Economists will say that the cost will be prohibitive; those of an acquisitive nature will bemoan the lower material standard of living that it may betoken. Because of the low intensity of solar radiation and the relatively tiny fraction of the whole which can be collected, the demand for land will undoubtedly be great – some put it as high as 3 million hectares.

But the advantages of the *Solar Sweden* plan would be enormous. In 'Solar Sweden' energy supplies would be secure; the arcane and Machiavellian manoeuvrings of the oil-supplying nations could be disregarded; environmental imperatives could be increasingly obeyed; the grizzly spectre of nuclear fission would no longer stalk the land. A post-industrial society – more decentralized, more ecologically conscious – would have been attained. The views of prescient men like Thomas Jefferson and John Stuart Mill would finally have been vindicated. All that is in doubt is that future Swedish Goverments will have the courage and foresight to pursue such a plan.

The Norwegian standard of living, measured by *per capita* GNP, is even higher than that of Sweden. Joblessness in 1979 is running at less than 1 per cent of the labour force – very low as compared with most industrialized nations. Even more importantly, Norway is the only Scandinavian country which is self-sufficient in energy.

The twin pillars of the Norwegian energy scenario are hydro-electricity and oil. Cheap hydroelectric power has been available in the country since the early 1900s and has proved an inestimable boon. All Norway's electricity is produced in hydro stations; half of the energy generated in the country is hydropower, and the latter has enabled Norwegian industry to develop with great rapidity. But hydropower is not unlimited. Most of Norway's available resources have already been utilized or are in the process of development, and the forecast is that by 1990 all viable sources of hydroelectricity will have been exploited. Meanwhile, the costs of harnessing rivers are escalating and this factor, combined with the objection of environmentalists, who in Norway traditionally wield a sizeable political clout, makes the future in this area less rosy than it was in the past.

Between 1900 and 1960 energy consumption in Norway rose by an average of 3 per cent each year. In the 'sixties and early 'seventies the rate of increase was even more spectacular, climbing to almost 5 per cent. Since then the rate has slowed considerably and the Government has put on record that it wishes this trend to continue. Between now and 1985 the average increase should not exceed 3.3 per cent per annum, while the industrial sector of the economy should limit the rise to 2 per cent.

When surveys for oil in Norwegian coastal waters began in the early 1960s it rapidly became apparent that significant deposits were present. Drilling operations which commenced on Norway's continental shelf in 1966 faced climatic conditions which were inhospitable, to say the least of it. The oil-bearing geological strata were deeply placed; innovative extraction methods were *de rigueur*; frequently the whole industry found itself operating on the pioneer fringes of technology.

Total proved recoverable reserves from the Norwegian area of the continental shelf are now put at about 1 billion tons of oil equivalent, distributed evenly between oil and gas. However, reserves could be much more extensive and one optimistic report suggests that if drilling were undertaken south of the 62nd parallel, the figure could rise to 4 billion tons. As of 1978 the Norwegians have four fields either in production or under development – Ekofisk, Frigg, Stratfjord and Valhall-Hod. By the early 1980s the annual production of these fields is likely to be 70 million tons oil equivalent – about seven times Norway's domestic needs.

With her small population (just over 4 million), high living standards and energy needs met largely through hydroelectricity, Norway is in a uniquely favoured position amongst the oil-producing nations. She has no need to proceed with rapid extraction and, indeed, caution has been of the essence of Norway's petroleum policy. The Norwegian Parliament, the Störting, made it clear in the 'sixties that oil would never become the *fons et origo* of the nation's economy. Oil concessions were granted with some reluctance, and the Störting decided to limit the annual production of oil to a figure of 90 million tons of oil equivalent (MTOE). Even this relatively modest total is unlikely to be achieved, official projections quoting a production rate of 76 MTOE for 1985 and 59 MTOE for 1990. The Government has repeatedly emphasized the environmental risks associated with oil development and in this way strikes a responsive chord in a country traditionally dependent on its fisheries and with a deep-seated awareness of the necessity to conserve marine resources. Indeed, since the mishap at the Bravo platform in the Ekofisk field in 1977 public enthusiasm to push ahead rapidly with further oil exploration has notably decreased.

Because of Norway's petroleum boom the search for alternative energy technologies is proceeding at a slow pace. Solar power might be important after 1990 for space heating, but it is thought unlikely that it will supply more than 0.5 per cent of the country's total energy demands by 2000. Little future is seen for wind, tidal and wave power or for geothermal energy during this century. Nuclear power is regarded as a potential energy source in the 1990s, by which time the price of electricity produced by the atom could be lower than that from thermal plants utilizing oil and gas. According to various authorities, nuclear power would be relatively easy to introduce into the Norwegian electricity system.

During the 'seventies the Norwegian Government announced that as a result of the beneficial effects of oil revenues on the country's balance of payments, it would increase capital transfers to the Third World and would raise still further the proportion of the GNP which it provides for aid to developing countries. The Störting has also stated that Norway intends to play an active role in the International Energy Agency and to strive for a more constructive dialogue between oil-producing and consuming nations. But by 1978 Norway's balance of payments gap was widening; private oil companies had made over-optimistic production forecasts; earnings from offshore oil and gas had been unexpectedly low; domestic consumption would have to be reduced along with imported goods. In the energy-hungry world of the late twentieth century even Norway, with her relative plenitude of oil, was facing problems. The influence of the country on global *realpolitik* might, after all, have to be less than her Parliament had once desired.

Denmark, unlike Norway, is massively dependent on energy imports. She consumes 16 million tons of oil per year, 90 per cent of it derived from Middle Eastern sources. Denmark's share of North Sea oil is at best a trickle and although a number of small gas fields have been discovered in the Danish sector of the North Sea, no evidence has been forthcoming to indicate that natural gas could supply anything more than a miniscule fraction of the country's total energy demand. Deposits of low grade uranium, amounting to some 16,000 tons, have been discovered at Kvänjefjeld in Southern Greenland and, provided that no formal change in the international status of the territory takes place, these reserves will continue to remain under Danish jurisdiction. Greenland's uranium ores have traditionally been regarded as too poor for commercial exploitation, but given the exigencies of the 'eighties and 'nineties, pressure to mine them may become irresistible.

In 1976 the Danish Government published its official energy policy for the next twenty years. An average annual increase in GNP of 3.5 per cent was forecast. Primary energy consumption was to rise by 50 per cent, and a massive increase in electricity production to a total of 9.5 gigawatts (GW)* was predicted. The hard energy path was to be favoured. By 1995, 48 per cent of Denmark's fuel was still earmarked from oil; 16 per cent would come from reserves of natural gas in the Norwegian and Danish sectors of the North Sea and 10 per cent from coal. Large centralized units of a capacity greater than 100 megawatts would be the sole source of power production; decentralization as advocated in *Solar Sweden* was not even considered. But the

* 1 gigawatt = one thousand million watts.

spectacular and controversial feature of the plan was its dependence on nuclear power for electricity generation. By 1995, five nuclear plants would have been constructed, four of them of 900 megawatts capacity and one of 1,300 megawatts. Between them they were destined to provide almost one-quarter of Denmark's total energy consumption.

The plan produced a bitter national debate centred around the primacy accorded to atomic power. Public interest was intense and opinion polls taken at the time indicated that if a referendum on the issue were held, about 60 per cent of the population would register an anti-nuclear vote and only 16 per cent would support the atom. An alternative energy plan laying much less emphasis on atomic power was subsequently compiled by a group of Danish scientists. Forecasts for economic growth and electricity production were similar to those of the official plan. Overall costs were obviously difficult or impossible to predict, but the overall conclusion reached was that the difference between the two systems would not be great. The alternative plan leant much more heavily on renewable resources. By 1995 solar energy and its variants – wind power and possibly biomass – would contribute at least 12 per cent to the total energy mixture. Oil consumption was forecast to remain high at over 50 per cent; the contribution from coal would rise to 12 per cent and from natural gas to 24 per cent. A notable feature of the alternative plan was its reliance on small decentralized units rather than massive power-generating leviathians for the combined production of power and district heating.

In 1900 there were 100,000 windmills operating in Denmark. Since then interest in wind power has diminished; but it is now having a rapid renaissance. According to the Danish Academy of Technical Science, at least 10 per cent of Denmark's energy needs could be met by wind power by the 1990s; by 2015 the figure could reach 50 per cent. The renowned but long defunct Gedser windmill is in the process of being reactivated and experimental generators in the 1 megawatt range are currently being constructed. The claim has been made that, even now, large horizontal-axis wind generators could produce electricity at prices competitive with fossil fuels and that with the technological improvements already in the pipeline, such costs could be rapidly reduced. Denmark's international energy grid which connects her to adjoining countries would be of great importance in relation to wind power. Surplus wind energy accumulating during the winter months could be stored in water reservoirs and utilized via the grid to provide electricity through existing hydropower plants for much of Scandinavia. Such a system would be especially valuable in summer when, of course, winds blow less strongly.

Other forms of alternative energy are now receiving attention in Denmark. Solar heating systems with flat plate collectors are being developed by a number of firms and prototypes are being tested on buildings. According to the alternative energy plan, 17 per cent of all the heat consumed in Danish buildings in 1995 could be provided in this way. Prospects for the production of wave power from the coasts around Denmark would seem to reasonably good, but research and development in this field is still in an embryonic phase.

A number of bioconversion schemes are also under consideration in Denmark. None is as ambitious as those outlined in *Solar Sweden*. The alternative plan has projected that crop residues, urban wastes and timber could provide 4 per cent of the country's heating requirements by 1985. About 2 million tons of straw are burned each year in Danish agriculture, and recently farms have installed straw-burning furnaces to substitute directly for heating oil.

Since Finland gained her independence from Russia just over sixty years ago, the country has been rapidly industrialized, a good social security system has been developed and a huge rise in living standards has been secured. Under the guidance of a series of outstandingly sagacious and prescient statesmen – including J. V. Paasikivi and K. Kekkonen – Finland has skilfully walked a neutral tightrope between East and West. But now, in the aftermath of the energy crisis, the Finnish economy has been plunged into deep recession, industries are operating at only half capacity, unemployment has risen to an unprecedented level of 7 per cent.

Finland is poorly placed in terms of indigenous energy resources. Fossil fuels, currently constituting about 70 per cent of her energy requirements, have to be imported and here she depends heavily on the Soviet Union, which supplies 60 per cent of her oil and most of her natural gas. Hydropower has a definite potential in Finland. Currently this source provides about 12 terawatt hours (TWh) per year of electricity, but there is no reason why this figure could not be increased by at least 50 per cent. More effective use of hydropower would necessitate the building of several small-scale plants, and doubts have been expressed both about their economic viability and their propensity to cause ecological damage.

There is enough peat in Finland to meet the country's total energy demand for at least forty years. Only the Soviet Union and Canada are more richly endowed with this natural resource. However, less than 10 per cent of Finnish peat is considered suitable for exploitation on economic grounds, and the production target for 1985 – 10-15 million cubic metres – represents only 5 per cent of the nation's demand for primary energy. At present peat is being used in Finland mainly to provide district and industrial heating and, to a lesser extent, in cogeneration schemes. Peat plants sited close to production fields have proved to be the most economic.

Four nuclear reactors are currently under construction in Finland, two being built by the USSR and two by Sweden. The forecast is that by 1981 Finnish nuclear generating capacity will exceed 2,000 megawatts of electricity and that by 2000 AD the total will be 5,000 megawatts. Finland, lacking indigenous resources and faced with high transportation costs for imported fossil fuels, obviously finds the nuclear option attractive and the projected capacity is quite large for a nation whose population by the end of the century is unlikely to be more than 4.8 million. On the other hand, Finland is chronically short of capital and this may prove a decisive constraint on further nuclear expansion. Alternative energy sources have not so far attracted much attention in Finland. Waste materials, particularly from the wood processing industry, have traditionally been used for energy production and attempts are being made to step up this process. Urban wastes have not so far been utilized to any extent, but their potential in district heating schemes is slowly being recognized.

Amongst the Nordic countries only Norway seems to have an assured energy future well into the twenty-first century. But innovative ability within Scandinavia is high, and were a plan along the lines of *Solar Sweden* to be introduced throughout the Nordic area the eventual outlook for these nations could soon become the envy of the rest of the world.

Chapter 6

Energy Futures for Britain, France and Federal Germany

Energy policy in Britain became a dominant theme only during the 1970s. Prior to that it had been played sporadically and in a subdued form by 'cellos and violas. Now, however, the orchestration has become emphatic, with violins, trumpets and trombones in the lead; and for the rest of this century and beyond the theme will undoubtedly demand *tutti* and *fortissimo*. Numerous energy futures for the UK have been promulgated in recent years. The aim of this section of the chapter is to discuss some of them.

By the late 'seventies world consumption of primary energy had climbed to 75,000 terawatt hours (TWh).* Britain, with 1.4 per cent of the earth's people, was using about 3.3 per cent of the total. Amongst industrialized nations the UK is notable in having a high usage of primary energy in relation to *per capita* Gross National Product. Only the USSR, the German Democratic Republic, Canada and Norway outstrip her in this respect. Variations of this kind in developed countries probably arise from a number of factors including climatic differences, the relative importance to the economy of energy-intensive industries and the efficiency of energy conversion procedures.

Much of the controversy in Britain as regards future energy policy centres around the possibility that an 'energy gap' will emerge before the end of the century and will have to be filled by nuclear power. Many forecasts, including that issued by the Government's Department of Energy, regard such a gap as inevitable. In a projection issued in 1976 the Department assumed that for the foreseeable future the demand for primary energy in Britain would rise by about 2 per cent per annum and that the demand for electricity would be even greater, increasing by $3\frac{1}{2}$-4 per cent per annum. Based on calculations

* 1 terawatt hour = one thousand million kilowatt hours.

of the amounts of coal, oil and natural gas which were likely to be available, the 'gap' could range from 370 to 750 TWh by 1990 and could reach 1,850 TWh by 2000 AD. As a result, economic growth would slow dramatically and the malign effect of energy shortages on living standards would become pervasive. The Department believed that only massive nuclear expansion could rescue the country from this imbroglio. Five gigawatts (GW) of nuclear generating power were being provided in 1975; this would have to increase dramatically – to 30 GW by 1990, to 104 GW by 2000, to 426 GW by 2030. As nuclear expansion proceeded increasing hegemony should be given to the fast breeder reactor which was scheduled to provide 370 GW by 2030. Nuclear fission did not feature in the official projection; generating capacity based on alternative sources was eschewed and policies of energy conservation received little or no attention.

In the early years of the Department's projection North Sea oil and gas were to be major contributors. The amount of oil ultimately recoverable from the region was put at 4,000 million tons (48,000 TWh) and of gas at 60 billion cubic feet (17,600 TWh). By the early years of the twenty-first century both fuels would be in a very short supply and extremely expensive. By then the main use of oil would be as a chemical feedstock, although some could still be utilized for transport. Assuming the National Coal Board's 'Plan for Coal' is fully implemented, coal production should reach 150 million tons (1,100 TWh) by 1990. Thereafter, as investment in nuclear power expanded, demand for coal would decline, falling to 110 million tons (814 TWh) by 2025. After 2000 coal would be diverted increasingly from electricity generation to the production of synthetic natural gas (SNG) and to liquid fuels necessary for transport.

The Department of Energy's projection came in for criticism from a number of sources, much the most weighty of these being the Royal Commission on Environmental Pollution. The Commission first drew attention to the considerable surplus of electrical generating capacity currently existing in the UK; on this ground alone the commitment of the country to a high nuclear future seemed highly inappropriate. The Commission also questioned a basic tenet of the Department of Energy's forecast, namely that electricity would penetrate the market to such a massive extent that by 2025 it would account for 60 per cent of the energy supplied to customers. Such a degree of penetration, which could only be based on coal and atomic power, might never take place because of the rising cost of electricity, now accepted as inevitable, would put a severe restraint on demand and would cause consumption to decline. North Sea gas, unless very heavily taxed, would be likely to remain competitive in cost for several decades; even when prepared from coal as SNG it would still be cheaper than energy derived from atomic fission. Moreover, the capital costs of the nuclear programme would be exceedingly high. For each job in an atomic plant £300,000 might have to be allocated, and by the mid-'nineties the country could be spending an astronomical 3.4 per cent of its GNP on electricity generated in this way.

Environmental considerations weighed heavily with the Commission in rejecting the 'high-nuclear, high-electric' energy future envisaged by the Government. New reactors would have to be constructed in coastal sites in order to ensure adequate supplies of cooling water. Amenity would suffer not only from the construction of the plants but also from the obtrusive paraphernalia of the nuclear fuel cycle, including large cooling towers, transmission pylons and overhead lines. Rural areas would be stamped with electricity generation as with the mark of Cain. Nuclear power would not only be hugely wasteful because of its 'technological overkill'; it could become a powerful catalyst for environmental depredation and ecological disaster.

The Commission proceeded to recommend an alternative energy strategy and sketched out its main ingredients up to 2025. The penetration of the energy market by electricity in the next fifty years was projected to be considerably less than that forecast in the Department of Energy statement and would be likely to account for only about 20 per cent of total consumption. Moreover, the admixture of power sources producing the electricity would be different. Nuclear reactors would, of course, contribute; but the proportion of electricity derived therefrom would be less. During the first two decades of the next century alternative energy sources would be making a sizeable contribution, and by 2020 solar power and its variants could be expected to account for as much as 260 terawatt hours.

The Commission accepted the statement of the National Coal Board that by the turn of the century coal production could be raised to 200 million tons per year and that it might be kept at this level for about 200 years. To achieve this target several new mines would have to be opened; there seemed little doubt that a large synthetic natural gas industry based on coal would develop. Environmental disruption from coal mining must, however, be kept to a minimum.

Modern techniques would help here; in particular, the fluidized-bed combustion method would reduce pollution damage. The Commission came out strongly in favour of combined heat and electric power (CHP) systems. The latter provided the possibility of matching the type of energy supplied to the needs of the user; the systems were particularly useful in relation to district heating and they constituted a vital ingredient of any rational programme of energy conservation. The argument that CHP has not so far proved economically attractive in Britain was not sustainable. The systems worked well in other Western European countries, notably Sweden, Federal Germany and in the Eastern bloc. With increased market penetration, the costs of CHP in Britain could be expected to fall dramatically.

The Commission's alternative strategy was designed to provide the same amount of electricity to consumers as did the official projection. A rise in primary energy demand of 2 per cent was forecast. The prediction was for a slight slowing of economic growth in Britain from the 2.7 per cent per annum recently to 2.5 per cent between now and 2000 and thereafter to 1.5 per cent. However, in spite of this modest diminution in overall economic activity, energy supply for the average person would be affected little if at all. By 2000 AD a rigorous policy of energy conservation should be in operation and the projected stabilization or decline of the UK's population would also have a beneficial effect.

The Government's Green Paper of early 1978[1] was the official reply to the Commission's report. It was critical of the alternative energy stategy, particularly beyond the year 2000. The Commission's predilection for CHP systems was considered to be unjustifiable because of the widespread dislocation which it was claimed would be caused in introducing them into heavily populated urban areas. The Commission was 'optimistic' if it supposed that fast breeder reactors could be avoided indefinitely. Future costs for renewable resources were completely unknown, their methodology often obscure and inchoate, their economic cutting edge when compared with atomic fission impossible to predict. Although the Green Paper indicated that the Government had now come round to the view that a dynamic and sustained programme of energy conservation was mandatory, its overall response to the Commission's report was still sceptical, full of doubts as to whether the alternative energy strategy outlined would meet its targets.

The Windscale Inquiry,[2] concerned with the request by British

Nuclear Fuels to build a new reprocessing plant in Cumbria, provided a good opportunity for alternative energy scenarios to be aired. One of the most comprehensive of these was provided by Dr Peter Chapman of the Open University in Milton Keynes. The burden of Chapman's argument was that the energy gap predicted by the Government was chimerical. It was based on an unrealistically high demand for fuel supplies, and it did not take into account society's capacity to adapt to a rapidly changing situation. The fact that the real price of energy was destined to increase markedly between now and 2000 would notably decrease demand; so would a broadly based energy conservation programme; so would zero or negative population growth with stabilization of numbers at an average level of 2.5 per household. Also, the consumer market was fast approaching saturation in terms of appliances. Three-quarters of households now had a motor car, half had central heating systems, two-thirds had washing machines, 95 per cent had television sets and 80 per cent had refrigerators. Chapman was much impressed with the prognosis for coal in the UK. Coal was the only major long-term source of hydrocarbon fuel and as such would undoubtedly be widely used in the steel and chemical industries. It was the best source of SNG, a fuel easily transportable and readily stored; it could be used to produce electricity for CHP stations, particularly in areas of high population density. Solar energy would find other uses, mainly in domestic space heating and in the provision of hot water; solar technologies like flat plate collectors and storage devices were expensive now but would become increasingly cost-effective. Wave energy looked particularly promising in Britain. Once installed, wave machines would provide electricity cheaply, and their environmental impact might well be less than had been previously predicted. As the petroleum era drew to its close alternative fuels for transport must increasingly be sought. Electric vehicles could be expected to come into wide use in the twenty-first century provided, of course, that the technology of high-energy batteries could be improved and that the latter could be manufactured on a commercial scale.

The overall energy scenario envisaged by Chapman for 2025 had coal, oil and solar power in pivotal positions. Primary electricity would be derived mainly from waves, tides, wind and hydropower. But a nuclear component equivalent to 50 MTCE* per year was also included, the installed capacity being about 25 GW. In Chapman's

* MTCE = million tons coal equivalent.

view an energy mixture of this type would have numerous advantages. It had a high degree of flexibility, readily permitting the substitution of one source for another; it allowed for a general programme of energy conservation; it would probably be highly cost-effective. But most important of all, by markedly reducing the nuclear component, the scenario would lessen the well-known risks associated with the plutonium economy.

The wide scope for energy saving in Britain has frequently been stressed in recent years and the environmentalists at Windscale made it a major rubric of their case. They demanded that elegance and parsimony in managing demand replace the present policy of blind expansion of supply. More than one-quarter of the nation's energy production currently went into people's homes. Houses were 'energy-guzzlers' on a gargantuan scale; only $1\frac{1}{2}$ million of Britain's 20 million homes were properly insulated; compared with other Western Europeans the British lived in houses which were near the bottom of the 'thermal efficiency league'.

Simple and familiar measures could effect vast economies. Walls and lofts could be insulated; draught-proofing, double glazing and cavity wall infill could be insisted upon; internal temperatures could be kept at a lower level than at present. According to Gerald Leach of the International Institute for Environment and Development in London, the adoption of such measures in typical post-war semi-detached houses (currently 30 per cent of total UK housing stock) would reduce the overall heating demand by over 80 per cent; in typical Victorian three-storey houses the savings would be even greater. Quite apart from insulation, new technological procedures – fluidized-bed heating equipment, electric or directly-fired heat pumps, solar water heating and, in the longer term, photovoltaic devices – would greatly reduce home fuel consumption. A vigorous conservationist policy pursued in the domestic sector alone could reduce Britain's primary fuel consumption by 15 per cent, and would have an even greater effect on the consumption of electricity.

Positive incentives to householders to improve their insulation should be stepped up. The precise form could differ – Government grants, tax relief, interest-free loans. Building societies might also consider withholding loans on properties with poor insulation and might make loans available specifically for domestic conservation measures.

Buildings outside the domestic sector – a highly diverse group including offices, shops, factories and hospitals – consume about 12 per cent of Britain's primary fuels and huge amounts of electricity. Less is known about the heat loss for which they are responsible but it can be safely assumed that their profligacy is spectactular. Again, major savings in this area could be achieved quite simply by 'good housekeeping' involving the use of measures such as reduction of lighting load, regulation of heating systems by day and night, improved thermal insulation, and much more rigorous temperature control through the use of heat pumps. In 1977 representatives from the Department of Industry visited 2,000 factories in Britain in order to investigate their energy practices. They estimated that a cost saving of over £400m per annum – nearly 10 per cent of the annual rate of industry's fixed capital investment – could be achieved by the use of simple and straightforward energy conservation technologies like those outlined above. A Government which had pledged itself to reducing national energy consumption by the year 2000 to a point 20 per cent lower than what it might otherwise have been given a continuation of the trends of the early 'seventies, should certainly be prepared to provide powerful incentives to industry to insulate its premises. Even more importantly it should ensure that all new buildings, whether commercial or domestic, should be insulated to the highest possible standard. The life of buildings is long and therefore it is urgent that action be taken now.

Transport absorbs about 15 per cent of the British energy budget; more importantly, it accounts for one-quarter of the total demand for oil. Improvements in motor car design could undoubtedly effect considerable energy savings. They include the manufacture of lighter vehicles and smaller petrol engines capable of operating on weaker mixtures, introduction of radial tyres, the phasing out of automatic transmission and its replacement by four-speed manual gear boxes. Fuel consumption by aircraft would also have to be scrutinized. Improvements in aerofoil design would be helpful; so would reduction in aircraft size, the fitting of auxiliary surfaces to wing tips, lowering of cruising speeds and on short-haul routes the reintroduction of turbo-prop machines.

In a further study, Leach and his colleagues concentrated on energy demand and conservation. They argued that 'official' energy forecasts grossly overrated future energy needs in Britain. They maintained that the Government need order no new power stations in the next decade; the fast breeder reactor was a costly irrelevance; indeed the whole nuclear power industry in Britain should be gradually run down and eventually dispensed with. The changes required included energy saving in industry, better insulation in houses, fewer energy-consumptive cars, the setting of realistic thermal standards for new houses and offices. Consumerism and the 'good life' need not be seriously affected, the authors argued. GDP could rise steadily; people could own more cars; domestic appurtenances need not necessarily be reduced in number.

Interest in alternative energy sources in Britain has waxed since the Yom Kippur War of 1973. Ideas in this area are very precious. They must win our fealty as well as our attention for upon them will largely depend the life-styles which we shall enjoy in the post-petroleum era.

A Select Committee of the House of Commons, reporting in 1977, argued that solar energy was the most pressing field for investigation in Britain. The cost of solar water heating could be reduced quickly and dramatically by manufacturing systems in bulk. Work should be commissioned immediately to develop suitable designs for buildings so that the use of solar energy could be maximized, and solar heat pumps should be speedily introduced into industry and domestically.

The Committee also gave strong support to wave power. The seas around Britain are amongst the best endowed in the world with this form of energy, the sites of greatest potential being the Atlantic Ocean to the west of the Outer Hebrides, the east coast of Scotland and north and south of the Cornish peninsula. Wave and solar power are, of course, directly complimentary, the former being at its peak during the winter months and coinciding with the highest demand for electricity.

The Committee concluded that wave power had the potential of contributing to the energy mixture to the tune of 150 MTCE by 2025. Various devices for the production of wave power are currently being tested and amongst these the Salter duck has been widely publicized. It is a cam-shaped device oscillating round a 'spine', it drives hydraulic compressors and is claimed to have a high degree of efficiency. 'Contouring rafts', devised by Sir Christopher Cockerell, are being sponsored by his company, Wavepower Ltd. There is also interest in oscillating water columns originally designed in Japan, and in a box-like structure known as the 'Russell Wave Rectifier' which is divided into high and low level reservoirs. The National Engineering Laboratory recently assessed the future of wave power. It was not wildly enthusiastic, maintaining that even if the immediate technical problems in harnessing the energy were solved costs are likely to remain very high.

Interest in tidal power in Britain has centred mainly on the Severn estuary which is believed to account for about two-thirds of the 30,000 million KWh per year potentially obtainable from UK tidal waters. Such a total, if ever reached, would represent 15 per cent of the current annual level of electricity generation and would produce a highly significant saving of fossil fuels, particularly oil and natural gas. But a Severn barrage would encounter difficulties similar to those of tidal power schemes elsewhere in the world. Capital costs for installation would be high; generating capacity is dependent on the lunar cycle and is therefore fluctuant; there could be baneful ecological effects including a radical modification in the tidal regime of the estuary and possible changes in siltation patterns.

A cogent argument for the widespread use of wind power in the UK has been made by the Astronomer Royal, Sir Martin Ryle. Wind power is the most highly developed of alternative energy sources in Britain, and Ryle considers that it will remain cheaper than wave energy, at least for the foreseeable future. The construction of wind generators of 1 megawatt capacity in coastal areas and in shallow offshore waters is recommended. If a sufficient number of these machines were built they could produce more energy than that projected by the Department of Energy for nuclear power by the year 2000. Also the technology for wind power has a much shorter lead time than that for atomic fission and therefore the energy could be made available more rapidly. Economics are said to be favourable, running costs being only about one-third of the nuclear alternative. Ryle admits that the visual impact of wind generators could not be avoided. But he considers that the overall environmental effect would be less damaging than that produced by large numbers of atomic stations with their ugly and disfiguring concomitants.

Ryle recommends that work begin immediately in Britain on a large prototype wind generator. The Department of Energy is castigated for its parsimony in this area compared with the largesse which it has heaped on the nuclear industry. The Electrical Research Institute has so far identified 1,500 sites, most of them in Scotland, with appropriate wind speeds, and the Energy Technology Research Unit of the Department of Energy has put the upper limit for a fully developed wind power programme at 10,000 generators each rating at 1 megawatt. Such a programme, if it ever became operative, would conserve fossil fuels to the extent of 7 MTCE annually.

The potential of peat in making a contribution to electricity generation in the UK is now receiving serious attention. About 10 per cent of the land surface in Scotland – more than $1\frac{1}{2}$ million acres – is covered by peat bog. Peat is already being used to generate electricity in other countries, particularly in the Republic of Ireland, Finland, the Soviet Union and Federal Germany. In Britain there is a growing feeling that peat is a neglected natural resource. Peter Dryburgh of Edinburgh University is one who believes that the UK could readily develop a fully integrated industry based on peat. Electricity generation, albeit important, would be only one facet of the programme, for peat is a versatile material useful in other areas such as gardening and horticulture. Moreover, a plenitude of products can be manufactured from peat, including insulation boarding, peat wax and activated carbon. Reclamation of the basal soil when the peat is removed is obviously of paramount importance and there is great potential here to make the reclaimed land available for agriculture and afforestation.

Governmentally-inspired documents about Britain's energy scenario contain many references to the positive correlation that exists between high material living standards on the one hand and increased energy consumption on the other. Yet such a link is tenuous to say the least of it. A corpus of evidence from international sources does not support it, and much informed opinion throughout the world now rejects the concept that Gross Domestic Product *per se* has much to do with welfare. The economist E. J. Mishan was amongst the first to assail this facet of the conventional wisdom. In his *Costs of Economic Growth* [3] Mishan spelled out the myriad of factors which destroy life's quality yet nevertheless may contribute to a rising GDP. They include the carnage on the roads due to the Mephistophelian activities of the automobile and the resultant increase in the workload provided for surgeons, undertakers and grave diggers, tobacco smoking with its attendant high mortality, the pillage of historic buildings and their replacement by roads, supermarkets and other forms of 'development', and the heedless use of energy resources in attempting to move more people and goods around in an ever more congested milieu.

In 1978 the then Energy Secretary Tony Benn entered the futures debate by providing likely estimates of Britain's energy mixture at the turn of the century. Expressed in MTCE his prediction was for coal 170, nuclear power and hydroelectricity 95, natural gas 50-90, indigenous oil 150, renewable sources 10. How Mr Benn will fare as a futurologist remains to be seen but certainly at present there is everything to be said for keeping all the energy options open and avoiding precipitate and irrevocable decisions. An energy policy, like any other edifice, is mainly bricks and there is as yet no consensus of view regarding its ingredients. Specialists are in open opposition one with another; generalists are equally split. Moreover, the strength of public opposition to some of the ideas being bruited around should not be underestimated. Coal mining in the Vale of Belvoir will be bitterly resented on environmental grounds; gas processing in Fife at Mossmorran is receiving increasing opprobrium. Nothing is more likely to incense the local populace than the suggestion that long lived radioactive wastes might be stored in their vicinity; opposition to the building of the nuclear power station at Torness in East Lothian could lead to a degree of civil disobedience not seen in Britain since the time of the suffragettes.

Little mention has so far been made of North Sea oil. As an environmentalist of over ten years standing I cannot end this section of the chapter without a threnody for it. Britain could gain lasting and immeasurable benefit from this uniquely valuable resource. But only if it is treated with the care and circumspection which it merits, only if the depletion rate is slow instead of proceeding with frenzied haste, only if something like the Norwegian paradigm is adopted whereby a strict annual ceiling is put on the recovery of reserves. Such a policy would have profound historical significance. It would buy the time for Britain to build a truly sustainable future, a future in which nuclear power would wither and die because there would be no need to nourish it, a future in which alternative energy sources could blossom and energy conservation become *de rigueur*.

The reality, however, is very different. Britain is in the course of squandering her geological heritage in a little more than two decades. The passing breeze of electoral expediency cannot be resisted; nor can the rosy vision which self-sufficiency in oil will provide for a brief period in the early 1980s. Nothing short of a miracle can now prevent the rapid exploitation of the British sector of the North Sea. For the policy has become a fashionable and pervasive orthodoxy, enshrined in all the energy scenarios quoted, supreme in academic circles, woven into the warp and the woof of parliamentary and legislative thinking.

A comparison can be made between North Sea oil and Spanish bullion. During the sixteenth and seventeenth centuries gold and silver flowed massively into Imperial Spain from flourishing ports in her American colonies – from Vera Cruz in Spanish North America, from Cartagena in Colombia, from Ammatique and Truxillo in Honduras, from Port Belo in Panama, from Callao in Peru. Between 1503 and 1595 there was a steady accretion in the receipts from the treasure, but during the first thirty years of the seventeenth century the picture changed. A vertiginous fall in the receipts took place and by 1700 they had shrunk to a mere trickle. Effects of the treasure on the Motherland had been far short of expectations. The great Spanish inflation had been fueled; an illusion of prosperity had been created and had fostered life-styles characterized by profligacy and extravagance; a gross maldistribution of wealth within society remained a prominent feature. The nation's economic vitality had been sapped; with all the treasure of the New World at her disposal Spain remained a poor country, just as Britain is today among the developed nations of the earth.

What judgement will historians of the next century pronounce on the political leaders in Britain in the 'seventies and 'eighties who presided over the exploitation of North Sea oil? Will they laud them for seizing the opportunity provided by the oil revenues to reduce taxes, attenuate inflation, pay off foreign debts and prop up traditional heavy industries? Or, as I fear is more likely, will they compare them to the rulers of Imperial Spain, castigate them for their Panglossian optimism, deride their *carpe diem* nonchalance and impugn them for their readiness to trade what is most precious for short-term gain?

The reaction of the French Government to the Arab oil embargo of 1973 was one of 'nuclear retaliation'. France embarked on a vigorous national programme of nuclear expansion with the American-built pressurized water reactor as its epicentre. When her domestic market faltered in the middle of the decade she became an aggressive vendor of atomic hardware throughout the world, often to politically sensitive nations. France is now the archetypal nuclear hard-liner; her nuclear programme is unrolling inexorably and seems the quintessence of singlemindedness. The President, Giscard d'Estaing, ignores his mounting anti-nuclear lobby or dismisses it with a few delphic phrases stressing national sovereignty and defence needs. Prestigious ecologists are derided by the French Establishment; 'green' candidates at elections are castigated and pilloried by conventional parties of left and right.

In 1974 the French Government announced that by 2000 AD the country would have 200 atomic reactors operating at fifty different sites. By late 1976 ten plants were in operation and the total generating capacity was 3,000 megawatts; 1981 should see thirty-two reactors with the megawattage increased eightfold. The plutonium economy has been embraced *à toute outrance* in governmental circles. This, of course, includes the fast breeder reactor, and currently a plant for commercial use – the Super Phénix Surrégénérateur – is being constructed at Creys Malville on the banks of the Rhône.

As early as 1970 an anti-nuclear lobby emerged in France and gatherings and sit-ins at proposed nuclear sites became almost routine. In 1971 there were 1,000 demonstrators at Fessenheim and 10,000 at Belgey; in 1973 Paris, Strasbourg, Toulouse and Montpelier staged anti-nuclear protests. In 1975 the 'appeal of the 400' was issued: a group of well-known scientists demanded a moratorium on the construction of further domestic power plants until the public were given the opportunity of debating the risks involved. Meanwhile demonstrations continued, and they showed an increasing propensity for violence, the latter reaching its apogee at Creys Malville in mid-1977 when ugly scenes erupted and *les forces d'ordre* behaved with a brutality seldom seen in Western Europe since the end of the Second World War.

Initially the nuclear debate in France was concerned with reactor safety and with the necessity for adequate consultation with the populace before a decision was taken to site a plant. But soon broader issues emerged and rapidly moved towards the centre of the stage. What was the governmental philosophy behind the nuclear programme? Was the Government prepared to face up to threats of terrorism and sabotage – similar to those already perpetrated at atomic plants at Fessenheim and in Finistère? Had the Government envisioned the possibility that paramilitary forces would be required to ensure the safety of nuclear materials in transit to atomic reactors? Was there not a possibility that the Fifth Republic might dissolve in a totalitarian imbroglio as a result of the Government's nuclear policy?

Environmentalists soon began to seek allies. They found common ground with pacifists, being able to draw upon experience of the latter in tactics of non-violent civil disobedience. They became much more politically conscious and began to contest elections at both local and national level, a trend which will certainly continue in the future. The environmentalist movement in France is slowly gaining ground, and when *Le Monde* ran a public oponion poll in 1977 80 per cent of those questioned took the view that ecology should have as important a place in educational curricula as do history and geography.

However, nuclear opponents in France will have great difficulty in bringing the Government to heel. They have only two alternatives at their disposal – to build a much stronger political base which will attract dissidents from conventional parties of right, centre and left, or markedly to raise the tempo of civil disobedience with presumably an ever increasing propensity for violence and social upheaval. The Constitution of the Fifth Republic looks askance at protest lobbies. The Government has a whole panoply of the legal authority whereby it can impose a nuclear programme if it wishes; checks and balances in the system are virtually non-existent; central planning decisions are sacrosanct and are not subject to public debate. Ultimately, if the anti-nuclear lobby persists with its activities, the whole constitutional order will inevitably be called into question.

Nuclear protagonists in France place much emphasis on the poverty of the country's other energy resources. Coal reserves are limited, probably not exceeding 1.4 billion tons, of which 0.8 billion are thought to be recoverable. French coal mines could at a stretch produce about 20 million tons a year until the late 1980s. But most of the coal is already earmarked for steam generation and coal required for other purposes, particularly for manufacturing steel, would have to be imported.

France has miniscule oil reserves, amounting to less than one per cent of the country's total demand. Drilling for oil is in progress in the Channel and in the Mediterranean Sea but the likelihood of substantial finds is small. On the other hand oil shale deposits in France are by no means negligible. In the Parisian region alone recoverable reserves are believed to contain about 1 billion tons of oil. However, the now familiar economic and ecological constraints dictate that the exploitation of shales in France will be difficult and it is unlikely to be undertaken to any marked extent in the foreseeable future.

Reserves of natural gas in France are only marginally more plentiful than those of oil. They are thought to amount to about 300 billion cubic metres and production is now running at some 10 million cubic metres annually. This level could probably be maintained till the early 'eighties but thereafter a reduction seems certain. In contrast to countries like the USSR French natural gas reserves are unlikely to be used in power plants, precedence being given to heating business premises and homes.

Exploitation of hydropower in France has been in full swing for several years. By 1972 hydropower was producing 58 TWh annually; by 1985, given further development, the total could reach 63 TWh, by 2000 70 TWh. La Rance in Britanny was the first tidal power installation in the world and is still the largest. However, since its completion in 1966 the scale of operation has been disappointingly small with a maximum output capacity of only 240 MW. The French Government has commissioned the construction of a new tidal plant at Mont Saint Michel but the project has not yet come to fruition.

French geothermal power is far from negligible; low and medium temperature energy from 'hot rocks' is available and the maximum output from French fields has been put at 20 MTOE. Geothermal power is currently being utilized directly to heat the studios and offices of ORTF, the television network in Paris. France is no stranger to solar power. Investigations on it began as early as 1949 when searchlight mirrors were used at Mont Louis to trap the sun's rays, and temperatures as high as 3000°C were attained. Research and development on solar energy and its variants is now being funded in France on a fairly generous scale. Moreover the Government has at last demonstrated some awareness of the potential of alternative energy sources by creating a new position entitled Delegate for New Energies (*Délégué aux Energies Nouvelles*) whose function is to co-ordinate research and development in this general area.

In spite of making ritual obeisance to alternative sources of power, France is being irresistibly propelled along a hard energy path. Nevertheless, within the straitjacket which such a policy imposes, considerable alterations in the energy mixture are projected between now and the late 1980s. By then the percentage of the total energy budget provided by oil is scheduled to have fallen from 65 to 40; coal will have dropped from 17 to 12, hydropower will remain static at about 6, gas imports are expected to rise, bringing its share up to 10 per cent. However, the most spectacular change will relate to nuclear fission power which is scheduled to rise no less than eightfold – from a current 3 per cent of total energy supply to a staggering 25 per cent. It is salutary to reflect that this momentous alteration is due to take place in less than ten years from now.

In 1979 Federal Germany still has one of the strongest economies in the world. The Deutschmark is riding high; inflation and joblessness have been contained; living standards continue to rise, albeit more slowly than in the past. An almost embarrassingly large balance of payments surplus exists. The Federal Republic's EEC partners with weaker economies – Italy, Britain and Ireland – are continually uttering fulsome panegyrics to German competitiveness and efficiency.

Yet the whole edifice of German prosperity could well be built on quicksands. Energy could rapidly become her Achilles heel just as is likely in other industrialized nations such as Japan, France and the USA. German's indigenous fuel supplies are modest except for coal. Middle Eastern oil has an ephemerality which must be giving politicians in Bonn sleepless nights. Above all the programme of nuclear expansion on which the Federal Government has put such stress is under acute political and environmentalist pressure and has had to be massively scaled down.

Even before the Yom Kippur War the German Government had decided that the growth of future energy supplies and the maintenance of high living standards could only be met through a 'forward' programme based on nuclear fission. In 1973 atomic power was meeting only 1 per cent of primary energy consumption. A radical change was called for. The Government decided that by 1985 nuclear capacity had to rise massively and should be generating between 45,000 and 50,000 megawatts. By then 15 per cent of primary energy consumption and 4.5 per cent of installed electrical capacity should be based on the atom, the American-manufactured light water reactor being the main vehicle. Meanwhile, research and development on other types of plant was to be actively pursued. A large fast breeder should be constructed at Kalkar and would be operative by 1983; a high temperature reactor with thorium as the basis of its fuel cycle was to be commissioned at Schiehausen and should be ready at about the same time. The German nuclear industry purred with contentment; a quantum leap into technical change was in sight and an all-nuclear future for the Federal Republic in the twenty-first century seemed assured.

Politicians in Bonn also began to take an increasing interest in the reprocessing of spent nuclear fuel. The electricity industry was instructed to draw up plans for a nuclear fuel complex at Gorbelen in Lower Saxony. The plant would be larger than that proposed for Windscale by British Nuclear Fuels and would have better facilities for the storage of long-lived radioactive wastes. The future availability of enriched uranium was also considered. Currently this material was being obtained mainly from the USA and South Africa. The Government was now determined to build its own enrichment plant and to utilize within it either the centrifuge technique which Germany had developed in association with the UK and the Netherlands or the fluid separation procedure which had originated in the Federal Republic and was now being utilized routinely in South Africa.

However, the nuclear euphoria in Germany has been of short duration. The Government has failed to take into account the widespread environmentalist opposition which had started in 1973 in rather limited form but mounted rapidly in the ensuing years. 'Citizen's groups', drawn from a wide spectrum of society and even including some members of the Bundestag, began to form all over the country. The movement started to flex its muscles and to show its mettle at sites of proposed nuclear constructions, particularly at Wyhl, Brokdorf and Grohnde. The effect at Wyhl was especially notable. Official approval had been given to proceed with the construction of a plant as early as 1974. The opposition used as its touchstone damage to local vineyards and when site prepartions started in 1975 local people occupied the area. Soon after, a large demonstration erupted in which police used dogs and water cannons to disperse the protesters. The scene now shifted to the court at Frieburg where the judge, taking due note of the intensity of the opposition, ruled that construction at Wyhl should not proceed until more elaborate safety precautions, including the encasement of the main reactor in a further six feet of concrete, had been considered. The court decision about the reactor at Brokdorf was even more far-reaching because it precluded further building at the site until the 'safe processing and storage of nuclear waste' had been assured.

The environmentalist lobby was gaining ground in Germany. By the end of 1977 installed nuclear capacity in the Federal Republic was much less than predicted four years earlier – a mere 6,500 MW

with a further 14,000 MW under construction. Pro-nuclear politicians in Bonn were ruefully admitting that if by 1985 total nuclear
generating capacity exceeded 30,000 MW the country would be very
fortunate indeed. Apocalyptic statements filled the air. An 'energy
gap' was now inevitable by the mid or late 'eighties; Middle Eastern
oil could not plug the dyke; nor could Dutch natural gas which had
already been squandered with extreme profligacy by the Netherlands
Government. Fuel rationing was a distinct possibility; economic
growth rates could shrink to less than 1 per cent per annum; joblessness would proliferate – so much so that the current figure of 1 million
unemployed would seem almost utopian in retrospect. Worst of all,
with living standards plummeting, social peace might not be maintained; draconian measures might be needed to enforce law and
order; the whole fabric of State authority might come under challenge and could collapse like a pack of cards.

The anti-nuclear lobby in the Federal Republic is better placed
constitutionally than in France. The West German Constitution,
modelled on the US pattern, is less *dirigiste* and more decentralized
than its French counterpart, making it more difficult for the Government to force a nuclear programme on a reluctant citizenry. Also all
the major political parties in West Germany – Social Democrats,
Christian Democrats and Free Democrats – are split on the nuclear
issue. In the long term some form of compromise between pro- and
anti-nuclear elements seems more probable in the Federal Republic
than in France, provided violence can be contained and the situation
can be prevented from spiralling out of control.

The only indigenous energy source present in West Germany in
reasonable quantity is coal. Coal has some strong supporters, and one
optimistic report goes so far as to suggest that it could meet the
country's entire energy needs for seventy-five years and that it could
do so without a serious fall in living standards. However, as in the rest
of western Europe, the saga of coal in the Federal Republic is of an
industry in relentless decline. In 1956 150 million tons were mined,
twenty years later the figure had plummeted to 90. In 1967 hard coal
accounted for 36 per cent of the country's primary energy; by 1976
this figure had been halved.

Belated attempts are now being made to revitalize the German coal
industry. With the Government's target of 30,000 MW of nuclear
capacity by 1985 becoming increasingly chimerical, imported oil and
gas becoming scarcer, more expensive and more politically sensitive

(especially following recent events in Iran), coal-fired capacity has very definite attractions, and during 1978 an agreement was reached between the electricity authorities and the coal mining industry for the supply of 30 million tons of hard coal a year for the next ten years. However, in the medium and longer term only a modest expansion of the German coal industry is feasible, and in addition to its use for electricity generation, increasing demands will be made upon it as a supplier of synthetic natural gas and oil. Also, problems associated with the revivification of a coal industry are depressingly familiar – high capital investment, ecological and social disruption, the recognition by miners that if they so desire they can apply a finger to a nation's jugular. Given this concatenation of circumstances, together with the all-too-obvious reluctance of most German politicians to take soft energy paths seriously and until very recently to proselytize for energy conservation, it can readily be appreciated why the siren song of nuclear fission has been sounding so loud and clear in governmental circles in the Federal Republic throughout most of the 'seventies.

NOTES AND REFERENCES

[1] *Energy Policy* (1978).
[2] *The Windscale Inquiry* (1978).
[3] E. J. Mishan (1967), *Costs of Economic Growth*, Staples Press, London.

Chapter 7

Perspectives on the Soviet Union

No event of the twentieth century has been more passionately debated than the Russian Revolution of 1917. It saw the emergence of a man, V. I. Lenin, who was quite exceptional by any standards. It established the Communist International, unique as a worldwide political movement; it gave grounds for the belief that at last the socialist millennium was about to dawn.

But the vision was ephemeral. The idealism soon evaporated and the promised land of liberty receded. Under the paranoid and despotic leadership of J. V. Stalin, Soviet Russia became an embattled, intensely nationalistic worker's state, brutalized, often hungry, ruthlessly conformist. This is not to deny the dramatic achievements of the Stalin era, particularly in the field of industrial production. But the achievements came at a terrible cost in human terms. Violence, repression and death became the accepted tools of politics. Sadism proliferated, cruelty prospered, vengeance against old colleagues ran rampant. All reached their apogee during the Great Terror and the notorious purge trials of the late 1930s and were perpetuated in the enormities of the Gulag system so vividly portrayed in the writings of Alexander Solzhenitsyn.

Sixty-two years after the Revolution the Soviet Union is accepted as a Superpower. She can be seen to have transformed a backward continent into a modern industrialized state. She houses 7 per cent of the world's population, possesses a plethora of natural resources, accounts for one-fifth of the earth's industrial output, is a leader in space research and modern forms of transportation. Above all, she boasts a military machine of awesome technical sophistication, enabling her to influence *realpolitik* in every corner of the planet.

Ambiguity about Russia's global intentions remain, and the enigmatic nature of her foreign policy will assuredly dominate the history of the final two decades of the twentieth century. Violently opposing viewpoints exist.[1] Some people believe that the Soviet Union has altered out of all recognition since Stalin's death. Russia, they say, is no longer basically hostile and dangerous, for it is led by men who are experienced, pacific, sagacious and moderate. Such individuals regard collaboration between the Superpowers as both feasible and timely, and they frequently castigate US 'military enthusiasts' still obsessed with an alleged armed threat from Russia and besotted with anticommunism.

The anti-Soviet view is based on a belief that the changes which have taken place in the USSR since the 1950s have been neither meaningful nor substantive. Proponents of this viewpoint believe that the central mechanisms of the state are much the same in 1979 as during the worst era of Stalinism; indeed that they differ only marginally from those created by Lenin in 1918. The Soviet leadership continues to stamp on pluralism and freedom. The power of the Politburo remains absolute; normal constitutional restraints do not exist; neither is there any control through popular representation. The citizen is the property of the state; the workman cannot strike. Peasants do not own their land and can only keep an exiguous part of the produce which they garner from it. Soviet foreign policy, far from being cautious and pacific, is both opportunistic and adventurist. During the Brezhnev years Czechoslovakia has been invaded, China and Romania threatened, a pro-Soviet Government has seized power in Angola, and the flames of war have been fed in the Horn of Africa. Supporters of this viewpoint are currently uttering dire predictions about Soviet intervention in Iran following the departure of the Shah.

The futures debate has a fascination for the Soviet politicians.[2] Although futurology as a term is frowned upon as being 'non-scientific', long-range forecasting (*prognozirovanie*) is evoking increasing attention amongst Marxist-Leninist ideologues, particularly in military circles. In contrast to the Western world where the future is often viewed in sombre terms, where constraints on economic growth are accepted by sentient people as inescapable, and where neo-Malthusian predictions about the population-food dilemma have gained wide credence, Soviet projections are invariably optimistic and frequently utopian. The contemporary world is painted in glowing terms: the outlook for mankind has never been brighter. The supreme objective of Soviet policy remains what it has always been since the Revolution – the creation of the 'material and technical basis of communism'. The objective is just as important to Leonid Brezhnev in 1979 as it was to Lenin in 1918, to Stalin in 1930, to Krushchev in 1960; and in order to attain this goal production must be seen to be continually expanding. How therefore can an economic philosophy embodying limits to growth have any appeal to the ortho-dox Marxist-Leninist? How can he look with favour on the transition to a more sustainable type of society? For his ideology maintains that the planet's natural resources still provide a huge reserve for develop-ment and that the only point at issue is how this development is to be directed and managed.

Two themes will concern us here. First the Soviet population scenario for the remainder of the century will be reviewed.[3] In the second part of the chapter consideration will be given to the Kremlin's policy in relation to mineral resources.[4]

In 1979 just under 400 million people are living in the seven countries of the Eastern bloc – Bulgaria, Czechoslovakia, the German Demo-cratic Republic, Hungary, Poland, Romania and the USSR. The population of the bloc exceeds that of the EEC by 110 million, North America by 130 million, Latin America by 30 million. Eastern bloc countries have three times more people than Japan, six times more than Britain, about half that of the world's most populous country, China.

The Soviet Union is by far the most heavily populated member of the bloc, accounting for over 70 per cent of the total. Two highly significant trends have dominated Russian demography in recent years – the overall decline in national fertility paralleling that in other developed nations, and the increasing proportion of total births taking place in Asiatic Russia, particularly in the Republics of Central Asia and the Transcaucasus.

The decline in fertility has been in full swing for almost two decades. The Soviet birth rate in 1960 was 25 per 1,000; by 1964 it had plummeted to 18.4, by 1975 it was 18.0 In 1959 the rate of natural increase of the population was 17.4 per 1,000. By 1965 it was down to 11.1 and during the 'seventies it has continued to fall, reach-ing 8.8 per 1,000 by the second half of the decade.

This overall picture must not be allowed to obscure the important regional variations that exist in Soviet fertility. Demographically speaking the USSR can be viewed as two nations. The Slavic-European part of the country, together with Siberia and the Far East, is experiencing a rapid decline in fertility. But in the southern tier inhabited mainly by a mosaic of nationalities mainly of Islamic origin, the population profile, with falling death rates and continuing high birth rates, is reminscent of that of a developing country in the second stage of the demographic transition.

Projections to the end of the century suggest that this discrepancy will deepen. In 1970 in the Baltic Republics – Estonia, Latvia and Lithuania – the birth rate was 16.2 and the rate of natural increase 6.1 per 1,000; the corresponding figures projected to 2000 AD are 13.5 and 1.7. The birth rate in Belorussia in 1970 was 16.2 and the rate of natural increase 8.6; the projections for thirty years later are 14 and 4 respectively. The large sprawling land mass constituting the Russian Soviet Federated Socialist Republic had a birth rate of 14.6 in 1970; this is projected to fall to 12.4 by 2000 AD. In the Ukraine the projected figure for the end of the century is 12.8 compared with 15.2 thirty years previously.

The figures contrast vividly with the situation likely to prevail in the Transcaucasian Republics – Georgia, Armenia, Azerbaijan – in Kazakhstan (the celebrated Virgin Lands of the Krushchev era) and in the Central Asian Republics of Uzbekistan, Turkmenia, Kirghizia and Tadzhikistan. The Transcaucasian birth rate in 1970 was 23.9 per 1,000 and the rate of natural increase 17.4. Projections for 2000 suggest that both these indices will remain high – 21.1 and 14.2 per 1,000 respectively. The contrast with Baltic and Slavic Russia is even more pronounced when the Central Asian Republics are considered. The projected birth rate for 2000 in that area is 34 per 1,000 and the rate of natural increase spectacularly high (20 per 1,000). According to one prestigious Soviet demographer, the average mother in Tadzhikistan during her lifetime is likely to bear three times as many children as her counterpart in Latvia.

Massive migration out of the Central Asian Republics to Slavic Russia would, of course, go far to mitigate the country's present and future ethnic imbalance. But there is no evidence that such a change is taking place for, although internal migration has been a notable feature of the Soviet demographic scene in recent years, such migration has tended to be within rather than between republics. Siberia has been painted by the Soviet leadership in glowing terms as a area of dazzling prospects, a veritable El Dorado with virtually unlimited natural resources. Migration into Siberia from all parts of the Soviet

Union has been actively encouraged and by 2000 AD the area is scheduled to house 100 million people. But the dream and the reality are far apart. By the early 'seventies the population of Siberia had reached a mere 26 million, and in the absence of draconian measures to enforce migration – a policy which seems unlikely in the post-Stalinist era – numbers of *Sibiryaks* are unlikely to exceed 35 million by the end of the century.

The changing demographic pattern of the USSR will undoubtedly have a profound impact. Already the regional differentials in fertility are producing ripples throughout the whole country, and the ripples will grow larger as the century reaches its close. Ethnic Russians, currently constituting 53 per cent of the population and concentrated mainly in the west of the country, are fearful lest their traditional hegemony is eroded. Their anxiety is not misplaced. For by the final years of the century the iron laws of demography will dictate that Slavs will be in a minority and that non-Slavic people – of Moslem, Armenian, and a whole variety of other backgrounds – will have attained numerical ascendancy.

But it is in relation to labour shortages and to the manpower situation for the armed services that the Kremlin finds current demographic trends most worrisome. During the 1980s the overall rate of increase of the labour force is unlikely to be maintained, and in the 1990s, although the pace of recruitment may rise slightly, it will still not match the situation of twenty years previously. During the 'eighties the increase in able-bodied citizens from Central Asia, Kazakhstan and the Transcaucasus will exceed that for the Soviet Union as a whole, while between now and 2000 the relative contribution of these areas to the national increase in the working population will be much higher than it was in the 'seventies. With the Slavic population the trend will be the reverse, the net contribution of the RSFSR to the labour force decreasing from 1980 onwards and that of the Baltic states after 1990.

There is every indication that the Soviet Politburo and the Communist Party are seriously concerned about the future of the country's civilian labour force both as regards industry and agriculture. In the latter the percentage employed is still much higher than in the West. But it is declining rapidly; so much so that by the mid-'seventies fewer than 30 per cent of the total number of civilians employed were in agriculture as compared with over 50 per cent in 1950. Various expedients are being considered to cope with labour force problems, and these received much prominence in the Tenth Five-Year Plan (1976-1980). An acceleration in the growth of labour productivity is demanded; increased mechanization is recommended; heavy manual work should be gradually phased out and policies designed to restrict the growth of employment in certain areas are receiving urgent attention. Since the early 'seventies foreign labour, derived mainly but not exclusively from other Eastern bloc countries, has been imported in an attempt to deal with the continuous bottlenecks which, in spite of omnipresent planning, continue to bedevil the Soviet economy. Bulgars, Czechs, East Germans and Poles have been constructing a pulp and paper complex in Eastern Siberia. North Koreans are cutting timber in the Khabarovsk Kray, while Finns and Italians are building industrial plants at various sites. This trend is likely to continue well into the twenty-first century.

The USSR maintains the world's largest standing army – currently estimated at 4.5 million. One and a half million youths are recruited each year at the age of eighteen for a mandatory period of twenty-four months' military service. During the 'eighties the supply of eighteen-year-olds is likely to fall, reaching a nadir in 1987, and because the nadir coincides with an impending labour shortage increasingly acute competition can be expected between civilian and military sectors. Moreover the ethnic composition of the young cohorts is likely to alter. Significantly, in 1975 17 per cent of them came from the five Central Asia Republics including Kazakhstan; by 2000 the share from that area will rise to almost 30 per cent. Many of these youths are not fluent in the Russian language, and given a situation in which manpower increments will come increasingly from non-Slavic republics, it is difficult to see how the traditional Great Russian dominance in the Soviet military can be maintained indefinitely.

At the World Population Conference in Bucharest in 1974 the Soviet delegate, in common with those from other Eastern bloc countries, minimized the global overpopulation crisis. The traditional Marxist-Leninist stance was adopted. Overpopulation was an artefact of capitalism which required 'enormous reserves of proletarians' to operate its system. 'Alarmist talk' about population problems was a capitalist plot spread by the calumniators and should be condemned. The Soviet delegate maintained that such a neo-Malthusian outlook merely diverted attention from the real social issues, particularly underdevelopment in the Third World. Explicit population policies were at best irrelevant, at worst inimical to progress. The Soviet delegate saw no need for them anywhere in the world.

Yet within the USSR itself a lively debate has been raging for years amongst demographers as to how governmental policies should impinge on population. A major point of contention concerns the extent to which family allowances and other subsidies should be paid to mothers in order to encourage child-bearing. Some population experts consider that a rising birth rate would give the Soviet Union an even more important role than at present in global affairs and for this reason actively proselytize for measures to boost it. Others, however, oppose this course of action. They argue that higher reproductive activity would reduce the number of women gainfully employed outside the home, would diminish their degree of involvement in the political process, and would run directly counter to traditional Marxist principles favouring female emancipation and women's rights.

However, neither group suggests that the liberal abortion law passed in 1955 after Stalin's death should be repealed. This is especially noteworthy when one recalls that in other Eastern bloc countries, particularly Romania, Hungary and Czechoslovakia, legislation *vis-à-vis* pregnancy termination has tended to move in a restrictive direction during the last decade. The abortion rate in the Soviet Union remains amongst the highest in the world. In the late 'sixties it was reported that 6 million abortions were being performed each year, and in 1973 in Moscow alone the figure for terminations was put at 200,000 – about the same as that for New York City which has been the pacesetter for the liberalization of the law in the USA. Repeated abortions on the same individual are said to be quite freqent in the USSR. It is obvious that the benefits of small families are clearly perceived by Russian women, particularly by those living in cities. A chronic housing shortage defies solution; economic necessity dictates that they hold down a full-time job. The Soviet medical profession, while making due obeisance to contraception, now accepts the inevitable. Doctors recognize that contraception, whether it be by Pill, cap or intrauterine device, is thinly spread and that because of its poor image vasectomy is not likely to be widely practised in the Soviet Union. For the foreseeable future, therefore, abortion will remain the preferred method of birth control.

Virtual unanimity exists amongst Soviet demographers that the gap between Islamic and non-Islamic populations should be narrowed, and that this should be achieved by increasing fertility in the

Slavic regions of the country. However, most of the available literature emanates from population experts of Russian descent who
obviously have a vested interest in advocating Slavic hegemony. Little
has so far been heard from authorities in Central Asia whose stance
one might expect to be quite different.

There is general recognition that whatever measures are adopted a
marked deceleration of population growth in Soviet Asia is highly
improbable. Therefore efforts must be made in the short and medium
term to mitigate as far as possible the effect of rapid growth of
numbers on material living standards. Rapid industrialization has
been suggested as the magic key to the future; so has a major expansion of agriculture through irrigation brought about by diverting the
course of rivers such as the Ob and the Irtysh which currently flow
into the Arctic Ocean. Migration of Islamic rural populations to
other parts of the Union would also be beneficial. But in the absence
of swingeing coercive measures this seems most unlikely because individuals born and bred in the southern tier of the country would be
exceedingly reluctant to move to the cold climate and culturally alien
atmosphere of regions such as Siberia.

The nationalities question is, of course, not new in Soviet Russia.
Indeed, immediately after the Revolution it was a major point of contention amongst the Bolshevik oligarchs. The nationalities question
will undoubtedly assume an ever-increasing dominance during the
next twenty years, vying in importance with such issues as the chronically poor Soviet agricultural performance and the maintenance of
détente. However, it is in the area of natural resources in which the
future of the USSR looks brightest and it is to this topic which we
shall now direct our attention.

In 1920 in an interview with the American Lincoln Eyre, Lenin
declared: 'In Russia we have wheat, flour, platinum, potash, and
many minerals of which the whole world stands in desperate need.
The world must come to us for them in the end, Bolshevism or no
Bolshevism.' There seems every likelihood that the view of the Soviet
oracle will be vindicated. The endowment of the Soviet Union with
natural resources is truly superb. In 1970 she had 57 per cent of the
world's coal, 45 per cent of its natural gas, 60 per cent of its peat, 46
per cent of its oil shales, 12 per cent of its hydroelectric power and 37
per cent of its oil-bearing area. The Soviet Union is the only major

industrial nation completely self-sufficient in energy. She has a plenitude of metals and at current rates of consumption and with present
methods of extraction her known reserves of gold, zinc, and lead will
last well into the twenty-first century and her copper till about 2050.
In Siberia she has so many rare elements – molybdenum and wolfram
are good examples – that the periodic table of Mendeleyev is brought
down to size. In addition, new wealth is constantly being discovered
in the USSR as more remote regions are explored for raw materials
and fuels.

Siberia is, of course, of crucial importance.[5] It is an area of 11
million square kilometres extending from the Urals to the Soviet Far
East, from the southern border of the nation to the shores of the
Arctic. Siberia has 60 per cent of Russia's timber and coal, 80 per cent
of her water power in giant rivers which, if joined, could encircle the
planet twenty times, natural gas fields which are reputed to be the
largest in the world, ample reserves of oil, at least for the immediate
future. Little wonder therefore that the native *Sibiryak* has an almost
childlike faith in economic growth and that to him the Cassandra-like
croakings of Western scholars and academics to the effect that the
world's resources are being rapidly depleted and will soon be exhausted seems like piling fiction upon fiction, paradox upon paradox.

Under the Tenth Five-Year Plan industrial production in Siberia is
scheduled to rise by 50 per cent as compared with 35 per cent for the
country as a whole. In 1980, the Plan states, 305 million tons of oil
will be extracted from the region along with 200 million tons of coal
and 155,000 million cubic metres of natural gas. By 1980 hydropower
stations will be generating 100,000 kilowatt hours of electricity, and
the world's largest hydrogenerator, Sayany-Shushenskoye on the
River Yenisei, will be in operation. By 1980 Siberian oil, gas, coal and
hydropower will account for about one-half of the energy demand
of the whole country. By 1980 power-hungry and fuel-intensive
industries – aluminium, petrochemicals, paper and pulp, and metal-
lurgy, to name but a few – will be moving increasingly to Siberia,
following the lodestar of vast and economically attractive electricity
stores.

But this is only the beginning. During the rest of this century and
well into the twenty-first the development and industrialization of
Siberia will proceed apace. Dams have always been part of the Soviet
mystique; they symbolize might and authority; they echo Lenin's
celebrated apophthegm, 'Communism is Soviet power plus the elec-

trification of the whole country.' The Kremlin's blueprint for the Siberia of the future envisages huge hydroelectric projects, new cities with the 'temples of kilowatts' hacked out of pine forests, massive expansion of existing reserves of coal and natural gas, utilization of nuclear power on a mounting scale, intensive railway construction (including the Baikal-Amur mainline which will open up remote mineral-rich areas of the Soviet Far East), and as mentioned previously, even the diversion of the waters of north-flowing rivers such as the Ob and the Yenisei so that they can flow southwards into the Caspian and Aral Seas, and thus succour the thirsty and less developed populations of these areas. At the 25th Communist Party Congress in Moscow in 1976 Leonid Brezhnev commented: 'What has been done and continues to be done in that forbidding territory is a feat in the true sense of the word.' He was stressing that the role of Siberia in Soviet economic development was already massive. But one does not need to have the messianic zeal of the loyal *Sibiryak* to predict that the impact of the region will be even greater in the world of tomorrow.

Soviet energy policy is currently in a state of transition. Since the late 1950s planners have been chiefly concerned with two issues – the acceleration and development of oil and natural gas resources in order to meet the growth of domestic demand, and the provision of export earnings which over the last twenty years have absorbed about 10 per cent of the nation's energy production. Energy specialists and government officials have also been grappling continuously with the eternal verity that some 90 per cent of the nation's energy resources lie east of the Urals while population and industry are still mainly concentrated in European Russia, which even now consumes about 80 per cent of all the country's energy. The general guidelines of the policy of the 'fifties remain today. But major modifications are in the offing and can be expected well before the end of the century.

It must be stressed that Soviet energy policy is grounded in hard technology. Official commentators play alternative energy sources in low key. Tidal power already makes a minor contribution to the energy budget, geothermal power is worth expanding, possibly wave power should be considered. But for the remainder of this century and well into the twenty-first the contribution of alternative energy sources will be picayune to say the least of it.

When the energy crisis erupted in 1973 Soviet officialdom purred contentedly. Amongst its protean manifestations the inability of capitalism to manage resources was especially obtrusive. On the other hand the Socialist countries, because of the alleged superiority of their system, would escape unscathed. Yet recent Soviet oil surveys have not been as optimistic as predicted, and Alexei Kosygin himself is on record as saying that the USSR cannot indefinitely 'fulfil the task of supplying everybody' with oil. On the other hand, the outlook for natural gas seems more promising and by the 'nineties this fuel, emanating mainly from Siberia, could account for as much as 35 per cent of the Soviet energy budget and could be earning sizeable export revenues. Long-distance transportation of gas and oil poses numerous problems. There are the sheer logistics involved in the building of pipelines, the development of high-voltage transmission lines and the construction of the all-too-familiar paraphernalia associated with the electricity industry. Even more worrisome, however, will be the political choices that will have to be made regarding exports of fossil fuels to Eastern European countries and possibly to other parts of the world.

At present peat and oil shales account for about 2 per cent of the USSR's total fuel requirement. The former is produced mainly in Belorussia, the latter in Estonia, and production of both is scheduled to rise. After a shift away from coal as an energy source in the 'fifties and 'sixties in tune with policies in other developed countries, coal is once again being perceived as a major contributor to meeting energy demand. The major production sites are the Donbas (covering an area of 60,000 square kilometres), Moscow and Karaganda basins. In Siberia the Kyznetsk, Pechora, Kansk-Achinsk and Lena basins are rich in reserves and are scheduled for rapid exploitation; even the island of Sakhalin has many coal fields.

Governmental support for nuclear fission power as a source of industrial and domestic electricity is mounting. The Kremlin projects a fourfold increase in nuclear power capacity between 1978 and 1980. In 1976 the Soviet Union had twenty atomic reactors producing about 6,200 megawatts of electricity. By 1981 the number of plants is expected to rise to thirty-seven, the megawattage to 20,000, and by this time the huge Atommash reactor at the confluence of the Rivers Volga and Don should be completed, reputedly facilitating the production of atomic power on an assembly-line basis. The Russians are amongst the staunchest supporters in the world of the fast breeder reactor and of the reprocessing of spent nuclear fuel. They have no anti-nuclear lobby within their own country and are on record as stating that those who oppose atomic power are also against détente !

Eastern European countries, partnered in the Council for Mutual Economic Assistance, are wary about future Soviet intentions in relation to natural resources. In particular, they are fearful lest the Kremlin play the 'energy card' for political reasons in order to maintain its hegemony. Such anxiety is not ill founded. The dependence on the USSR for oil is total in the case of Czechoslovakia and Bulgaria; the German Democratic Republic obtains 95 per cent of her oil from Russia, Poland 90 per cent, Hungary 75 per cent, Yugoslavia 25 per cent. Even in countries not in the CMEA but importing considerable quantities of energy from the USSR – Finland is an obvious example – changes in Moscow's energy policy could produce social and political upheavals.

Soviet ideologues and commentators have consistently maintained that the causes of the 1973 energy crisis were 'social and political' rather than geological.[6] The veteran statesman Andrei Gromyko proclaimed that the crisis was 'not natural', and Alexei Kosygin, in the course of a fulsome panegyric lauding the virtues of the socialist planned economy, compared the tranquillity *vis-à-vis* resources in the Eastern bloc with the turbulence, disorder and uncertainty in the capitalist world. Nevertheless, early in 1975 Soviet oil prices to other CMEA countries were raised appreciably and, although they still remained well below world levels, effects on Eastern bloc countries were dramatic. East Germany, the most industrialized member of the bloc, and with highest *per capita* GNP, was particularly bitter, stating bluntly that because of the price hike she would be unable to guarantee delivery of manufactured goods to the Soviet Union under the Tenth Five-Year Plan.

Between now and the end of the century Soviet officialdom will be much preoccupied with the resources question and in particular with how to counter shortages. Improved efficiency will be urged on the workforce; limits will be set on non-essential consumption. The Kremlin has an alluring and almost childlike faith in scientific achievement, this dating back to the early days of the new Soviet state. Lenin's confidence in technology was boundless. He fervently believed that the industrial miracle, the technological fix, would overcome economic problems, eliminate human foibles, agitate the sluggish waters of bureaucratic apathy. After all, had not Maxim Gorky, philosopher, communist benefactor and close confidant of

Lenin for many years, written in *The Russian Peasant* (1922) that the Soviet citizen of the future will 'learn the meaning of electrification, the value of the scientific agronomist, the use of the tractor and the necessity for having in every village a qualified doctor and a paved road'? And were these prophecies not proved to be correct by the time the world moved into the second half of the twentieth century? Small wonder, therefore, that Soviet official policy has its pennon firmly nailed to the mast of technological wizardry, that ambitious programmes for the exploitation of new reserves are already underway, that space research will be prosecuted with increasing vigour and that, even before the end of the century, serious attempts will be made to harness the 'innumerable riches' lurking in the ocean bed.

Pari passu with the accelerative thrust of technology a strong dynamic to obtain foreign capital for investment can be anticipated. Western credit will be sought; raw materials will be traded; policies redolent of S. Y. Witte, the hard-driving Tsarist Minister of Finance in the late nineteenth century, will be prosecuted. No ideological gymnastics are required for such a course of action; in no way do such practices imply even a hint of apostasy, much less an end to the class struggle. After all, Lenin himself, even before the Revolution, stated that under the Bolsheviks most capitalists would be able to work both profitably and honourably, and in the early 1920s he lauded the capitalist for having the secret which could 'make the economy bloom'. Lenin took especial pleasure in the Rapallo Treaty of 1922. To him this represented the first major success of Soviet diplomacy. The two pariahs amongst the European powers, Germany and Russia, came together, but even more importantly agreement was reached that an advanced Western nation would assist the USSR with its industrial and commercial problems. Given this background, therefore, Soviet-Western negotiations on trade are likely to burgeon over the next twenty years and Russian efforts to attract foreign investment will almost certainly meet with mounting success.

All this is not to say that compensation agreements in which Western Governments and corporations participate do not pose profound political problems for the Kremlin. This is especially so in view of the size of the debt CMEA countries owe to the West – amounting to $48 billion by the late 'seventies. However, in a world becoming increasingly resource-hungry, mutual self-interest would seem to dictate that, far from contracting, such arrangements are likely to expand. Soviet resource policy has traditionally been constructed on the tripod of self-sufficiency, national security and the control of indigenous resource sites. There is no reason to expect any notable divergence from this stance in the foreseeable future. Marxist-Leninist ideologues are particularly scathing about the *Limits to Growth* controversy. To them preoccupation with an environmental apocalypse is ideologically determined; it is yet another expression of the decadence of bourgeois society, which, like the sorcerer's apprentice, wishes to get rid of the industrialization to which it owes its power; it indicates yet again the profound pessimism of the capitalist world and its lack of trust in the future of mankind. Ecological Cassandras of the West proclaim that the planet must pay for its own *hubris*; civilization will be both victim and executioner.

To Marxist-Leninists the MIT *Limits to Growth* study commissioned by the Club of Rome represents the all-too-familiar attempt of 'monopolistic circles' to capture and enslave the ecological movement. The study itself is dubbed naïve, simplistic and singularly lacking in rigour. It creates a semblance of penetration into the human prospect for the twenty-first century, but at the same time it diverts cognition and attention from the 'real roads' that constitute the only possible solution to such global problems. To the orthodox Marxist-Leninist, *Limits to Growth* recalls La Rochefoucauld's maxim: '*La verité ne fait pas tant de bien dans la monde que ses apparences y font de mal*' (The truth does not do as much good in the world as its semblances create evil).

In spite of these criticisms of *Limits to Growth*, Soviet bureaucrats do posit that global resources are not unlimited. Leonid Brezhnev himself has subscribed to this view. But the danger of resource depletion is not considered to be imminent, and, moreover, Marxist-Leninist doctrine dictates that the socialist world will by its very nature be immune from it, or overcome it with ease. This is not to say that occasionally material shortages may not obtrude. But the overall superiority of the planned economy to cope with inflationary increases and to damp down unemployment will rapidly provide the necessary correctives.

On the other hand, say the Marxist-Leninists, the resource crisis in the capitalist world can only deepen. This is because of its 'inherent contradictions', of the 'monopolies' that dominate it, of the catastrophic consequences which will inevitably ensue from the capitalist mode of production. As predicted by Marx, the resource crisis will be a major factor in the overthrow of the system. Then the classical strategic purpose of Communism will have been achieved, and a world Communist society will have been established. The utopia will have dawned; the realm of necessity will have been replaced by the realm of freedom; the threat of global war will have vanished forever. The State will be unnecessary and will simply wither away. Marx's celebrated dictum enunciated in his *Critique of the Gotha Programme* will have come to pass: 'From each according to his ability, to each according to his needs.'

To many in the West the very word 'Marxism' sends a *frisson* of fear down the spine. Its shrill, abrasive, ritualistic slogans are anathema; it conjures up a vision of massive totalitarian repression, of non-existent human rights, of the practice of medicine scarred and polluted so that healthy people are dubbed insane and confined within psychiatric hospitals. Yet of a global population of just over 4,000 million, more than 1,300 million people are denizens of nations which claim their inspiration from Karl Marx. We may not approve of their system and their policies, but at least it behoves us to loosen our ideological carapace, to pay attention to the pronouncements of their leaders and to determine whether or not we have anything to learn from their experience.

NOTES AND REFERENCES

[1] One of the best recent summaries of such views is contained in *Encounter* (1978), March, April and July numbers. George F. Kennan, US career diplomat, former ambassador to Moscow and author of the celebrated 'containment' policy for the USSR sees beneficial changes occurring in the Soviet Union. Richard Pipes, Professor of History at Harvard University, and Leopold Labedz, editor of a prestigious American periodical, take a strongly anti-Soviet line, not dissimilar to that espoused by people like Margaret Thatcher and Lord Chalfont in the UK.

[2] See John Erickson (1977) for discussion.

[3] For this section I have drawn extensively on articles by Murray Fesbach and Stephen Rapawy (1976) and David H. Heer (1977). For the Soviet viewpoint I recommend I. Frolov (1978), 'Socio-philosophical Aspects of Demography', *Social Sciences*, Vol. 9, No. 4, p. 149.

4 Much the most authoritative articles on Soviet resources which I have read are those by Daniel S. Papp (1977 and 1979, *Resources Policy*, Vol. 5, No. 1, p. 51).

5 See, for example, A. Aganbegyan (1978).

6 For the Marxist view on this issue I recommend E. Fyodorov and Yu Fyodorov (1977), 'Human Problems of International Co-operation', *Social Sciences*, Vol. 8, No. 2, p. 190, and V. Zagladin and I. Frolov (1977).

Chapter 8

Food Prospects for the Next Twenty Years

Lin Yutang, the Chinese philosopher, once wrote that 'a full belly is a great thing; all else is luxury'. Paul Ehrlich, ecologist, favourite of the media and erstwhile passionate advocate of a global redistribution of wealth and resources, did not think that many bellies would remain full. In 1968, in his polemical book *The Population Bomb*, he declaimed: 'The battle to feed all of humanity is over. In the 1970s the world will undergo famines – hundreds of millions of people are going to starve to death in spite of any crash programmes embarked upon now. At this stage nothing can prevent a substantial increase in the world death rate. . . .' The 'sixties were the epoch which saw the emergence of the lifeboat ethic and of triage, the former being the brainchild of US population expert Garrett Hardin.[1] Hardin compared the earth to a lifeboat with huge numbers of hungry poor people swimming towards it. The main characteristic of the lifeboat was its exclusivity. Only the affluent and the well-nourished could be accommodated; the poor would swamp the vessel and should therefore be permitted to drown. Triage figured in the writings of the US agronomists, William and Paul Paddock, and the concept was given free rein in their much-quoted book *Famine 1975*. The idea was far from new. Triage stemmed originally from the cruel dictates of military medicine, dating back to the carnage of the First World War, to the trenches of Flanders and France, at places like Ypres, Neuve Chapelle, Loos, the Somme, the Aisne, and Passchendaele. Triage recognized three categories of wounded – minor casualties who with relatively simple treatment could rapidly be restored to full active duty, 'walking wounded' requiring attention at a hospital base, and severely wounded in need of extensive and radical surgery. The last group was dubbed expendable; scarce resources should not be allocated to them and they should be allowed to die.

To the Paddocks, global famine constituted the supreme dilemma of the second half of the twentieth century, and they proceeded to apply triage to their vision of the future. They concluded that India, Haiti and Egypt could not be saved; population growth in these countries had far outstripped agricultural potential; to dispatch food to them from North America would be about as useful as 'throwing sand in the ocean'. Libya and the then-Gambia were placed in the category of 'walking wounded'. Their agricultural resources were reasonable, their balance of payments situation moderately healthy; they could buy food in world markets and should be encouraged to do so. Whither then should food aid from USA be directed? According to the Paddocks to nations in which the imbalance between food and population seemed manageable in the long term and where there appeared to be a reasonable likelihood that the practice of birth control would take root and that agricultural research would prosper. Pakistan and Tunisia were two of the countries so categorized.

Lifeboat and triage were brutal and shameful concepts. They were an affront to human dignity, redolent of genocide; they represented a crude form of social Darwinism not dissimilar to Adolf Hitler's odious concepts of racial purity enunciated in *Mein Kampf*. Fortunately the progenitors of lifeboat and triage proved to be exceedingly bad forecasters. To date, over ten years later, no country has had to be effectively 'quarantined', no nation definitely consigned to Armageddon. However, that is not to say that justifiable anxiety has not prevailed in recent decades. Famines were endemic in the Indian subcontinent and Sahelian Africa during the 'sixties and 'seventies. It is insufficiently recognized that much of this could have been avoided. For it stemmed to a not inconsiderable extent from the determination of international agribusiness, centred particularly in North America, to keep world food prices artificially high by persuading farmers to take fertile land out of production in exchange for subsidies and so to ensure that the poor of the earth continued to go hungry. Yet in spite of this inexcusable behaviour the apocalypse was avoided. 'Hundreds of millions of people' did not starve to death, as predicted by Paul Ehrlich, and by the end of the 'seventies more and more sentient individuals were recognizing the presence of countervailing forces which, if given free play, could push history in the opposite direction, could increase food supplies in Third World nations faster than the rate of population growth, and, even before the year 2000, could lift from mankind's shoulders a burden as ancient as the human race itself.

Students of the global food situation divide themselves naturally into two categories. The *populationists* have traditionally hogged the media. Overbreeding in the Third World has been endemic for years and as a result there are too many mouths to feed. Improved agricultural production in the area – a *sine qua non* for improvement – can only take place if birth control technology becomes pervasive; coercive measures to restrain population growth (as was tried in India in 1976) may be necessary. According to this view the rich countries are also culpable because they waste the world's grain supplies by consuming so much food in the form of meat. René Dumont, the outspoken French ecologist, has referred to the rich white man as a 'veritable cannibal'. By his dietary habits and particularly through his propensity for meat consumption he is literally eating the children of the Sahel, Ethiopia and Bangladesh, and he continues to do so in the late 'seventies with an undiminished appetite.

I find myself much more in tune with those who take the *distributionist* view of the world food situation.[2] To them hunger is a scandal rather than a scourge reflecting the failure of current political and economic systems. It is the rich and powerful in the world whose interest in limiting the needs of the poor, the downtrodden and the destitute is most acute. Some people even see food as a new form of power, a weapon for subjugation, an extra dimension of Western diplomacy and one which was used particularly in the Nixon-Kissinger era of the early 'seventies. The Green Revolution (see p. 142), far from mitigating the situation, is seen as being a potent factor in its perpetuation. The 'distributionists' cast US agribusiness in a Mephistophelian role and none has attacked it more strongly than the International Union of Foodworkers which incorporates over 120 national trade unions and has a membership well in excess of two million. According to the IUF, US agribusiness bears a unique responsibility for the world food crisis. The main goals of the multinational companies through which the system operates are *not* to increase food resources, *not* to contribute to its global redistribution, *not* to adapt existing technologies to the conditions of particular Third World countries. They are indeed quite different. Markets must be increased; commercial outlets must be maximized; profits must soar and in all of these policies the vampirical tendencies of the developed countries must be encouraged and stimulated. In some areas of the Third World the conduct of the multinational companies can only be described as reprehensible. The most egregious example is, of course, the use of advertising policies to encourage African mothers to eschew breast-feeding of their babies – far and away the best method in that part of the world – for formulation milk feeding. Such policies are now recognized to have contributed directly to infant malnutrition in many parts of Africa.[3]

'The first condition for producing food is to have land.' Susan George's truism, which emphasizes the backwardness of land tenure systems in developing countries, should be kept continuously in the forefront of our consciousness. In most of the poor countries land is concentrated in inordinately few hands. For example, in Latin America 17 per cent of the landowners own 90 per cent of the land, and in Africa 75 per cent of the populace have access to only 4 per cent of the land. Regarded at the global level and based on figures issued by the Food and Agricultural Organization in the 'sixties (the data are unlikely to have changed markedly in the last fifteen years), 2.5 per cent of landowners with holdings in excess of 100 hectares control nearly three-quarters of the earth's total land area and what is even worse, the top 0.23 per cent of landowners control over 50 per cent of the terrain.

If poor people in the rural areas of the Third World are to be fed properly they must be given access to their land. It is as natural for a peasant to desire land of his own as it is for night to follow day. So far nations with centrally planned economies – China, Cuba, and the Republic of Vietnam immediately spring to mind – have been most successful in this respect. On the other hand the landowning classes in most of the poor countries have shown a singular and almost pathological reluctance to promote any form of egalitarianism and have consistently refused to make even the most minor of concessions.

'The contrast is too acute between the wealth and luxury of one class and the destitution and degradation of the other. One man works hard and has to recruit his exhausted strength in cramped quarters. . . . Another man who does nothing has allotted to him acres . . . nay, miles . . . of breathing ground all for himself. . . . One man labours and yet starves; another lounges and still feasts. One set of men strive all the days of their lives in the vineyard and yet, amid the plenty and profusion which they themselves have helped to produce, sink unhonoured into a pauper's grave. Another set of men enter into the precincts of the vineyard only to partake of its most luscious fruit, and they live and die amid the pomp and prodigality of millionaires.' This was David Lloyd George, at the height of his radicalism, speaking at Bangor in Wales over eighty years ago. How apt his words are to the poor and landless of the Third World in the final quarter of the twentieth century. The peroration at Bangor was masterly and is, perhaps, equally applicable to the situation in the Third World today: 'But as sure as justice and mercy are eternal attributes in the government of the world, that system which macadamizes the road to luxury for the few out of the hearts of the many is doomed. . . .'

Irrespective of whether one takes a populationist or distributionist stance *vis-à-vis* the global food situation the amplification of food production in the poor countries is undoubtedly vital to the problem of feeding humanity. Yet the difficulties and complexities involved must not be underrated. A break with the past will be necessary; we shall require the touch of a creative Brahma so that our Procrustean desire to tailor our wants to modes of established thought will be reversed. Amplification of agricultural production will mean, above all, the abandonment of subsistence farming which in its classical form involves only man, his animals, his seed and his exiguous stretch of land. In the late twentieth century subsistence farming – totally at the mercy of soil fertility and climatic caprice, eschewing science and technological innovation – can only be regarded as a blatant anachronism.

It must however be stressed that all developing countries do not have to import food. Some actually export it, Argentina and Thailand being prominent members of this group. China was virtually self-sufficient in food during the whole of the Maoist hegemony; whether it will remain so under a new leadership dedicated to economic growth and consumerism rather than sustainability is a matter of intense speculation and will be referred to later in this chapter. In the early and mid-'seventies OPEC had vast monetary reserves – nearly $90,000 million – in petrodollars. The members of the cartel were buying food in world markets with abandon, and they were delighting themselves by reminding us of the old maxim that sooner or later the beggar seeking bread at the gate will appear at the door armed with a document authorizing him to buy the mansion. But, as already stressed in Chapter 3, by the late 1970s OPEC's position was much less favourable; Iran, a major producer, was in ferment; other members of the cartel were running heavy balance of payments deficits. Their outlook as buyers in world food markets for the last two decades of the century is unpredictable; much will depend on global factors over which they have little or no control.

For the foreseeable future food deficits will be especially prominent in a specific group of Third World countries. Extreme poverty is their lot; they are the victims of the niggardliness of nature and their productivity in terms of crops and animals is miniscule. For them self-sufficiency in food seems chimerical, about as realistic as advocating chastity in a brothel. Most of these countries depend for their export trade on a single cash crop or on a miniscule number of raw materials. Their foreign exchange reserves are derisory, and their *per capita* Gross National Product abysmally low.

As well as being very poor, many of these nations have small populations. Latin America in 1978 had only five countries – El Salvador, Honduras, Grenada, Haiti and Bolivia – with a *per capita* GNP of less than $500; and in all of them numbers were less than 5 million. In Africa, of 37 states in the same economic bracket, 29 (80 per cent) had fewer than 10 million inhabitants; in Asia the corresponding proportion was 9 out of 23 (39 per cent).

The plight of most of these countries is directly linked to the policies of the ex-colonial powers. Many of them are geographical aberrations with frontiers artificially created. Also, most of them have gained their independence very recently. The UN informs us that thirty-six of the world's poorest countries became independent after 1945 and of these no fewer than twenty-nine after 1960. As appendages and helots of the colonial system these areas were cosseted and hedged in by a plethora of protectionist measures. Suddenly they had to face the icy blast of the free market and the ex-colonial powers had left them singularly ill-equipped for the ensuing economic blizzard. They had neglected basic crops and animals; they had established few centres of excellence in which agricultural research could be prosecuted; they had totally failed to establish proper systems of marketing and supply. The colonial powers were the progenitors of confusion and disarray and when they departed they took with them most of their skills, knowledge and expertise. For the newly free nations the days associated with the attainment of independence were heady indeed. But can one wonder, given the nature of their legacy, that disillusionment rapidly set in?

The post-colonial era soon saw the emergence of local élites – privileged individuals, sycophantic, eager to collaborate with their former masters for even the most picayune slices of cake. It also saw the attainment of authority by many individuals who were singularly ill-informed about agriculture. Lawyers, engineers and particularly military officers were now in the saddle. The iron fist of despotism was prominently displayed; the swell and pomp of authority seemed to have an almost mesmeric effect on aspirant and practising politicians. One of the results was that the ruling classes began to show a crass and blatant insensitivity to communities which were predominantly agrarian. Urban dwellers – more clamorous in their demands than the traditionally passive peasants – had favours showered upon them; the countryside wilted and atrophied. Governmental leaders became fixated with technological legerdemain; the glamorous Western-style appurtenances of modernization – dams, national airlines, industrial plants, atomic reactors – became the true symbols of success.

Within agriculture itself the priorities were often wrong. Undue emphasis was given to crops exportable for cash; the latter could be edible or non-edible and included coffee, cocoa, rubber, tobacco, jute, sugar, peanuts and bananas. The main characteristic of a cash crop is that the people who produce it are not the same people who eat or utilize it. The burgeoning of such cash crops means that too little land has been devoted to the growing of staples essential to feed the indigenous population – wheat, rice, corn, legumes and a variety of root crops, to name a few.

Third World leaders, through bitter experience over two decades, are now coming to learn that the rest of the world does not owe them a living. Food independence, sturdy self-reliance – these must be the hallmarks of their nations in the 'eighties and 'nineties. Food 'aid' from developed countries, particularly the USA, is slowly starting to have a somewhat pejorative connotation. It is acceptable on a short-term basis and in times of acute crisis but, regarded in the long sweep of history, its overall effect can only be debilitating. It is like a crutch to the hypochondriac whose lameness is illusory; it is a palliative, never a cure. By providing a *point d'appui*, food aid can sap initiative, stultify the political will to develop indigenous agriculture and even serve as an excuse for not galvanizing leaders of developing countries into much needed action on their home food front.

There is no doubt that a huge potential exists for increasing agricultural productivity in the Third World. Most of the area snuggles between the tropics of Cancer and Capricorn; overall temperatures are warm, rainfall generally abundant, albeit seasonal. Throughout much of the year there is an extravaganza of solar energy absorbed by plant pigments through the process of photosynthesis, converted into chemical energy and eventually built up into the complicated organic substances necessary for growth.

Yet the door to this El Dorado has not been effectively prised open. For to gain entrance to the halls of plenty various things must happen. Local self-reliance has already been referred to. There must also be a massive transfer of capital from rich to poor countries. Huge areas of the Third World are starved of capital investment and need it urgently. Take the Sudan as an example. It has a low population density (less than ten persons per square kilometre), and although its numbers are currently increasing by 3 per cent per annum and could double in twenty-five years, it will certainly not show any form of the overpopulation syndrome during the remainder of this century. The southern region of the Sudan is potentially one of the richest farming areas in the world. It has good soil, limitless sunshine, adequate water resources. Why then is it not one of the earth's most bounteous granaries? The answer is, of course, poverty. The *per capita* GNP is less than $300, and without a proper economic base the country is effectively emasculated, sutured off from the mainstream of world events. The Sudan cannot drain its foetid swamps; it cannot harness its rainfall, grow more than one crop per year, or make a serious attempt to replace its nomadic cattle breeders with less mobile and more sophisticated farmers.

In *Sex and the Population Crisis* I commented on the huge gap in agricultural efficiency which existed between rich and poor countries. During the last ten years the gap seems to have widened rather than narrowed. In most of the developing countries the productive capacity of the land remains very poor; fertilizers are used sparingly – even more so in the years immediately following the Yom Kippur War and the subsequent escalation of oil prices. Poor quality livestock are ubiquitous; agricultural mechanization has scarcely begun; transport facilities are miniscule, 'farm-to-market' roads being in particularly short supply. The Third World continues to face an acute shortage of trained agronomists: the juggernaut of agrarian reform alluded to above has scarcely begun to roll along the road.

The measures which should be taken are obvious. The pace of agricultural development in the Third World must be forced *à toute outrance*. The area must become enveloped in a wave of economic activity, for this alone is likely to facilitate rural development, increase crop and animal production and favour multiple rather than single cropping. Storage facilities for grain must be vastly improved and must preclude its consumption by insects, rats and other living organisms. A proper marketing organization is a *sine qua non*; agricultural schools and colleges need to be established and appropriate research vigorously prosecuted therein.

Development of water resources is at the hub of any scheme to increase agricultural production. Israel is always cited as the quintessential example of what can be achieved by the application of modern irrigation techniques and certainly the country has raised its farm output eight-fold in the thirty years of its existence as a state. Other areas are even more promising. The Indus-Ganges-Brahmaputra plain sprawls through India, Pakistan and Bangladesh, and it has been estimated that, given adequate irrigation facilities along with sophisticated farming practices, its 40 million hectares* could provide agricultural yields up to 20 metric tons of cereal grain per hectare per year and so could supply about four-fifths of the current cereal output of the world! Even Sahelian Africa – an area synonomous with drought and famine – could, by prudent use of its groundwater resources and rivers, provide crop water for over 2 million hectares. The capital costs of these ventures would be prodigious. But if they came to fruition the gains for mankind would be immeasurable.

We are now rather better organized at the international level to cope with food problems. The global framework for this development was laid by the UN-sponsored conferences of the 'seventies – on population, food, water and other natural resources. The rhetoric at these conferences was often bromidic, sometimes flamboyant, frequently euphoric and bristling with the impeccable sentiments and platitudes which are the hallmark of actors on the international stage. Doubts continue to exist about the usefulness of such exercises. Are they capable of evoking the high qualities of statesmanship which alone

* 1 hectare = 2.271 acres.

could make it possible for diamonds to shine amongst the untidy dross of the years? As a result of these meetings is there any likelihood that individual nations will co-operate rather than compete with one another in their attempts to solve problems of a global nature?

The proceedings of the World Food Conference in Rome were poorly reported in the press. Nevertheless the Conference did come up with a series of substantive suggestions which, if put into practice, would markedly improve the global food situation during the 'eighties and 'nineties. The establishment of a World Food Council to co-ordinate the activities of the myriad of international agencies already working in the areas of food and agriculture was agreed, and the Council, consisting of representatives of the Ministries of Agriculture of some forty nations, had its first meeting in 1976. It remains to be seen whether the Food Council will be useful or will become yet another elephantine bureaucracy. Also whether it will be able to eschew the siren song of US agribusiness and instead make it its passive tool. Only time will provide an answer to these important questions.

Another brainchild of the Conference – and probably one with considerably more potential – was the International Fund for Agricultural Development. IFAD had as its aim the improvement of agricultural production in the Third World. By 1977 its capital had reached the £1,000 million mark and it was ready to become operational. IFAD has a unique political structure; it gives equal voting rights to developing recipient countries and to donor nations, the latter being drawn both from the OECD and from OPEC. Within IFAD a pivotal role is perceived for the main oil-producing countries. After all the OPEC countries themselves are in the process of development and as donors would seem to be much more acceptable to other Third World countries than the industrialized and acquisitive nations of the West.

The Food Conference also stressed that a warning system to cope with famines was an urgent necessity. Such a system should have at its disposal a plenitude of sophisticated technology, including weather satellites and economic and climatic indicators. It should be the watchdog *par excellence*; its view should be global but it should direct its attention particularly to areas of the world – the Indian subcontinent and Sahelian Africa are the obvious examples – which are most vulnerable to food shortages. A monitoring system of this type should undoubtedly be given the highest possible priority, and it ought certainly to be fully operative by the early 'eighties.

What are the prospects for the much vaunted 'Green Revolution'? Certainly the new dwarf strains of wheat and rice developed by the Rockefeller Foundation in Mexico and the Ford-financed International Rice Research Institute in the Philippines boosted agricultural production in some areas of the Third World to unprecedented heights. Indian wheat output doubled between 1968 and 1972; Pakistan had an exportable rice surplus in 1970; even the Philippines, whose record for agricultural production had been abysmal and whose population growth was still running at about 3 per cent per annum, hovered temporarily on the threshold of food self-sufficiency. Also the Green Revolution tended to show the Asian peasant farmer up in a different light. Far from being the conservative and lethargic prototype so frequently depicted by the Western media, he now took on the mantle of energy and innovation when seen to react appropriately to a specific and supposedly beneficial stimulus.

Proponents of the Green Revolution – people like Lester Brown, Director of the Washington-based Worldwatch Institute and dubbed by Susan George through his 'disarming candor' her favourite Revolutionary – regard the process as a watershed in agricultural practice.

They stress that, for the first time, 'scientific' as opposed to traditional subsistence farming is making its appearance in the developing world. Given adequate inputs of fertilizers and pesticides, along with access to large amounts of crop water, the opportunity is being provided for breeding new crops adapted to the needs of intensive agriculture in poor countries. The widely spread plant varieties of the past can be dispensed with; now there can be densely packed plant populations which can use solar energy more effectively for respiration and transpiration. Multicropping on a large scale has at last become a viable proposition. Suddenly expenditure to control plant diseases and kill off insect pests has become attractive from the economic point of view.

What is the status of the Green Revolution looked at from 1979? There is no question that it has had a limited success in a number of Third World countries and that the high-yielding varieties of grain could probably be transferred to other areas, particularly in Africa and Latin America. But there are a number of profoundly disturbing features about the Green Revolution which augur badly for its future. American agribusiness has become pervasive throughout the process, with the result that only the rich farmers are tending to benefit. They do so because they can afford the purchase of the expensive inputs – fertilizers and pesticides, high-pressure sprayers, mechanical dryers for crops, motorized equipment – all of these being denied to their poorer counterparts. Lester Brown, however, has no doubt as to how the revolution should proceed. He believes that the USA should be the paradigm; she provides a 'useful guide' and other nations should certainly follow her lead. Supplying farmers in the Third World via the Green Revolution could be 'big business', and only US agribusiness with its concomitant multinational corporations is fitted to undertake this task.

Quite apart from the malign influence likely to be purveyed by multinational companies in promoting the Green Revolution there are other worrisome points. Ecological balance and nature itself could be affected by these high-yielding grains; local varieties of food crops could become extinct and their genetic characteristics obliterated forever. Diets could be affected in a baneful manner. The new cereal seeds are high in carbohydrates and relatively low in proteins, and they could have the effect of forcing Third World denizens off their normal protein supplements which they consume for example in pulses, ground nuts and soya beans. Even in Mexico, where the Green Revolution has been in existence for the longest time and is most deeply embedded, there is still no definite evidence suggesting that it has raised overall *per capita* food consumption significantly.

Social impacts of the Green Revolution have been mixed. There have been some good effects in a limited number of poor countries; in others it has assumed the guise of a poisoned chalice. To its credit it has tended to raise marketable surpluses and has thus improved the diet of urban residents. But by seriously increasing inequalities between farmers, by stirring up rivalries which previously did not exist, and by tending to make the rich richer and the poor hungrier it has certainly had an inimical influence. The World Bank has been particularly critical of the Green Revolutionaries for modernizing the methodology of the already better-off farmers and neglecting the needs of the poor. The Bank's director, Robert McNamara, has vehemently criticized the 'limited transfer of benefits from the modern to the traditional sector.' In his opinion, 'disparities in incomes will simply widen unless action is taken which will directly benefit the poorest.'

The Green Revolution therefore is no panacea for the world's food problems during the next twenty years. That it can play a useful role is not in question. But that role must be subsidiary to agrarian reform, to redistribution of land and wealth and to curtailment of privilege amongst the élites within Third World countries.

China is the most populous nation on earth and is also the putative leader of the Third World. Her experience in agriculture since the establishment of the People's Republic in 1949 obviously merits careful scrutiny. In particular the question is continuously being asked as to whether the Chinese exemplar can be transferred to other developing nations with different social, economic and political systems.

Mao Tse-tung consistently emphasized self-reliance, austerity and spartan living. Maoist doctrine had as its lynchpin that the road to the Communist utopia lay through the peasants. The Soviet model, stressing the importance of heavy industry and pandering to the industrial proletariat, was eschewed from the start. In the Russia of Lenin and Stalin planning had started with steel; in Maoist China it started with grain. To Mao food self-sufficiency constituted the whole basis of political and economic independence; and after the schism with Russia in the 'fifties there were even stronger reasons for seeking it.

By the early 1970s Mao seemed to have attained many of his objectives. Between 1970 and 1975 agricultural production in China rose by some 3 per cent per year; at the same time population growth rates were declining, so at least the plough was keeping up with the stork. Chinese agriculture under Mao became very labour-intensive and the image was of huge numbers of people constructing terracing and building drainage and irrigation works. However, Mao did not neglect what he called the 'modern leg' of agriculture, and between 1966 and 1975 the output of fertilizers in China was estimated to have risen from 10 to 30 million tons. Mao was always at pains to emphasize that the Chinese pattern of agricultural development in no way precluded the creation of industry. The two facets were interdependent; it was only logical that they should grow and flourish together.

The new Chairman, Hua Kuo-feng, has given a different twist to Chinese policy. The leadership, spurred on by the dynamic Vice Premier Teng Hsiao-ping, is driving strongly for increased economic growth. In Teng's view, the country must be prepared for another great leap forward and before the end of the century China must be transformed into a 'great powerful modern socialist country'. To achieve this, rapid modernization must take place and China must be opened up with maximum speed to Western ideas, technology and finance.

The new leadership is currently aiming at a 4.5 per cent annual increase in agricultural production. They intend to lift the country to a higher tier of agricultural technology and productive efficiency; to quicken the pace of hydrological innovations like flood control and irrigation schemes; to give priority to research on plant breeding so that new types of crop can be introduced. Synthetic fertilizers must be used more widely, although the benefits of organic farming – a relic of Maoist days – should not be neglected.

During the next twenty years the demand for food is likely to rise considerably in China. Rural-urban migration will be hastened in the wake of policies of economic growthmanship and within the cities themselves richer and more varied diets will be demanded. Consumption of meat is almost certain to increase and this will impose stresses and strains on the grain market. If the Chinese leadership is in too much of a hurry to stimulate agricultural production a chaotic situation could arise in which it would be necessary for the country to make heavy demands on world food markets in order to feed her large and growing population. This has been avoided since the inception of the People's Republic; it could only have an inimical influence on the global situation during the next twenty years.

Between 1950 and 1974 four factors contributed to a doubling of world food production – increasing utilization of hybrid corn, a massive expansion of irrigation, a sixfold rise in fertilizer use, and advances associated with the Green Revolution. We cannot, however, look forward to a further quantum leap forward in food technology during the next twenty years. Experiments are being made in a number of areas – some of which are discussed below – but it would be over-optimistic to expect dividends in this century.

Raising the photosynthetic activity of crops would be a major advance. Plants do not use solar energy efficiently, and enormous amounts of air have to be processed in order to obtain the carbon dioxide which they need. The assimilation rate of carbon dioxide into the photosynthetic cycle is limited by a variety of factors – rate of entry through leaf stomata and across membranes, solubility in cell fluids, concentration into the vital green pigment chlorophyll. Possibilities for improving the plant's ability to utilize carbon dioxide by affecting any of these parameters are under investigation but no major advances have so far been reported.

The breeding of crops that would extract nitrogen preferentially would be of inestimable value. The atmosphere, of course, contains large quantities of nitrogen but a great deal of fossil fuel energy is necessary in order to convert it into a food that can be used by plants. Leguminous plants – peas and beans for instance – have micro-organisms which live symbiotically on their roots and enable them to 'fix' nitrogen from the atmosphere directly; this is the basis of so-called 'green manuring'. If strains of these organisms could be produced which retained their nitrogen-fixing capacity and could live symbiotically with crop plants like cereals, the requirement of the latter for synthetic fertilizers would decrease greatly. But work of this type requires the solution of many long-standing problems in genetic engineering and no immediate breakthrough seems likely.

Quick solutions to the world's food dilemma cannot be expected either through unconventional forms of agriculture or from farming and harvesting the sea. Modest progress continues to be made in both areas. The eventual pay-off, if it ever materializes, will be in the twenty-first century. Hydroponic methods, particularly the nutrient film technique, are particularly alluring for they offer the possibility that eventually crops will be grown with less water, fertilizers and other inputs, that crop diseases will be tamed or eradicated, and that arid, inhospitable land will be made fertile.

During the 'seventies the production of farmed fish, particularly carp, increased significantly, Asian countries – China, India, Singapore and the Philippines – taking the lead in this field. But too little capital was invested in the enterprise, and financial constraints are likely to persist for the foreseeable future. During the next two decades the imbalance between national aspirations and sovereignty on the one hand, and fishery resources on the other, will almost certainly become an increasingly contentious issue in many areas of the world.[4] One cannot look to fish farming to palliate this situation; certainly it is no antipyretic designed to take the heat out of any political fever that might erupt.

Likewise synthetic foods are not destined to play a major role during the next twenty years. They could be used on a modest scale, mainly as additives in parts of the world where protein deficiency is endemic and diseases such as kwashiorkor and marasmus are widespread. But synthetic foods must be bought before they can become comestibles, and the poor of the earth have no money and their governments almost no capital. Developing countries would be rash and ill-advised to look to exotic foods to solve their short- or medium-term problems. Instead, in their quest for self-sufficiency and better living standards, they must firmly affix their pennon to the mast of scientific agriculture employing methods already available.

New foods will undoubtedly feature in the twenty-first century and the area is one with great potential. Single-cell proteins can now be grown in a petroleum-based medium; cellulose derived from trash, paper, wood and agricultural waste can be changed to glucose and the latter converted into protein by bacterial action. Certain food wastes and bi-products now discarded or used only as animal fodder could be converted into human foods or used as additives. Among the latter are skimmed milk, whey, oil, seedmeal and fishmeal. Meat analogues produced from soya beans are slowly penetrating world markets. This is the celebrated 'meatless meat' which lends itself to large-scale preparation and which has a very high protein content.

Up till now the history of synthetic foods has been far from happy. Acceptability is the touchstone of their success, and so far mankind has proved singularly resistant to the blandishments of officials and entrepreneurs who wish to purvey them. Man's taste in foodstuffs is complex, sophisticated and often unpredictable. It is frequently governed by caprice; but at the same time it shows an intense conservatism, a preference for familiar flavours and consistencies, an almost pathologically hostile reaction to additives in any form. The case of Incaparina is classical in this context. Incaparina is largely made of cotton seed; it contains corn and is liberally larded with Vitamins A and D. It was introduced into Guatemala in 1957 with the massive fanfare of publicity generally reserved for a major scientific breakthrough. Not only would Incaparina alleviate nutritional deficiency in Guatemala, but it would soon solve the problem at the global level. However, the reality was very different. Incaparina had a cool reception from the local inhabitants who disliked its taste and refused to eat it. Twenty years later Incaparina has been consigned to the 'rubbish heap of history'; its effect on the world's starving millions has been nil.

It is a truism to state that the earth's equilibrium is very delicately maintained. Nowhere is this more so than in the realm of agriculture. The congeries of events to which we are exposed present a multiplicity of ingredients, and many of these are mutually antagonistic, with forces and counterforces, with currents being continuously neutralized by countercurrents. And just as there seem to be a number of factors which, over the next twenty years, will tend to promote an increase in agricultural production in the poor countries, so there are many countervailing influences which could act to frustrate or totally preclude such a favourable outcome.

I have discussed some of these malign influences elsewhere.[5] Ecological stress is, of course, paramount, pride of place going to the macabre troika of soil erosion, overgrazing and deforestation. About one third of the earth's surface is already arid; deserts continue to spread with alarming speed and the soil fertility of adjacent areas is falling rapidly. At the southern edge of the Sahara about 70,000 square kilometres of land are in the process of being desertified; in the Indian sub-continent and in parts of Latin America desertification is spreading like a highly malignant cancer. The causes of desertification are manifold, factors such as population pressure, destruction of vegetative cover and the traditional pattern of nomadic existence all playing distinctive roles.

Eric Eckholm and his colleagues at the Worldwatch Institute in Washington have provided a detailed description of the energy crisis which uniquely affects the Third World, that of firewood.[6] Firewood is, of course, the mainstay for cooking in the poor countries. Rapid population growth has been a major contribution to its depletion; trees and population are now manifestly out of balance and afforestation schemes, however avidly prosecuted, are notoriously slow to come to fruition. The price of wood is soaring in world markets and is an important factor in the genesis of inflationary pressures. Also, as emphasized by Eckholm, the problem is being exacerbated by the invasion of potential farmland by urban extension, and the squalid, disease-ridden shanty towns which have proliferated on the periphery of Third World cities are certainly a vivid and volatile testimony to the deterioration and depredation of the rural environment.

We are consuming oil at a prodigious rate. This point is well brought out in a recent book by Maurice Green, *Eating Oil* (1978). Green hammers home the point that food production is crucially dependent on fossil fuel energy. Scientific farming and modern agricultural practice are increasingly dominated by energy-intensive inputs. Petrol and diesel fuels are used to power tractors, combine harvesters, and many other forms of machinery; propane fuels grain dryers; milking machines and other forms of stationary equipment are driven by electricity; fertilizers, pesticides, herbicides and insecticides are all synthesized by processes which are massively energy-intensive.

Food at the farm gate has a long way to go before it reaches the dining table. And in rich and poor countries alike the energy expended in activities such as processing, packing, transporting, distributing and cooking is greatly in excess of that involved in food production. In rural India twice as much fuel is utilized to cook the rice as is used in the crop itself. In the USA 13.8 per cent of the total energy derived from fossil fuels goes into processing, distribution and preparation of food, as compared with 3.1 per cent into primary agriculture. In the UK the corresponding figures are 22.8 and 4.6 per cent.

The finite nature of fossil fuels is, of course, no longer in doubt. Before the mid-'nineties oil and gas reserves will have reached their peak production and will be beginning to decline. During the 'eighties fossil fuel costs will rise steeply as the gap between supply and demand yawns widely. All this poses awesome questions. Can energy-intensive agriculture as practised in the West be extended at any reasonable level to the poor countries, particularly to those with no indigenous resources, no capital and massive balance of payment deficits? Indeed, is it possible to continue this type of farming indefinitely anywhere on this planet?

The purpose of farming was once described as 'the capture of solar energy', and there is no question that solar power could be of crucial importance for the agriculture of the twenty-first century. Yet for many decades farmers have been progressively weaned from the sun. They have been forced to eschew organic farming and so have become increasingly divorced from the great biological and ecological cycles whose purpose it is to drive and support agriculture. Farmers' self-reliance has been steadily eroded as they have become the helots of the multinational companies, the acolytes of the petro-chemical industry. Even worse, the future of the small farmer has been increasingly jeopardized by his exposure to the wildly fluctuating market forces which dominate capitalist economics and over which he has no control. It is high time that farmers all over the world reversed this trend and reestablished their natural and necessary links with the sun. There is no need for this to be a *fin de siècle* phenomenon occurring at a time when the earth's oil supplies are virtually exhausted. Instead the change should be proceeding now and with maximum possible speed.

In *Syndromes of the Seventies* I reminded readers of the idealistic vision of Lord Boyd Orr, the first Director General of the Food and Agricultural Organization. Boyd Orr saw in his imagination the burden of famine lifted from the shoulders of mankind, and he urged the acceptance of 'a great world food scheme which will bring freedom from want to all men.' But Boyd Orr, had he been alive today, would have been disappointed with the performance of the warriors against hunger. They have been poorly equipped for the fight; their vision has been that of the tunnel, their penchant for narrow nationalism a transcendent feature. The voice of idealism has not triumphed; no generalissimo has yet emerged to organize an appropriate global strategy. Solomon once said, 'Where there is no vision the people perish.' The warriors against hunger should take note.

Now at the end of the decade of the 'seventies we stand at a crossroads. It is as though we are resting ourselves in a quiet pool between two waterfalls. The past is littered with the detritus of failure; yet the future is not unpromising in certain respects. Only one thing is certain, namely that if the global food situation is to be ameliorated during the next twenty years, the political will for change must clearly be seen to exist.

How will political leaders react to the challenge? Will they rise to the occasion, show high qualities of statesmanship and as a result will a new harmony sound from the celestial spheres? Or will they show themselves to be little men of the past confronted by big events, overwhelmed by the future, unable through lack of imagination, inadequate cerebral endowment, avarice or sheer bigotry and prejudice to keep up with the accelerative thrust of global events? Judging by their previous track record I must admit to a certain pessimism. But if the second option prevails then political leaders of the final two decades of this century must expect that future generations will impugn them before the bar of history and say of them, as did Churchill of the Baldwin administration in the 'thirties, that they were 'decided only to be undecided, resolved to be irresolute, adamant for drift, solid for fluidity, all powerful to be impotent.'

NOTES AND REFERENCES

[1] Garrett Hardin (1968).

[2] By far the most powerful and cogent exposition of this viewpoint I have read is Susan George's *How the Other Half Dies* (1976). I thoroughly recommend it.

[3] See *New Internationalist* (1973), No. 6, August.

[4] The 'Cod War' between Britain and Iceland is a good example.

[5] See *The Death of Tomorrow* (1972), Heinemann, London, Chapter X, and *Syndromes of the Seventies* (1977), Peter Owen, London, Chapter 5.

[6] See Erik P. Eckholm (1975), *The Other Energy Crisis: Firewood*, Worldwatch Paper 1, September; Erik P. Eckholm (1976), *Losing Ground*, Norton, New York.

Chapter 9

Population Still Dominant

Overpopulation was my entrance to the global *problematique*. My interest in it started when I strayed into the shanty town in Santiago in Chile in 1959. Later I wrote in *Syndromes of the Seventies* that never before had I witnessed such degradation, poverty and squalor. But the outstanding impression was of the people everywhere, the majority of them young, most of them malnourished and frankly starving. I never forgot Santiago.

During the 'sixties I lectured whenever I could on the population issue. The 'seventies were occupied with writing as well as with speaking. In *Sex and the Population Crisis* I registered my frustration as an endocrinologist that although reliable methods of birth control, particularly the Pill and the vacuum suction technique of abortion, had become freely available, the predicament was still appalling; man remained 'locked in mortal combat with his reproductive processes'. Time was not on the side of governments and international organizations. If they failed to act, posterity would pay the price and the reckoning would inevitably be grim.

In *The Death of Tomorrow* I dubbed overpopulation 'the supreme dilemma of our time – the most tangled crisis which our planet has ever faced'. I stressed in particular its pervasive effect. It has had a baneful environmental influence, which has been especially obvious in industrialized countries; it has contributed 'to the pall of pollution over big cities, to the contamination of rivers, lakes and seas, to the littering of the earth's surface with all manner of debris'. It has had a pivotal role in the depletion of precious and non-renewable resources, particularly metals and fossil fuels. The surge of human numbers has been a major factor in forcing the inflationary spiral ever upwards. The human misery that flows from excessive urbanization is incalculable. Global famines have followed the lodestar of overpopulation, so have conditions conducive to the outbreak of armed conflict both within countries and between nation states. Overpopulation,

152

that 'strange malady of modern life', has haunted our every activity; there has been no escape from it throughout the length and breadth of the earth.

I predicted that the overriding impression of the early twenty-first century would be that the world was bursting at the seams with people. The most striking increase would, of course, take place in developing countries. By 2000 AD one in five people on earth would be Chinese, one in six Indian, one in eight African, one in ten Latin American. The relative position of the developed world *vis-à-vis* population would be much weakened. For example, the USA and the USSR combined would house less than 10 per cent of the world's people, the EEC countries only 5 per cent. It was, I wrote, in the Third World, 'amongst that seething mass of fecund, starving, illiterate, underprivileged and intensely pathetic people that our planet will have its tryst with destiny. It is there that the fate of mankind will be decided; it is there that civilization as we currently perceive it, may take its final lurch into oblivion'.

Writing in 1972, these apocalyptic forecasts did not seem misplaced. By the early 'fifties a certain degree of death control had been achieved in the Third World. In some regions in that area – Latin America was the most prominent – death rates began a vertiginous descent and soon came to resemble those in the industrialized world. But although the Medical Revolution with its battery of vaccines, antibiotics and other highly potent drugs, had conquered or emasculated many of the infectious diseases which had decimated the planet for millennia, birth rates had scarcely been affected by the onslaught. The yawning gap between birth and death rates remained and was at the kernel of the population explosion. Family planning programmes were receiving a good deal of publicity and in some areas were being assiduously practised. But their effect seemed minimal. Each year over 70 million people were being added to the planet – more than the combined dead in the First and Second World Wars, one and a half times the population of Britain. The earth was experiencing the greatest explosion of numbers in recorded history.

A change in reproductive habits in some of the industrialized countries compounded the problem. Western Europe experienced its 'baby boom' after World War Two, and it had been confidently predicted that these nations would settle down comfortably to the pattern of low fertility which had been a feature of the interwar period. But this did not happen. Between 1955 and 1965 countries in that area – particularly the UK, France, Federal Germany and Italy – experienced a surge in procreative activity. Convincing reasons for this trend have never been adduced. Perhaps it was the swansong of pronatalism in the West, a nostalgic interlude before the economic constraints imposed by child-bearing and child-rearing came to obtrude harshly into the public consciousness. Certainly it was an era in which optimism did not seem misplaced. The consumer boom was gaining momentum; 'getting and spending' were being practised as never before. Britain trimmed her sails to the prevailing breeze, and in 1959 the Conservative leader Harold Macmillan campaigned and won a general election on the straight materialistic slogan 'you've never had it so good.' No one, least of all the politicians, seemed to be aware that by our profligacy with finite resources we were in the process of damaging the planet irreparably and giving a plethora of hostages to fortune. The environmentalist lobby was virtually non-existent in the 'fifties. *Limits to Growth* would have been laughed out of court or regarded as an eccentric form of *opera bouffe*. Economic recession and spiralling inflation – the now familiar 'stagflation' – were for the future; no one had the temerity to suggest that within as short a period as a decade they would join forces to put fertility firmly into a straitjacket.

The horsemen of demography were in full gallop during the 'fifties and 'sixties. In 1950 global numbers stood at 2,500 million; by 1960 they had climbed to 3,000 million and by 1969, 600 million more people had been added. A notable landmark was reached in 1977 when the total passed the 4,000 million mark. The demographic divide between rich and poor nations has been much in evidence at the end of the 'seventies. The industrialized world houses one quarter of the world's people and fertility rates there have been plummeting for over ten years. Western Europe has pushed its birth rate down to 12 per 1,000 population, the Soviet Union down to 18, the USA to 15, Japan and Australia to 17.

The Third World presents a totally different scenario. Seventy-five per cent of the earth's people are living there, 85 per cent are being born there. Much more importantly from the point of view of the future, 90 per cent of the additions to the planet between 1980 and 2000 will take place in that area. Population-wise, therefore, the hinge of history is moving ineluctably away from the West and towards the Third World, a situation which will undoubtedly be portentous for mankind. It could, for example, be a factor in exacerbating the acrimony of the North-South confrontation (see also Chapter 1); it could put increasing strain on polyglot organizations like the British Commonwealth of Nations and the French Community which draw their members from rich and poor worlds alike.

Yet although the momentum of population growth in the poor countries remains formidable by any standards and will continue to do so for the foreseeable future, the demographic map within the region itself is changing with great rapidity. As the world enters the 'eighties, East Asia has witnessed a particularly significant fall in its population growth rate, largely due to herculean efforts in China during Mao Tse-tung's hegemony. Elsewhere in the developing world, a mixed bag of states – Tunisia, Egypt, Costa Rica, Panama, Colombia and Mexico are notable – have succeeded in reducing their birth rates. Islanders have been particularly successful in curbing fertility. Singapore cut its birth rate from 30 to 18 per 1,000 in twelve years, Hong Kong from 29 to 19, Cuba from 35 to 25, Barbados from 26 to 21; in Taiwan, Sri Lanka, Fiji, Puerto Rico and Mauritius the story has been similar. Even in Haiti, for long the fief of François Duvalier, who operated a regime as obnoxious and atavistic as any in the world, the long march towards population control seems to have begun. Most of these islands (Haiti is the obvious exception) now have broadly-based family planning services and high literacy rates. Female emancipation and women's rights have become important issues, and serious attempts are being made to redistribute wealth on a more equitable basis. There seems every reason to suppose that these trends will continue into the 'eighties and 'nineties.

Demographic forecasting is a twentieth-century phenomenon. Its track record has not been a happy one and much obloquy has been heaped on its head. Yet demographic forecasts – essentially based on extrapolation of current fertility levels surrounded by a 'high' and a 'low' band – remain indispensable. In the short term, they can provide reasonable forecasts about the likely development of school-age and working populations; they can avoid the trap of forecasting fertility on the basis of transitory and 'fashionable' behaviour patterns; and by drawing the attention of politicians and officials to likely trends and their consequences they can become a focus for action. Demographers are much more cautious than in the past about their vaticinations. The limitations of the analytical tools which they employ are freely admitted; the fallacies and frailties of extrapolation in relation to mortality and migration as well as to fertility itself are well recognized.

Probably the most widely quoted projections for global population trends are those issued annually by the Washington-based Population Reference Bureau which relies mainly on UN sources. According to the Bureau's *Bulletin* of 1978, world population is likely to rise to just over 6,200 million by 2000 AD. The forecast for Africa is for an increase from 430 to 820 million, for Asia from 2,430 to 3,660 million, for Latin America from 344 to 600 million. Rates of increase in the developed world will of course be appreciably slower – in North America from 240 to 290 million, in Europe from 480 to 538 million, in the USSR from 260 to 310 million.

China, with numbers forecast to exceed 1,200 million, will be the world's most populous nation in the year 2000. Second place will be held by India with numbers in excess of 1,000 million. Two other Third World countries – Indonesia and Brazil – will have topped the 200 million mark and in at least four – Nigeria, Bangladesh, Pakistan and Mexico – numbers will lie between 100 and 200 million. Some smaller countries in the developing world are scheduled to show spectacular population rises between now and the end of the century – Algeria from 18 to 36 million, Sudan from 17 to 33, Ethiopia from 30 to 50, Tanzania from 16 to 33, Iraq from 12 to 24, Turkey from 42 to 70, the Philippines from 46 to 84, Peru from 17 to 31.

Projections from sources other than the Population Reference Bureau put the global total in 2000 somewhat lower. The World Bank favours a figure of 6,000 million; two Chicago-based demographers, A. O. Tsui and D. J. Bogue, 5,800 million, the Worldwatch Institute in Washington 5,000 million. The heterogeneity of these forecasts is obvious. But they do not mask the fundamental point already made in Chapter 1 that world population growth probably reached its zenith in the early 'seventies and is now declining slowly. The rate in 1970 was 2 per cent; by 1978 it was down to 1.7 per cent with a corresponding lowering of projections for 2000. There is of course no question of the population explosion 'petering out', as some optimistic writers have recently predicted. But a persistence of the current trend would be highly advantageous. A less cataclysmic view of the twenty-first century might then be justified; an era during which pessimism about numbers has been paramount might slowly give way to a more hopeful epoch of 'wait and see'.

But if one looks further ahead, it must be stressed that any expectation of an early stabilization of population, at the level of 2 children per family, is quite chimerical. One of the well-recognized character-istics of population growth is its intrinsic momentum, and in recent years – and particularly since the end of the Second World War – the momentum has been very considerable indeed. So much so that, if the industrialized world reached replacement level by 1980 and the developing countries by 2000 – forecasts so wildly optimistic as to verge on the preposterous – the inertia of the demographic process would dictate that world population would not reach a plateau until the total had risen to 8,000 million. The probability is much greater that replacement level will not be achieved till 2020 at the earliest. If so, the earth will be called upon to support 11,000 million people before stabilization is finally achieved in the mid or late twenty-first century.

Of that 11,000 million a very large proportion will be dependant on their fellow citizens. In 1979 nearly half the world's population was in the dependant age groups – below 15 or over 65 – and was deriving its support from people of working age. Europe was the earth's most 'elderly' continent with 12 per cent of its 480 million people aged 65 or over. North America had 10 per cent, the USSR 9 per cent, Oceania 7 per cent. In 1979 the 'oldest country' in the world was the German Democratic Republic with 16 per cent of its denizens aged 65 and over. Austria, Federal Germany and Sweden had 15 per cent in this age bracket, Belgium, Norway and the UK 14 per cent, France, Luxembourg, Hungary and Switzerland 13 per cent. Ireland notched 11 per cent, Spain, Portugal and Finland 10 per cent.

Individual countries in the developed world have aged at different speeds. In Britain it took sixty years (from 1905 to 1965) for over-65s to increase from 5 to 12 per cent. The comparable time in Sweden was 105 years (between 1855 and 1960), in France 170 years (between 1790 and 1960). Japan had 5 per cent of its population over 65 in 1950 but by 1995 the figure is expected to have risen seven points to 12 per cent.

Sociologist David Tuckett[1] has vividly described the dilemma which Western countries face in terms of their ageing populations. In the case of Britain, Tuckett concludes that 'if past population trends are maintained and if the present hospital construction programme and medical admission policies are continued, then by 1992, 94 per cent of the non-maternity beds for women and 75 per cent of all beds for men, in non-psychiatric hospitals, will be filled by patients aged over 65'. Such a prospect is daunting by any standards.

Between now and 2000 an unprecedented change in *global* age composition is also assured. In 1970 over-60s in the world numbered 304 million: by 2000 they are projected to rise by over 90 per cent to 580 million. When the over-80s are considered the change is even more dramatic. This group contained 26 million people in 1970: by 2000 it will have increased by 120 per cent to exceed 57 million – a rate of accretion half as much again as that for the world's population of all ages.

It has been generally assumed that only the industrialized countries need feel concern about their ageing populations and that the main problem in Third World countries is their explosion of youth. However, such a view is no longer tenable.[2] Developing nations are now experiencing steep increases in their numbers of old people and this emerges most clearly when absolute numbers are taken into account. Between 1970 and 2000 over-60s in the Third World are expected to rise from 150 to 347 million (130 per cent) and for the over-80s the increase is from 10 to 26 million (158 per cent). These figures give some indication of the force and tenacity of the geriatric tide in the poor countries.

Within the Third World the most striking changes in age composition will take place in Asia and Latin America. Over-60s in South Asia are expected to rise by 137 million (150 per cent) in the next twenty years. East Asia's over-60s numbered 78 million in 1970; the projection for 2000 is that the figure will double to approximately 158 million. East Asia's over-80s are forecast to increase by 170 per cent by the late 1990s, by which time this region will have the largest number of people in this age bracket anywhere in the world. The trend in Latin America is the most impressive of all. Over-60s are forecast to rise from 16.3 to 41 million between 1970 and 2000 and over-80s from 1.2 to 2.6 million during the same period.

Western society is becoming increasingly youth-orientated, with a consequent downgrading in the status of old people. So argues Professor James Williamson of the Chair of Geriatrics at Edinburgh University. Developed countries provide poorly for the requirements of old people. Instead of being perceived as a natural and inevitable part of human life, old age is regarded as an epoch where losses proliferate – loss of youth, loss of vigour, loss of sexual interest, loss of finance, loss of any definite societal role.

Difficulties of the elderly are being compounded by increasing pressures for retirement at a fixed age. Some look on retirement with pleasure and equanimity because of the opportunity which it provides to indulge in pleasure-giving activities. But to others, attuned all their lives to a 'work ethic' and deriving considerable satisfaction and fulfilment from their jobs, retirement can be an unmitigated disaster with huge lacunae of leisure time which are difficult or impossible to fill. According to Williamson, a much more flexible system is needed. Some people should be permitted to continue working well beyond the age of sixty or sixty-five; others should retire earlier or move to a less demanding and responsible work when pressures mount and they are unable to cope with them. *Pari passu* there must be radical changes in the whole educational structure. At present education is packed into a few short years in early life and thereafter for most people there stretches an illimitable desert. This can no longer be tolerated. Instead education should be a lifelong process and in this way many of the traumata associated with retiral would be mitigated.

Governments of industrialized countries have varied greatly in the political will which they have demonstrated in caring for their elderly. In the field of pensions the British record has, alas, been one of niggardliness and parsimony, in which inadequate assistance and sustenance have been provided for deserving old people. Even now the British pension seldom exceeds 25 to 30 per cent of average earnings, this comparing most unfavourably with rates of 50 to 60 per cent paid in Britain's EEC partners, France and Federal Germany.

In other ways, however, successive British Governments since the end of the Second World War have given notice that they are not prepared to see their geriatric population wither on the vine. The UK National Health Service has undoubtedly been of inestimable value to this age group. Personal social services for the elderly including home helps, 'meals on wheels', and aids for the disabled, are slowly increasing. Local authorities now view with greater sympathy requests from elderly people to maintain some quality of life by making alterations to their homes – improving insulation, providing hand-rails and grips, installing new baths and toilets, widening doorways for wheelchairs. Day centres and clubs increase social contacts, reduce loneliness and encourage leisure activities. Such facilities have improved during the 'seventies and the process is likely to continue.

Housing is crucial to old people. They have to spend more time at home than their younger counterparts, and if they are severely disabled they are virtual prisoners of their environment. Developed countries now and developing nations for the whole of the twenty-first century are unavoidably committed to looking after mounting numbers of old people. Yet only recently have the basic requirements for adequate housing of this age group come under any sort of scrutiny.

According to Williamson, houses for old people should satisfy four criteria. Design, layout and furnishing should be appropriate; and for this to happen experiment, research and much innovative thought are mandatory. The house should be alongside those inhabited by other age groups so that feelings of alienation from the rest of the community are reduced. When rehousing is necessary this should be in a familiar area thus preserving contact with relatives and friends. Lastly, for certain groups of old people, particularly the lonely and disabled, 'flatlet schemes' – so-called sheltered housing – would seem to offer a number of advantages, particularly the blend of security with continuing independence.

J. M. Keynes wrote in 1929 that in the course of two generations, 'elderly people . . . will be nearly 100 per cent . . . and middle-aged people . . . nearly 50 per cent more numerous than in the recent past.' The prospect did not please Keynes because he saw no way of coping with what he termed 'the able-bodied retired'. Many modern writers share his qualms and view an ageing society with disapprobation, distaste and even rancour. They claim that it will be dull and stagnant, that nostalgia and conservatism will proliferate and that the society will be singularly ill-adapted to react to changing circumstances.

Are these gloomy lucubrations justified? Recent history scarcely bears them out. Throughout the twentieth century the average age of people has been rising steadily, particularly in the industrialized countries. Nevertheless the engine of change has been continuously fuelled, and has been hurtling along the track at an unprecedented pace. The past eighty years, far from being dull and stagnant, have witnessed events which can only be described as seismic, and the epoch is likely to go down in history as amongst the most tumultuous and convulsive in man's experience.

In 1972 the US Population Commission published its report *Popu-*

lation and the American Future. It was a sober and scholarly document, exhaustively and critically researched; it remains a classic of the decade. The Commission had this to say about ageing: 'We are led to the conclusion that the age structure of the population is unlikely to be decisive in the form of social organization which will emerge. . . . There are many advantages of population stabilization which seem clearly to outweigh any fears of an older population.' The statement carried authority and prescience, and although it referred to the situation in the USA, it is equally applicable to most other parts of the world.

As mentioned previously, the population troika is made up of fertility, mortality and migration. *Homo sapiens* has always been a migrant, and with the discovery of the New World by Europeans the tempo of migration greatly accelerated. Between the sixteenth and twentieth centuries, over 60 million Europeans went overseas. The chief countries of emigration were Ireland, Austria-Hungary, Germany, Spain, Poland and Russia, and the main destinations the USA, Canada, Argentina, Australia, Brazil, New Zealand and South Africa. This period of history is commemorated by Emma Lazarus' inspiring words inscribed in bronze on the Statue of Liberty:

> 'Give me your tired, your poor,
> Your huddled masses yearning to breathe free,
> The wretched refuse of the teeming shore.
> Send these, the homeless, tempest-tost to me,
> I lift my lamp beside the golden door.'

During the twentieth century, however, barriers against free movement of peoples have been growing continuously. Eastern bloc countries and China discourage permanent emigration. Many other nations – about 120 on a recent UN count – restrict incoming migration. Australia, New Zealand and Canada – countries which historically have encouraged in-migration – tightened controls during the 'seventies. The USA still accepts more newcomers than any other nation, but here also the tide of immigration is now definitely on the ebb. The EEC has a liberal immigration policy amongst its member states; moreover in the past twenty years large numbers of people from non-EEC nations – Spain, Portugal, Greece, Turkey, Yugoslavia, Morocco and Algeria are examples – have been permitted to enter the Community. Now, however, with the world recession continuing and unemployment soaring in Europe as elsewhere, the presence of these alien workers is being increasingly resented. Nevertheless, with the projected expansion of the Community to include Greece and eventually other Southern European states as well, it is difficult to see how curbs on immigration could be realistically enforced.

Forecasting future patterns of migration for the rest of this century is a matter of extreme difficulty and will mainly depend on the attitudes of individual governments. When the world was relatively empty, migration provided a very necessary safety valve. Now that it is grossly overcrowded, the efficiency of the valve has been seriously impaired. Yet traditionally, migration was the stepping stone whereby man solved his resource problems and sought a better quality of life. This was true of the early nomads, of colonists throughout the ages, of oppressed people fleeing from intolerance, hatred, bigotry and prejudice. Given the fact that, when pressed hard enough, individuals are prepared to operate outside any law which may be imposed – recent Mexican emigration to the USA is a good example of this – can we ever envision a situation in which a virtual surcease on migration is imposed? And what would be the effect of such a ban in a world in which gross disparities of wealth and opportunity exist between developed and developing nations? The late President Houari Boumedienne of Algeria once commented, 'No quantity of atomic bombs could stem the tide of billions . . . who will some day leave the poor Southern part of the world to erupt into the relatively accessible spaces of the rich Northern Hemisphere looking for survival.' If the former Algerian leader's statement turns out to have a prophetic quality – and one cannot afford to discount his views completely – the effect of this mass migration on mankind would be nothing short of seismic.

With the attainment of zero or negative population growth* in an increasing number of industrialized countries, the governments of these nations could theoretically manipulate migration to maintain a particular rate of growth.[3] This would be particularly so if the government in question perceived a falling population as a threat. A country could, for example, juggle with its migration quotas so that any deficit in births in the previous year could be rectified. But at best

* In a nation with negative population growth deaths per year exceed births.

this would be a hazardous procedure bristling with problems. The tuning would have to be inordinately fine and moreover the immigrants would presumably be of different colours, nationalities and cultural backgrounds. Any economic benefits which might accrue from boosting the labour force in this way could well be rendered nugatory by the chaos and turmoil arising from the attempt of the immigrants to adapt to an alien environment.

The remarkable decline in fertility in industrialized nations during the 1960s and 1970s has meant that population forecasters have had continuously to lower their projections for the future. The British scene is typical in this respect. In 1964 the Office of Population Censuses and Surveys was forecasting that by 1990 numbers in the UK would exceed 66 million; by 1968 the projection for 1990 was down to 64.5 million and by 1976 it had plummeted to 57.3 million. It is salutary to record that in little more than a decade 9 million people were summarily 'lopped off' the projection. The baneful effects of such innacurate forecasting in areas such as health, housing and particularly education need no emphasis.

The OPCS is naturally very cagey about one of the most contentious political issues in contemporary British politics – the number of coloured people likely to be resident in this country by the end of the century. In 1972 immigrants from the Indian subcontinent, Africa and the West Indies numbered 1.4 million and constituted 2.7 per cent of the total population; by 1976 numbers had risen to 1.8 million and 3.3 per cent. What about the likely situation in 2000? Judging by immigrant experience elsewhere in the world – Puerto Ricans in New York City are often quoted – it seems unlikely that 'differential fertility' will be a serious contributor to changes in the relative sizes of groups of different ethnic origin in Britain. Between 1972 and 1976 average family size was decreasing significantly in West Indian women and rather more modestly in women from the Indian subcontinent. This process can be expected to speed up over the next twenty years as the coloured population ages, as their death rate rises and as social mores impel couples towards a procreative pattern characteristic of their new country of residence. Prominent political figures bent on criticizing the pluralistic type of society now evolving in Britain seldom take note of this trend. Such individuals are undoubtedly treading a dangerous path, for they stand the risk of being engulfed in the whirlwind which they may loose and of being borne along by storms over which they are powerless to exert any form of control.

According to the OPCS, low birth rates and a tendency towards an ageing population will persist in Britain well into the 'eighties. Two factors may then operate to reverse these historical trends. The first is that people over retirement age will be composed mainly of individuals born during the interwar period – an epoch when fertility was relatively low – and numbers in this group will be declining both relatively and absolutely. The second factor is that children born in the late 'fifties and early 'sixties, when procreative activity was quite high, will themselves be reproducing and consequently a slight rise in birth rates can be expected.

In 1979 Britain's population is delicately balanced with births and deaths about equal. However, at least four European countries – Austria, Luxembourg, the German Democratic Republic and Federal Germany[4] – are now in negative growth. With a continuation of current fertility trends Belgium, Czechoslovakia, Denmark, Hungary, Norway and Sweden will reach zero or negative growth early in the 'eighties and Bulgaria, Greece, Finland, Italy and Switzerland will follow by 1990. In 1979 the US is reproducing at a rate of 1.8 births per female; and according to the 'low' projection of its Bureau of the Census numbers could eventually stop growing at a figure of 253 million in 2015. However, even if fertility climbs back to replacement level (2.1 per children per woman), the US population is likely to reach only 260 million in 2000 and 283 million in 2015. These figures are much lower than those being confidently bruited around only a few years ago.

During the next twenty years, haphazard fertility in developed countries can be expected to decrease significantly. Contraceptive practice will certainly become more widespread in all social classes; sterilization will gain in popularity with both sexes, abortion will be more readily obtainable as intransigence and bigotry on this issue gradually fade. Today's predilection for the two-child family could well continue, although one-child marriages are likely to become more frequent. The trend towards later marriage (even now many women wait until they are almost thirty) and postponement of births for longer periods of time after marriage will undoubtedly persist. Unless soaring unemployment and resultant financial hardship produce a major clamp-down on procreative activity in the industrialized world, birth rates in that area seem unlikely to alter dramatically over the next two decades. A level close to or just below replacement is probable because in the public view this will represent the sort of family size which will be in tune with perceptions about the quality of life in the future. The level is unlikely to be altered by political rhetoric of a pronatalist character or by the mild and trivial economic inducements customarily offered by Western governments in an attempt to boost fertility. That is not to say, however, that fluctuations in birth rates will not take place. Certainly they will, and they are likely to be irregular both in amplitude and periodicity, accurately mirroring the reaction of couples to the differing social and economic forces with which they are confronted.

With the advent of zero population growth in many Western countries quite soon, there is increasing speculation about the demographic characteristics of such a steady state. Only three facets seem certain – birth and death rates low and in balance each year, a decrease in the percentage of youth, and a rise in the proportion of the elderly. Any other ingredients can only be guessed at. Lincoln Day, a demographer at the Australian National University, postulates that in a stationary population in which death rates remain low, the sex ratio will shift slightly, with the excess of males over the age of fifty gradually diminishing. He argues that because of this change, pressures to marry for purely demographic reasons will be eased. Day doubts whether marriage patterns themselves will be affected. In the steady state marriage could be almost universal or quite rare; it could occur early or late and, if the divorce rate was high, several times in a lifetime.

The concept of the steady state has traditionally received much opprobrium because of its alleged propensity to produce a cataclysmic fall in the labour force. Existing employees, on retirement, would have too few workers to support them; occupational and state pensions would be thrown into disarray or placed in jeopardy. All the evidence so far adduced suggests that such fears are grossly exaggerated. The US Population Commission did not regard this as a major problem and instead extolled the social and environmental advantages which would flow from keeping the labour force within reasonable bounds. The Government-appointed Population Panel in the UK concluded that, even by the end of the century, the ratio of workers to non-workers would still be quite acceptable and might even be better than in the early 1970s when the average family size exceeded two children. Other authorities have gone even further. They totally reject the view that foreseeable demographic developments in the industrialized countries in the direction of population stabilization will have an adverse effect on the labour supply. If shortages do occur, they argue, institutional, social and economic factors, rather than change in population structure and dynamics, must take the blame.

One of the most fascinating areas for speculation in a stationary population concerns the status and role of women. Once the steady state is established, lowered fertility will be a *sine qua non*; furthermore, in the transition to sustainability, a larger proportion of childless women can be anticipated. This changing fertility pattern is likely to arise both through greatly increased dissemination of sophisticated birth control methods and as a consequence of later marriage – with postponement of child-bearing and a higher likelihood of female infertility at a stage of life when ovulatory cycles become less frequent. One does not have to be a clairvoyant to predict that in a stationary population, substantially less of a woman's life will be spent on activities related to reproduction and child care. The effects of this on society as a whole will certainly be profound. Husband-wife relationships, marriage patterns and divorce rates will all be affected; so will the composition of the labour force;[5] so too will the future of the Women's Liberation Movement, which is likely to show an even greater tendency than at present to seek improvements in status and expectations for females.

The move towards a stationary population in the developed world is greatly to be welcomed. Yet insufficient attention has been paid to this benison. Instead several countries – France and Federal Germany have been amongst the most vociferous – have indicated that they feel very uncomfortable about the current trend towards low fertility, and political leaders have been issuing dire warnings about the effects likely to ensue if numbers continue to fall.

Alarm bells need not be sounded on this issue. Our finite planet can ill afford a high degree of procreative activity in the rich nations. For each birth there places a disproportionate strain on the earth's diminishing resources. The situation of course reaches its apogee in the USA where the amounts of land, water and fertilizer required to support the average American are almost five times greater than are necessary for citizens from Third World countries like India, Nigeria, Colombia and Peru. Moreover, many industrialized nations –

Belgium, the Netherlands, Federal Germany, the UK and Japan immediately spring to mind – are amongst the most heavily settled on earth. In all of them, an acute imbalance between population and indigenous resources exists; in all, a steady deterioration of the environment together with an ineluctable erosion in the quality of life are taking place.

The advantages which would accrue to such overcrowded countries from reduction of numbers would be manifold. Pressures on land would ease; housing might become less costly and more readily obtainable; land erosion by motorways and other large roads rendered necessary by the heavier traffic which population growth engenders, would be less pervasive. With fewer consumers, urbanization at the expense of the agricultural sector would slow; food imports would be reduced and the thrust towards greater self-sufficiency given more of a cutting edge.

There would be benefits too in the field of education, particularly in the medium and long term. Smaller classes in schools and an increase in individual tuition would be more feasible in the steady state; an improvement in the quality of the instruction might take place. In the field of employment, with the spread of automation and mechanization, the reduction in the need for manpower to achieve the same level of productivity will undoubtedly be progressive and, although the provision of full employment in industrialized nations has come to be regarded, except by wildly optimistic and anachronistic politicians, as totally fanciful, nevertheless a certain amount of steam could undoubtedly be taken out of this socially explosive issue.

International implications are also important in this connection. Overpopulation in industrialized countries is a crucial factor in their trading vulnerability and in their inordinate sensitivity to world shortages of food, raw materials and energy. Population pressures in these nations are stoking the fires of monetary inflation and contributing to the overall global economic malaise. In developed societies with static or diminishing populations, such effects, although still present, are likely to be less pronounced.

During the next twenty years, man's habitat will alter in an unprecedented fashion. World population in 1900 was 1,500 million and 13.6 per cent of people lived in cities; by 1978, of a world population of

4,200 million, town dwellers constituted 40 per cent. By 2000 an event of high portent will have taken place because, for the first time in human history, urbanites will outnumber rural denizens.

The rise in the number and the change in the pattern of distribution of large cities during this century has been spectacular. In 1900 there were only eleven cities with populations in excess of one million. By 1950 the total was seventy-five and just under half of them were in Europe. By the late 'seventies, however, a radical transformation had taken place. Cities with populations in excess of one million were now sited mainly in the poor countries; there were seventy-five of them in that area in 1978 with a forecast of a further two hundred by the end of the century.

Most metropolitan areas in the Third World are growing at truly phenomenal rates, much greater than that of the host country itself. For example, the population growth rate of the Philippines is 2.5 per cent; but Manila, the capital, is expanding at 12 per cent per annum with numbers likely to double in a decade. The rate of increase in Ghana is 2.9 per cent as against the capital Accra at almost 8 per cent. The population of Bombay is forecast to rise from eight to nineteen million by 2000, that of Karachi from five to sixteen million, of Jakarta from five to eighteen million, of Calcutta from ten to twenty-two million, of Cairo from six to sixteen million, of Seoul from eight to twenty million. One could give numerous other examples of this urban stampede. It is also projected that by the end of the century places hardly known today will house a million or more inhabitants. They include such unexpected names as Asmara in Ethiopia, Kitwe in Zambia, Kananga in Zaire, Maraçaibo in Venezuela and Danang in the Republic of Vietnam.

Third World urbanization reaches its maximum in Latin America. The South American continent is already 60 per cent urbanized, comparing most unfavourably with Africa and Asia where only a quarter of the population live in cities. In Brazil the urbanization problem is as intractable as anywhere on earth. On average, cities in that country are growing by 7 per cent per annum. Already five – Rio de Janeiro, Sao Paulo, Recife, Porto Alegre and Belo Horizonte – have topped the million mark. Rio had almost seven million people in 1970; a projection for 1985 is for 11.4 and for 2000, 22 million. Sao Paulo was reputed to house 8 million people in 1970; numbers could rise to 17 million by 1985 and to 26 million by 2000. In other Latin American countries the trend is the same. Bogota could top 6 million by 1985; Lima, with a population of a mere 175,000 in 1929, had 3 million people in the late 1970s and could double its numbers again by 2000. Population growth in Mexico City has been gargantuan – 1 million in 1930, 8 million by 1970, and a mind-boggling forecast of 32 million for 2000.

Nigeria's capital, Lagos, has become a monster. In 1932, numbers were thought to exceed a million; 1976 saw the 3 million mark passed. Currently Lagos is Africa's fastest growing city with a forecast of 20 million inhabitants by the first decade of the twenty-first century. Young people are flooding into Lagos from the countryside and from outside Nigeria in search of education and jobs. Half the city's inhabitants are under fifteen years of age; procreation is running rampant; demography's iron law dictates a huge population burden for the future. Already the malign effects of overpopulation dominate Lagos – massive overcrowding, inadequate housing, appalling sanitation, soaring infantile mortality rates, chaotic traffic, pervasive water shortages, ubiquitous power cuts, port facilities clogged or stretched beyond endurance. How much worse will all this be twenty years from now?

Each day in the Third World, 75,000 people migrate from rural areas to cities. Why is this so? At the hub of the problem is misplaced development, Governments having allocated scarce resources preferentially to cities and having left the countryside to moulder, stagnate and decay. The result has been a massive *cri de coeur*, a 'vote with the feet' against boredom, despair, lack of opportunity, unfulfilled aspirations. Migrants to shanty towns recognize that they face severe hardship; suffering, degradation and misery are widespread – in some cities more than others. But the flame of hope still flickers; conditions may improve; warmth and glow may be brought to grey and drab lives. For cities are where the action is. Educational facilities are better, medical services more readily available, jobs more plentiful. The resourceful migrant can often find employment in the 'informal economic sector', also termed 'the bazaar economy'. He can, for example, become a street peddler or sweeper; he can involve himself with transport, with personal services of all kinds, with the establishment of 'mini-businesses' of a quite extraordinary variety. The trancendent feature of the shanty towns is the tenancity shown by human beings in the face of daunting odds, people confronting a concatenation of circumstances with a degree of ingenuity and innovation remarkable by any standard.

Up till now most Third World Governments have treated their informal economic sector as a pariah and have refused to deal with it. Even after the Habitat Conference in Vancouver in 1976, at which strenuous efforts were made to reverse this policy, intransigence still prevails. By forcing a tight-fitting carapace on their informal sector, Governments of developing countries are depriving themselves of a huge amount of productive effort which could be much more efficiently utilized. By acting in this way they are manifestly out of tune with the tides of contemporary history.

It is a coruscating irony that, just when mankind may have reached a critical turning point *vis-à-vis* population as a result of falling birth rates worldwide, it must now face another devastating explosion – that of its labour force. Growth of the labour force is a direct result of the entrance each year of millions of able-bodied young people into working age groups. It can be likened to a prism reflecting previous reproductive performance and its composition is in a state of continuous flux, as it mirrors different patterns of work participation by men and women at the global level.

Unemployment is a crucial issue for the next twenty years. It reminds one of a gigantic rock in a rushing stream, creating the swirls and eddies of economic, social and political controversy. And of all the accompaniments of the overpopulation syndrome, the degree of joblessness is amongst the most difficult to forecast. No area is more uncertain: nowhere is prophecy more hazardous, opinon more divided.

What views hold sway? [6] First there is the 'business as usual' school. They espouse the philosophy of economic growth and regard unemployment as a cyclic phenomenon which will ultimately be self-correcting. The group of futurologists headed by Herman Kahn at the Hudson Institute in the USA are even more optimistic. [7] They predict a new *belle époque* when the whole vast fabric of society will be in the process of beneficent transformation and when civilization will move to its desired goals with dignity, majesty and speed. They envision the emergence of several super-industrialized states well before the end of the century. Purses will clink, economic growth rates soar and affluence abound. The creation of a plethora of new and exciting jobs in an epoch of unprecedented technical innovation will be the basis of the political and social stability which they predict.

Environmentalists are, of course, much less sanguine. Some perceive a crisis situation with violence, unrest and revolution following the lodestar of massive unemployment. Others, concentrating mainly on energy profiles, espouse a rather less apocalyptic view. They stress that a change in global energy policy would greatly ease the employment situation. Were the hard energy path – capital intensive, labour-destructive, dependent on finite resources of fossil fuels and uranium-235 – jettisoned and replaced by the utilization of alternative energy sources, such a policy would lead to the creation of a wealth of new jobs, particularly if the use of alternative energy sources were combined with a massive and sustained programme of energy conservation. Yet another group of people view the likely employment scenario characterized by increasing joblessness with serenity and equanimity. They welcome the advent of an age of leisure, with man freed from demanding and remorseless toil. John Stuart Mill is their prophet, his famous aphorism that there would be just as much scope for improving the art of living when man 'ceases to be engrossed by the art of getting on' their guiding star.

Joblessness will, of course, reach its zenith in the Third World.[8] The International Labour Office forecasts that the Asian labour force will have expanded by 51 per cent by 2000 AD, the African by 74 per cent, the Latin American by 87 per cent. Spectacular increases are projected in individual developing countries. Mexico, Peru, Venezuela and Algeria will double their workforce in the next twenty years; Nigeria's will rise by 19 million, Turkey's by 12 million, Pakistan's by 20 million, Indonesia's by 34 million, Brazil's by 33 million, Mexico's by 21 million, India's by 5 per cent per annum. ILO is on record as forecasting that 1,000 million new jobs, mainly in the Third World, will have to be created by the year 2000. Such a figure has, of course, no conceivable overlap with reality in a world in which constraints on economic growth will bite increasingly. Instead, the unpalatable fact must be faced that in many of the poor countries a whole generation of children will be destined to grow up and proceed directly from school into retirement.

At first sight, developed nations will fare better in the race for jobs. Declining birth rates will help; palliatives such as extending education into adult life, lowering retirement age, shortening hours of work, cutting the working week, can be more readily applied and even now are being actively canvassed. Also, the numbers involved are much less formidable. Thus the North American labour force is projected to increase by only 30 million (28 per cent) between now and 2000, that of the USSR by 20 million (15 per cent), that of Western Europe by 30 million (14 per cent). Individual countries in which the expansion of the labour force is likely to be less than 10 per cent include Italy, Federal Germany, Finland, Greece, Hungary and Bulgaria.

Yet these rather optimistic forecasts take no account of what has been labelled the Second Industrial Revolution. At its hub is the specialty of micro-electronics; its pivots are the computer and the microprocessor. A degree of automation is now becoming feasible which was undreamt of by the visionaries of previous decades. Micro-electronics have provided the spur for a quantum leap for humanity into a quite unforeseen form of technical change. Undoubtedly the benefits to society that will accrue from microprocessors will be manifold. But this must not be allowed to disguise the fact that the technology could become the rationalizer *par excellence,* the innovation with the potential to throw literally millions of people out of work.

This is no place to recount the saga of the silicon chip. The details are already well known to many people – the development of the transistor thirty years ago, the ready synergy between transistors and computers, the scientific triumph of the semi-conductor integrated circuit, the rapid thrust towards miniaturization culminating in the assemblage of a quarter of a million chips on one transistor. Robert Noyce, a pioneer in this field, wrote in *Scientific American* in October 1977: 'An integrated circuit and chips . . . a quarter of an inch square can now embrace more electronic elements than the most complex piece of electronic equipment that could be built in 1950. Today's micro-computer . . . has more computing capacity than the first large electronic computer, ENIAC. It is 20 times faster, has a longer memory, is thousands of times more reliable, consumes the power of a light bulb rather than a locomotive, occupies 1/30,000 of the volume and costs 1/10,000 as much.' The summary is excellent, stressing as it does the basic qualities of the most remarkable feat of technology which mankind has ever devised. Microprocessors are reliable and flexible and they have the capacity to displace man's thinking, judgement and intuitive powers. Already microprocessors have infiltrated widely; and they will continue to do so – so much so that by 1986, the number of electronic functions incorporated into products of all kinds can be expected to have risen a hundredfold. No field of manufacturing or service industry will be immune from the long arm of the microprocessor: blue- and white-collar workers, intellectuals and non-intellectuals alike will be affected. Never before has a powerful technology advanced with such breathtaking speed. In an era in which inflationary pressures are rampant and prices are soaring, the vertiginous decline in the cost of electronic hardware has been nothing short of miraculous. Since the early 'sixties, the price of each unit of performance has been reduced by a hundred-thousand-fold; with an ever proliferating market and a continuing innovative thrust, further stunning reductions in cost will come as naturally as night follows day.

With the advent of the chip the vision of the post-industrial society – more leisured, less thrusting, with a better quality of life –shimmers tantalizingly on the horizon. Futurologists have, of course, been adumbrating the post-industrial society and stretching out to their nirvana for years. The routes recommended have been very different. John Stuart Mill saw the road through the economics of the steady state, J. M. Keynes in his *Economic Possibilities for our Grandchildren*, and Herman Kahn and his colleagues in *The Next 200 Years*, through continuing and rapidly accelerating economic growth.[9] However, irrespective of these forecasts, in the eighth and ninth decades of this century, it is the short- and medium-term effects of the chip which must be faced, and one of the possible results of its presence will be a high degree of structural unemployment in industrialized countries.

The sequelae to such a state of affairs could be ominous. Luddite reactions could be stimulated along with a degree of social and political upheaval beside which the Depression years of the 'thirties could pale into insignificance. One need not stress here that to individuals imbued with a strong 'work ethic', unemployment can be a shattering experience. Self-esteem is reduced, confidence eroded; boredom proliferates and the carapace of depersonalization grips tighter as social contracts narrow. Moreover, the sociological and medical effects of unemployment have been poorly researched and Western nations are ill equipped to deal with the magnitude of the problem. Senator Hubert Humphrey, one of the most far-sighted statesmen in this field, warned the US Congress shortly before his death that unemployment 'has a strikingly potent impact on society. Even a one per cent increase ... creates a legacy of stress, of aggression and of illness affecting society long into the future.' Dr Harvey Brenner, prestigious physician at the Johns Hopkins Hospital in Baltimore, has echoed these sentiments. Brenner claims that the increase of 1.4 per cent in US unemployment between 1970 and 1975, affecting $1\frac{1}{2}$ million people, caused 20,000 deaths from heart and kidney disease, 500 deaths from liver cirrhosis due mainly to excessive alcohol consumption, 920 suicides and 420 homicides.

Alexander Solzhenitszyn once wrote that, if we care only about re-producing our species and crowd the earth senselessly, we shall merely create a 'terrifying society'. In an era in which the global population growth rate is slowing, the type of society envisaged by Solzhenitszyn may seem to have receded somewhat. But a concomitant of over-population, that of joblessness, certainly has not, and the micro-electronic revolution will force this issue increasingly into the public mind. Governments of industrialized countries must be fully aware of the dilemma which they face. Micawberism – all too rife in political circles – must be discarded; the 'men of brains' must be summoned to debate the issue and seek solutions. The Second Industrial Revolution is here to stay and we must all learn to dance to a new tune. Those who underrate the significance of the microprocessor can only be compared to kings who sit by the sea plaintively commanding the tide not to rise.

NOTES AND REFERENCES

[1] David Tuckett (1976), *An Introduction to Medical Sociology*, Tavistock, London.

[2] See W. M. Beattie (1978).

[3] See C. F. Westoff (1978), 'Marriage and Fertility in the Developed Countries, *Scientific American*, Vol. 239, No. 6, p. 35, for a thoughtful appraisal of this issue.

[4] In 1976 Federal Germany had 733,000 deaths and 603,000 births. A recent television programme entitled 'Are the Germans Dying Out?' reflected governmental anxiety. One German demographer declaimed, 'Beneath the blankets we are a dying people.' (See C. F. Westoff (1978), op. cit.)

[5] For Europe as a whole the International Labour Office has projected a three-fifths participation of women of reproductive age in the labour force for 2000 AD.

[6] A good description of the different viewpoints is provided by James Robertson (1978), *The Same Alternative: Signposts to a Self-Fulfilling Future*, published by the author, London.

[7] See also Epilogue, p. 207.

[8] See, for example, Edward Goldsmith (1978) for a discussion of this theme.

[9] The two visions of the genesis of the post-industrial society are well des-cribed by Michael Marien (1977), 'The Two Visions of Post-Industrial Society', *Futures*, Vol. 9, No. 5, p. 415.

Chapter 10

The Prognosis for Birth Control

The crucial importance of birth control in a grossly overpopulated world needs no emphasis. Yet the saga of research and innovation in this field in recent years has been uneven and erratic. Some mountains have been successfully scaled; elsewhere, however, the foothills of discovery have scarcely been glimpsed. What then is the current situation? How do we stand? What new methods for birth control are likely to become available in the eighth and ninth decades of this century?[1]

In the late 'seventies abortion constitutes one of the most widely used methods of birth control, and it is unlikely that any population has attained a low level of fertility without its utilization on a considerable scale.[2] Over the past twenty years liberalization of abortion laws globally has proceeded at a pace which has probably been more rapid than that of most other major social changes. Christopher Tietze, a recognized American authority on abortion statistics, states that 36 per cent of the world's population now live in countries in which the termination of pregnancy is legal on request virtually without restriction. For another 23 per cent of humanity, broad social grounds such as inadequate housing, poverty and marital status are recognized as valid reasons for legal abortion. Twelve per cent of the world's women can have their pregnancies terminated legally to protect their health, in case of rape and incest, and where there is a likelihood that the foetus will be malformed. However, the remaining 30 per cent are much less fortunate. They reside in countries which still operate highly restrictionist laws and in which pregnancy termination is either totally proscribed or is permitted only to save the life of the mother. Contemporary society deserves to be severely castigated for the fact that as we enter the eighth decade of the century the majority of the world's abortions are still performed illegally. Indeed, in some areas – Latin America is the outstanding example – the incidence of illegal abortion is actually increasing, particularly amongst

175

women in the lower socio-economic groups.

Illegal abortion can, of course, be a highly perilous procedure. Untrained personnel frequently participate, equipment is poor, conditions insanitary; a plethora of complications can ensue including perforation of the womb, vaginal bleeding and surgical shock from rapid and massive haemorrhage. As late as 1970 it was estimated that 150,000 women throughout the world were dying each year as a result of illegal abortion. Since then documentation from many countries has shown that the shift from illegal to legal abortion has been reflected in a decline in abortion mortality. Overall, the outlook for the future *vis-à-vis* pregnancy termination is not unpromising, since the probability remains that the current trend towards liberalization of laws will persist. In *Syndromes of the Seventies* I argued that the anti-abortionists were in the process of being trounced globally, and that liberal abortion was here to stay – 'The pro-abortionists have breached the ramparts; the citadel is theirs for the taking' – I have no reason to alter this world view three years later, even in the presence of resurgent Islam to which liberal abortion is, of course, anathema.

One of the most exciting events in birth control during the 'seventies has been the introduction of compounds know as prostaglandins. The latter are widely distributed throughout the body and have a multiplicity of actions. In relation to reproduction, prostaglandins are thought to be involved in the processes whereby the egg is shed from the ovary, transplanted to the womb and implanted therein. But an even more important effect which they possess is to cause uterine contractions and thus to act as abortifacients. In the early days of prostaglandin research, the material was given into veins and muscles. However, this caused unacceptable side-effects – especially nausea, vomiting and sweating – and had to be abandoned. The route of administration subsequently favoured was directly into the amniotic sac (the innermost membrane surrounding the developing foetus) and prostaglandins given in this way soon gained recognition as an auxiliary method of pregnancy termination after the tenth week. However, in early pregnancy they remained inferior to more traditional methods of vaginal evacuation by dilation and curettage, and for the past ten years or more by the vacuum suction technique.

Early abortion by prostaglandins is increasingly exercising the minds of those interested in fertility control. Quite recently definite progress has been reported. Prostaglandin analogues have now been made in the form of vaginal suppositories which can be administered by the patient herself and thus obviate the necessity for hospital admission. International trials conducted through the World Health Organization suggest that the vaginal administration of these materials is likely to be just as effective as vacuum aspiration in terminating a pregnancy during the first four weeks. High hopes are being held out for the eventual applicability of the method on a large scale, and it is also forecast that by 1980 a prostaglandin analogue will have been developed which can be taken by mouth.

Research is also in progress on better methods for using prostaglandins as abortifacients later in pregnancy. Repeated administration of vaginal suppositories containing prostaglandin analogues every three hours throughout the day is reputed to be more efficacious than giving the material into the amniotic sac. Promising results have also been reported by the single administration of a long-acting vaginal suppository containing such an analogue. Another new birth control method is under study, the aim of which is to prevent prostaglandins from acting on the reproductive system, particularly on the ovary and uterus. This work is still at a very early stage. However, a number of such materials have now been discovered and some have been shown to be effective in animal experiments. The application of these compounds to human reproduction could be an exciting and challenging exercise.

Intrauterine devices have a long history. One of their earliest applications was to prevent excessive fertility in camels: Arabian and Turkish camel drivers were in the habit of inserting a round stone into the animal's uterus before setting out on a long desert journey. Currently attempts are being made to improve the efficacy and reduce the side-effects of this method of birth control.

Excessive bleeding following intrauterine contraception has always been a major problem. However, there is now some hope that bleeding can be lessened by utilizing devices impregnated with the female sex hormone, progesterone, or with chemically related substances. Another quite different group of chemicals known as diamidines affect blood clotting and might be incorporated into devices thus reducing bleeding. Pain and spontaneous expulsion of devices are also well-recognized disadvantages of intrauterine contraception. Both result from increased uterine contractions, and a number of compounds are currently being tested which, when incorporated into a device, might damp down such contractility.

Vaginal rings and devices which can be inserted into the neck of the womb are also receiving attention. Both types of method are intended to provide contraceptive protection over long periods of time; in both, the protection is designed to be reversible. Rings can be inserted and removed by the user with the minimum of instruction. Some rings release female sex hormones, particularly progesterone, and their aim is to effect contraception without preventing the shedding of the egg. Recent evidence, mainly from Swedish sources, suggests that rings so impregnated can give good menstrual cycle control and may not cause the irregular bleeding which traditionally has been a prominent feature of this type of medication when given by mouth. If work in this area prospers, a vaginal ring for widespread use could be available by the early 1980s.

Devices for insertion into the neck of the womb are still at an early stage of development. The main aim of this research is to develop a reservoir whereby a drug with contraceptive properties can be released over long periods of time. *Pari passu* with work in this general field the search is being continued for substances which are capable of killing the male sperm and which could also be incorporated into vaginal rings and uterine devices. Such compounds are potentially very numerous and many of them are currently utilized in spermicidal preparations available commercially.

The Pill remains the touchstone of contraceptive practice. Oral contraceptives are now available in more than 150 countries; at least 80 million women around the world are taking them. In industrialized nations the risks of the Pill are now well recognized and documented, special attention having been given recently to hazards in older women and in heavy smokers. However, in developing countries with much younger populations and with a burgeoning demand for this form of birth control, a series of important questions remains to be answered.

Health Authorities in Third World countries wish to know whether the side effects and hazards identified in Western women with the Pill will occur with equal frequency in *their* populations which have different cultural, dietary and reproductive habits. What, for example, will be the effect of the Pill on lactation, a mechanism of crucial importance for achieving spacing between successive births?[3] How will malnourished and anaemic women and those with parasitic infections fare on the Pill? Also – and this is repeatedly asked – can family planning personnel without previous medical experience be rapidly trained to manage problems which arise in relation to Pill administration and usage? The Chinese and, to some extent, the Tanzanian and Cuban exemplars suggest that they can. However, evidence in other cultural settings is needed.

Long-acting contraceptives are in considerable demand, particularly in Third World countries. Most of the preparations contain the two female sex hormones, oestrogen and progesterone; injections can be given at monthly, two-monthly or three-monthly intervals. Since its inception this form of treatment has been beset by a multiplicity of problems. Over ten years ago I listed some of them.[4] Menstrual cycles were of variable length; heavy bleeding was a frequent complication, absence of menstrual flow unduly protracted. There was a significant pregnancy rate under treatment, and on stopping the medication the delay in the return of fertility could be unacceptably long. Yet over more than a decade, the pace of change in this field has been glacial. And to expect the difficulties of the method to be ironed out in the foreseeable future seems to savour of a degree of optimism which can only de described as Panglossian.

A few new approaches to long-term contraception are currently being tried; what success they will have remains à matter for conjecture. A 'biodegradable delivery system' is now available, in which normal body processes are supposed to break down a mixture of female sex hormones. The purpose is to develop an implant to be sited under the skin and which would be reliable, devoid of side-effects and capable of abolishing fertility for at least three months and preferably for one year. The aim is, of course, impeccable; the practice will no doubt be exceedingly difficult.

The name of C. Djerassi of Stanford University in California will forever be enshrined in the annals of biomedical research. For it was largely due to Djerassi's pioneering and meticulous chemical work that the Pill was introduced into clinical practice. Recently Djerassi looked at the future of oral contraception.[5] He is not optimistic that any major change in the chemical composition of the Pill will take place in the short or medium term, and instead he forecasts that in 2000 AD much the same type of compounds will be in use as are currently being marketed. To support his contention, Djerassi cites the long-term nature of the epidemiological studies required to determine whether a contraceptive agent could be responsible for the production of a major disease such as cancer. Information of this type is only now beginning to emerge in relation to the Pill, and many years and possibly decades will have to elapse before definite conclusions can be drawn. If such studies show no cancer risk or even a reduction in the incidence of certain forms of malignant disease, the compound will then be presumed to be safe; and the obvious reaction of Health Authorities will be to maintain its supply to the public, rather than to introduce newer and less tried forms of medication. Economic factors also support this viewpoint. In the USA and other technologically advanced countries the time lag between the initial discovery of the medication and final governmental approval for its use after exhaustive testing in animals and human volunteers may be as long as fifteen years. Djerassi's comment is that 'the potential return on the large financial investment by one of the multinational pharmaceutical companies for developing any fundamentally new steroid oral contraceptive is small and risky'. It should be stressed that such a *modus operandi* is not confined to the capitalist world. Marxist China is totally self-sufficient in the manufacture of its steroid contraceptives. Yet here also the search for new compounds receives low priority, the main thrust being towards the production of compounds of known efficacy.

Djerassi obviously has an affection for multinational companies and he cites events in Mexico to buttress his predilection. Formerly, Mexico satisfied one half of the world demand for hormonal contraceptives because the country possessed in abundance the plant steroid diosgenin which could be extracted from various species of *Dioscorea*, and which was far and away the most versatile of all raw materials for the production of these materials. By the mid-'sixties, multinational pharmaceutical firms were well established in Mexico and were producing diosgenin at highly competitive prices. Then the Mexican Government, increasingly resentful about the activities of companies over which it had no direct control, proceeded to nationalize the collection of *Dioscorea*. The immediate result was a precipitous rise in the cost of diosgenin with alternative new materials rapidly becoming economically competitive. Leaves and roots from *Solanum Aviculare* began to be cultivated in New Zealand, *Solanum Marginatum* in Ecuador. Djerassi likens the rise and fall of the Mexican steroid industry to a Greek tragedy and unequivocally blames the final outcome on the Mexican Government's nationalization policy.

The medicinal value of plants has long been known to indigenous populations, and some of the most valuable drugs in medicine – digitalis is the classic example – have been derived from this source. A wide-ranging folklore exists on the fertility-regulating proclivities of plants. For example, in Mexico, *Montanoa Tomentosa* is still used to terminate early pregnancy, in Paraguay a local plant is widely employed for contraceptive purposes; Chinese motherworth continues to be utilized throughout the Far East as an early abortifacient and a plant native to Bangladesh, and now growing in the Kew Botanical Gardens in London, is reputed to have the same effect. However, at the time of writing, the specific substances in the plants which produce those effects have not been identified and their chemical composition is still a mystery. This whole area of research is undoubtedly one of great promise for the future, and it would seem especially germane to developing countries whose self-sufficiency in methods of fertility control could be greatly boosted, and whose Health Authorities would then be in a position to provide drugs, the source of which was already familiar to the local population.

A method of birth control which would act very early after fertilization of the egg by the sperm would have obvious attractions. The availability of such a technique would, for example, greatly diminish the necessity for abortion. The woman could merely swallow a pill when she noticed her period was late or, alternatively, she could take the medication each month and so prevent the implantation of the fertilized egg in the uterine wall. Various lines of research are being followed in this area. They include attempts to interfere with the function of the uterine wall by blocking receptors in it which would normally accept the fertilized egg, interfering with the function of the egg itself, and inhibition or suppression of the activity of a structure in the ovary known as the corpus luteum (yellow body) which, if fertilization takes place, is crucial for the development of the tiny embryo. An assessment of the feasibility of developing satisfactory 'anti-implantation' methods should be possible during the 'eighties and thereafter the marketing of suitable materials might follow quite rapidly.

Vaccination dates back to the 1790s, when Edward Jenner developed a system of protection against smallpox which involved the injection of a very similar but relatively harmless virus *vaccinia* (the cowpox) into one of his patients. For many years no one knew how Jenner's vaccine worked; now, however, immunologists understand its mechanism of action. When the body detects a foreign substance – commonly known as an *antigen* – it reacts against it by producing an antibody which combines specifically with it. This often has the effect of destroying the foreign protein, utilizing the body's own defence mechanisms.

Usually the body does not manufacture antibodies to its own naturally produced antigens. But there are occasions when it can, and an antigen in question which has relevance to fertility control is known as *Human Chorionic Gonadotrophin*. HCG is the archetypal hormone of pregnancy and it is produced by the placenta (afterbirth), a structure rich in blood vessels and linking the growing baby with the mother's womb. HCG appears in large quantities in the blood and urine of pregnant women; after the delivery of the child, it vanishes rapidly from the body. During the 'seventies the potential of a contraceptive method designed to block HCG by using the body's own antibody-producing system was recognized. HCG became the hub of anti-pregnancy research.

The basic aim of pregnancy vaccination was obviously to disrupt the production and function of the mother's HCG. But this proved difficult in practice and the problems which arose were manifold. Firstly, HCG was not normally interpreted as a foreign body because it was so similar in its structure to another substance, the luteinizing hormone (LH), secreted by the pituitary gland in the skull and mainly responsible for the shedding of the egg at the middle of the menstrual cycle. Because of the similarity between these two materials, researchers who succeeded in making HCG antigenic by various manipulations found that the antibodies which they had raised did not distinguish between HCG and LH, but merely cross-reacted. This had the effect of lowering LH levels in body fluids and interfering with the normal rhythm of the menstrual cycle.

Detailed laboratory studies on HCG and LH were then undertaken. Both hormones could be cleaved chemically into two pieces designated respectively the *alpha* and *beta* subunits. In the two hormones the *alpha* subunits were identical, but the *beta* units differed significantly The way was now open to take the *beta* subunit of HCG, stick it on to another antigen molecule to act as the immunological carrier and produce antibodies which did not cross-react with

LH. In American experiments on baboons this manoeuvre was sucful. The *beta* subunit of HCG retained its specificity and females vaccinated with it remained consistently non-pregnant in spite of being surrounded by males of 'proven fertility'.

The stage seemed set for clinical trials with the new vaccine and India with its mammoth overpopulation problem was obviously the ideal site. Clinicians at the All-India Institute for Medical Sciences in Delhi started administering the beta-HCG subunit coupled to tetanus toxoid to fertile women. But the work did not prosper. Adequate antibody concentrations were not raised; there was a worrisome lack of knowledge about the basic function of HCG in pregnancy. To a chorus of recriminations from other researchers, including accusations of 'jumping the gun' with respect to the vaccine, the Indian doctors discontinued the clinical tests and retired demurely to the laboratory in order to undertake further animal experimentation.

However, this slight hiccup should not dim the prospect of eventually being able to immunize women against pregnancy. Approaches other than that involving HCG are now being tested. They include the use of different protein materials from the placenta, antigens from sperm and compounds derived from ovarian follicles. Undoubtedly the push for a pregnancy vaccine will continue, and if the research is eventually crowned with success it could constitute one of the greatest biomedical achievements of the whole century.

The regulation of fertility in men is, of course, just as important as in women. Condoms and sterilization by vasectomy are now well established. But the need for a male Pill remains clamant all over the world. Although this area of work should be receiving the highest priority, enthusiasm for it has been singularly lacking; industrial firms have shown little interest; research funding for male contraception at the global level has been exiguous by any standards.

Although no great leap forward has occurred in male contraception in recent years (nor are any on the horizon), there are some promising leads which should be avidly pursued. Mixtures of male and female sex hormones given by mouth or by injection can reduce sperm formation. But often the side-effects – excessive weight gain, breast enlargement, above all diminished sex drive – have made the treatment unacceptable. An agent called cyproterone acetate, which has the propensity to lower blood levels of the male sex hormone, testosterone, and to decrease sperm formation, offers distinct possibilities of a male Pill suitable for general use. But cyproterone acetate, too, is not devoid of side-effects and these include weakness, tiredness, dizziness and depression. More important, the contraceptive efficacy of the medication is also in doubt, women having intercourse with males taking the drug reporting a small but significant incidence of unplanned pregnancies.

The search for other compounds to act as male contraceptives continues. A spectre from the past – a material called Inhibin, believed by endocrinologists when I was a medical student in the 1940s to suppress the secretion of the pituitary follicle-stimulating hormone – has had a renaissance during the last few years. No one has determined its chemical composition; reliable methods for its estimation do not exist. Yet in spite of these large lacunae in our knowledge, serious and experienced researchers are on record as saying that Inhibin may be the substance *par exellence* which will interfere with sperm formation, but at the same time will be devoid of side-effects and will cause sex drive to be retained in all its pristine glory.

When male sperms are released from the testes, they cannot fertilize eggs until they have passed through a structure known as the epididymis, a relatively long and nodular organ which covers the back of the testicle. The precise changes which sperm undergo during their journey through the epididymis are unknown at present, but obviously the possibility of interrupting the process of sperm maturation at that site would be an attractive method of male contraception. No compound has yet been shown to have this ability, although a number are currently under test.

The touchstone of male contraception is acceptibility. Traditionally, contraceptive use has been perceived as an exclusively female responsibility. This is especially so in the Third World countries, where male *machismo* reigns supreme and is the focus of adulation. However, there is now some rather tenuous evidence that ingrained attitudes of this type may slowly be changing. A recent WHO survey reports a surprising degree of willingness on the part of men to share in the responsibilities of family planning, even in developing countries. Males were also asked to give their views about individual methods of birth control. They much preferred the condom to vasectomy. Should a male Pill eventually become a reality they would wish to administer it themselves; long-acting preparations would be preferable; sexual pleasure should not be interfered with and orgasm should continue to be enjoyed to the full.

Probably no one in the world has done more to ensure that family planning programmes are properly implemented in the developing world than Dr Malcolm Potts of the International Pregnancy Advisory Services centred in London. Potts has repeatedly stressed that in the poor countries demand for family planning far exceeds supply, and that the political will to implement radical change in this field is weak. Family planning clinics from Santiago to Bangkok, from Rio de Janeiro to Kuala Lumpur, from Manila to Sao Paulo differ little. They are costly enterprises, manifestly capital intensive, usually culturally inappropriate. They are much too doctor-dominated; paramedical staff are insufficiently utilized; choice is often limited to a single contraceptive method.

Potts recognizes two groups of family planners which he designates the *demandologists* and the *culturologists*.[6] The former are the activists; they eschew slow-working remedies; they are driven to seek immediate and ideal solutions. They blame the under-utilization of family planning on defects in the services themselves and argue that the only way to ensure that a birth control programme will operate efficiently is to inundate the area with contraceptives and to ensure ready access to sterilization and abortion. The culturologists, on the other hand, are much more cautious. They stress the need for education; their approach is all too often tailored to a Procrustean bed; when criticism erupts, their reaction is pusillanimous.

Potts' predilection is obviously for the demandologists. He claims that their record is good and he cites various examples, including the Howrah in Calcutta, where squalor, poverty and degradation reach their apogee, yet where contraceptive inundation programmes have produced dramatically high acceptance rates. He lauds the aim of using community resources and of building on existing skills, particularly at the village level. Big international organizations sponsoring family planning have opprobrium heaped on them by Potts for their anachronistic approaches, for their fixation with the shibboleths of a bygone era, for their casuistry and lack of candour, and for developing 'conjuring skills' through which they portray weak and ineffectual programmes as if they were both meaningful and successful.

The surgical aspects of fertility control – sterilization and abortion – are of paramount importance and have been insufficiently utilized.

Potts notes that huge numbers of sterilizations will have to be performed before the end of the century just to make up for the neglect of the past. Abortion is safe, cheap and effective. Also it is greatly desired by women, who will travel long distances to obtain it. Abortion can be readily taught to paramedical personnel; barefoot doctors in China seem to perform it without difficulty; others could receive similar instruction.

More and more people are now becoming convinced that a social marketing approach to family planning will be mandatory in the future. We have already seen that between now and 2000, dazzling new developments in contraceptive technology are scarcely to be expected, welcome as they would obviously be. So we must make the best of the tools we have available and this, therefore, is an *a fortiori* argument for adopting with maximum possible speed properly-managed community-based programmes operated mainly by para-medical and auxiliary personnel.

The social marketing model typically has a small management cadre, research promotion and distribution coming within the purlieu of specialist agencies. The model enables contraceptives to be channeled at very low cost from urban wholesalers to village shops where they can be sold over the counter at nominal prices. The number of service outlets is continually increasing; and when measured by the hard criterion of cost-effectiveness social marketing has already proved its worth. The Preethi condom programme in Sri Lanka was an undoubted success; so, to a more limited extent, was the Nirodh programme in India.

The total amount of money spent globally on fertility control is not known with certainty. Potts puts the figure at $4,000 million per year, but this is little more than an inspired guess. At the time of writing, developed countries transfer about $500 million per year to the Third World for family planning programmes. Such parsimony is to be greatly deprecated when compared with expenditure on projects such as Concorde – that supreme *folie de grandeur* – and a pervasive arms trade which must rate as by far the most pernicious of all human activities. The Population Council in New York recently provided information on family planning funding in twenty-eight developing countries. Mauritius, with a *per capita* expenditure of $1.28 US, headed the list; next was Costa Rica, with 86 cents. Uganda was lowest (1.4 cents), Rhodesia second bottom at 4 cents.

Reproductive biology claims only about 2 per cent of global

governmental expenditure on medical research, and during the second half of the 'seventies the proportion devoted to the specialty actually declined, having reached a peak of $100* million in 1973. If even current levels of activity are to be maintained in 1980, at least $200 million will be required. But present investment is considered by many to be grossly inadequate and, if the field is underfinanced now and the inflationary tide continues to flow, as it almost certainly will, the situation will undoubtedly become even more precarious. The Ford Foundation has estimated that a realistic effort in 1980 would involve the expenditure of at least $500 million, and that this expenditure should rest on the well-recognized tripod of basic research, contraceptive development and safety studies in animals.

The former US President, Woodrow Wilson, once said of human leadership that 'great reformers do not, indeed, observe time and circumstances. Theirs is not a service of opportunity. . . . They are the early vehicles of the Spirit of the Age.' The field of reproductive biology needs a continuous stream of 'great reformers', researchers who will hold high the torch of creativity, people who will not become obsessed with achieving academic acceptance at the expense of practical relevance. Ideas live: men die. But probably in no other branch of biomedical research are ideas and initiative of such transcendent importance for the future well-being of mankind.

NOTES AND REFERENCES

[1] Some of the information in this chapter was derived from the World Health Organization's Sixth Annual Report, *Special Programme of Research, Development and Research Training in Human Reproduction*, November 1977. I am grateful to Dr A. Kessler, WHO, Geneva, for permission to quote from this document.

[2] See World Health Organization (1978), *Induced Abortion*.

[3] See R. V. Short (1976).

[4] John A. Loraine and E. T. Bell (1968).

[5] See R. V. Short and D. J. Baird (eds.) (1976), *Contraceptives of the Future*, The Royal Society, London, p. 175.

[6] See D. M. Potts (1976).

* Expressed in terms of constant dollars (1970 = 100).

Chapter 11

The Paramountcy of Environmental Medicine

We live in an era in which the technological capacity of medicine is very powerful. We have at our disposal a huge battery of drugs, highly sophisticated aids to diagnosis and an ever widening spectrum of treatments. Actual and incipent developments within medicine widely discussed and routinely receiving wide coverage by the news media include the implantation of live, cadaveric and mechanical organs, genetic and other forms of human 'engineering', techniques designed to influence thought and behaviour, and, within the general ambit of fertility, topics such as *in vitro* fertilization (test-tube babies) and the pre-selection of sex.

The era of 'engineering medicine' has been associated with a huge increase in hospital personnel. This has been especially marked in industrialized countries. Since the end of the Second World War, the overall British labour force has increased by only 10 per cent. But during this time numbers of hospital doctors, nurses and administrative staff have risen by 100 per cent and of hospital technicians by 150 per cent. Currently, Britain is spending nearly 6 per cent of her Gross National Product on her National Health Service. In the USA, where medical care has traditionally been and continues as a legitimate field for intense entrepreneurial activity, costs are soaring. In 1950, America spent 4.6 per cent of her GNP on medical services; by 1975, the figure was 8.3 per cent and if the present tendency towards high-technology medicine continues unchecked, the forecast for 2000 is a staggering 12 per cent.

Engineering medicine has been greatly lauded; yet its success rate has been modest to say the least of it. The outstanding feature of twentieth-century medicine has been to increase life expectancy at birth, and this has been due chiefly to the elimination or emasculation of infectious diseases like smallpox, malaria, yellow fever, cholera and diptheria which formerly ravaged large areas of the planet. On the other hand, life expectancy at the age of forty-five has changed little during the last fifty years, and the enthusiasm for engineering medicine contrasts vividly with the rather meagre advantages which have accrued to health through its application.

Given such a state of affairs it is scarcely surprising that in some quarters demands for a 'demedicalization' of society are growing in intensity. Within this general field, the most trenchant critic of the medical profession is, of course, Ivan Illich. Illich's *Medical Nemesis* opens with the dramatic statement that 'the medical establishment has become a major threat to health'. Illich contends that modern medicine does more harm than good and that many of society's ills can be attributed to iatrogenesis – the impairment of health due to medical intervention. Medicine has become altogether too heroic. It has destroyed the privacy of the individual, transformed pain and sickness into a mere technical exercise ripe for the deployment of a formidable array of laboratory expertise. Doctors are enslaved by a false paradigm; they have become helots to a system espousing un-fettered economic growth within which the ethos of engineering medicine is deeply embedded.

Illich's thesis is essentially destructive and it can be readily criti-cized. He grossly underrates the spectacular advances which have occurred in the diagnosis, management and above all, prevention of disease during this century; he has an almost mystic faith in the skills and expertise of non-medical personnel and he even has the temerity to suggest that poor people in the Third World should eschew the benefits which modern medicine would bring them. David Horrobin in his *Medical Hubris* has given the most detailed and sentient reply to Illich so far. Horrobin, a doctor himself, agrees that the present state of medicine is defective in many respects but his prescription for ameliorating the situation differs radically from that of Illich. Accord-ing to Horrobin, doctors should show more rather than less heroism; science within medicine should proliferate rather than contract, although this does not necessarily mean a corresponding expansion of high technology. Horrobin's critique of the medical profession is basically that doctors, having acquired a mighty empire 'in a fit of absentmindedness', have since shown themselves singularly ill-equip-ped to manage it.

Illich's *Medical Nemesis* nevertheless remains a classical polemic. Had it been hedged around with all the restrictions and reservations which are usual in rational thought, its influence might well have been less. Instead its very elements of sophistry, exaggeration and sheer distortion have been highly effective in transmitting its message. *Medical Nemesis*, by highlighting the medicalization/demedicalization issue and by attracting the attention of people much more capable than Illich of analysing health needs, has already become a touchstone for change, a catalyst for thought about fundamental and philosophical principles, in fact, a key medical document of the late twentieth century. Another point in Illich's favour is that his views are likely to become much more acceptable in the steady state society of the future than in the growth-orientated world of the late 'seventies. I forecast this in *Syndromes of the Seventies* when I wrote that in association with the trend towards global sustainability, 'engineering medicine, with its proclivity for resource depletion will appear less attractive. The successor . . . could well be ecological medicine in which the role of the environment in the causation of disease will assume primacy, and the subtle and arcane manner in which environmental factors derange bodily functions will be the focus of mounting interest.'

The word 'environment' means different things to different people. To the ecologist it is synonymous with the 'web of life', that complex series of fragile and closely interrelated systems within which plants, animals and *homo sapiens* exist. The meteorologist equates the environment with the atmosphere, the public health expert with sanitation, the sociologist with human relationships and man-made institutions. But irrespective of definition, two points cannot be disputed. The first is that the global environment is being constantly assailed by man as the engine of economic growth is further fueled. The second is that some of the alterations which are being produced are so crude and blatant that eventually they are likely to become both irreversible and catastrophic.

Assaults on human health from environmental causes are commonplace and the medical literature of the 'seventies is replete with examples of them. Population pressures, industrialization and burgeoning affluence are combining to cause atmospheric pollution over big cities and to produce diseases like bronchitis and emphysema, not to mention those that result from specific air contaminants. Health hazards mount as streams, rivers, lakes and more recently whole seas – the Baltic and the Caspian are examples – become contaminated. Dangers exist from atomic radiation, pesticides, detergents and some of the 100,000 chemicals which are thought to be in use in Western societies. Dietary habits are recognized to be bad ; tobacco smoking is on the upgrade in Third World countries; addiction to alcohol is increasing; promiscuity, with its concomitant of venereal disease, damages health on a mounting scale. In big cities stressful living predisposes to delinquency and violent crime while the cacophony generated by industry and transport makes life intolerable for great numbers of people.

What diseases are most likely to kill us in the eight and ninth decades of this century? They are, of course, two in number – heart attacks and cancer.* In both, environmental factors are crucial; both are theoretically preventable. The rest of this chapter attempts to place them within the framework of environmental medicine.

Disease of the blood vessels affecting the heart – the coronary arteries – is the leading cause of death in the developed world. A third of deaths each year in the USA result from it, and more than half of these are in the age group of 35 to 65. In Canada, coronary heart disease is the most frequent killer in men over the age of 40 and in women after they reach 50. In the UK it is the foremost cause of death in middle-aged men, accounting for 40 per cent of fatalities between the ages of 45 and 64.

The term *ischaemic heart disease* implies a major reduction of blood supply to all or part of the heart; in the vast majority of cases it results from localized arterial narrowing (arteriosclerosis). Arteriosclerosis is basically a process of 'furring up' during which fatty substances resembling porridge form in arteries and obstruct blood flow by encroaching on the lumen. Arteriosclerosis affects predominantly the aorta and its major branches, notably the coronary arteries supplying the heart and the carotid system supplying the brain. Arteriosclerosis is a lifelong process and by the time the patient consults the doctor, the disease is usually in an advanced stage. This means that treatment must of necessity be palliative rather than curative.

Coronary artery disease can apparently be present for many years without affecting blood flow to the heart or producing any symptoms. In some individuals, however, progressive gradual narrowing of an artery causes angina pectoris, a characteristic form of chest pain which occurs during exercise or emotional stress; in others, the sudden, total obstruction of a narrowed vessel leads to the death of a

* Stroke is becoming increasingly frequent and is now moving into third place. Environmental factors are undoubtedly of importance here also.

portion of the heart muscle and to the clinical picture of an acute heart attack (coronary thrombosis; myocardial infarction).

A general milieu of overindulgence in food and tobacco seems to favour the development of coronary heart disease. The latter has been dubbed the archetypal malady of the modern industrialized state, a disease associated *par excellence* with the 'trappings of affluence', an accurate index of man's maladaptation to his environment.

The geographical variation in ischaemic heart disease is striking and immediately suggests the importance of environmental factors in its causation. For countries which keep accurate records – and these are not yet in the majority at the global level – rates in both sexes are highest in Finland, South Africa, the USA, Scotland, Australia, New Zealand, Canada, Israel and the Republic of Ireland. Rates are lowest in countries such as Thailand, Ecuador, Guatemala, El Salvador, Taiwan, Paraguay, Peru, Jordan and Hong Kong. Differences between nations at opposite ends of the spectrum are considerable; for example that between Finland and Thailand in the age group 35 to 64 is five-hundred-fold.

As societies develop, become more industrialized and affluent, and adopt Western-type life-styles, their susceptibility to coronary heart disease increases. For such countries – and they include Hong Kong, Singapore, Taiwan, South Korea and Papua New Guinea – coronary heart disease is likely to be a major health problem well before the end of the century. However, development *per se* is obviously not the only answer, for in the most advanced country of all, the USA, death rates from coronary heart disease have actually been falling.

Within individual nations there are fascinating variations in the incidence of coronary heart disease, again pointing to the importance of environmental factors. For example, in the USA the highest concentrations are to be found in the industrial heartland and manufacturing belt of the country while the lowest rates are in the rural South and South-West. In Australia the incidence is highest in the South-East, particularly in cities such as Melbourne and Sydney. UK death rates from ischaemic heart disease tend to be higher in the north than in the south of the country, especially unfavourable areas being Scotland, Tyneside and Northern Ireland. South Wales also has had a high mortality rate and forms an exception to this generalization: so do some of the London boroughs. Even within cities in the UK and elsewhere, patterns of mortality for coronary heart disease vary considerably. Glasgow, which has an overall mortality rate for ischaemic heart disease higher than that in the rest of Britain, nevertheless contains wards in which rates are below the national average. Death rates in Chicago are much higher in the centre of the city than in its burgeoning suburbs.

Risk factors in relation to coronary heart disease have been much studied in recent years. There is compelling clinical and epidemiological evidence indicating that high blood pressure is associated with premature arterial degeneration and that this is probably the most important single causative factor. The precise mechanism whereby a rise in blood pressure causes fat to be deposited in arteries is still a matter for conjecture, but at present the balance of opinion suggests that the fundamental damage is to the inner lining of the vessel. One of the salient points about blood pressure in relation to the risk of coronary heart disease is that the incidence of the latter rises smoothly with the blood pressure level. So far no definite 'cut-off point' has been demonstrated where the height of the blood pressure influences either the present or future course of the malady.

A plenitude of studies now support the view that cigarette smoking is harmful to coronary arteries. Smoking causes arterial constriction and increases the permeability of arterial walls, mainly, it is thought, through the accumulation of carbon monoxide in the blood. Light smokers suffer less from ischaemic heart disease than heavy smokers; the cessation of the habit is associated with a reduction in the incidence of heart attacks. Much painstaking research has been devoted to identifying the component in tobacco which constitutes the greater risk to coronary arteries. Nicotine, lead, tar and carbon monoxide have all been implicated but the precise cause remains to be discovered.

There are few more contentious subjects in modern medicine than the relationship of dietary fat to coronary heart disease. An immense research effort has gone into this area, particularly over the past two decades. That some relationship exists is not in doubt. Yet its nature remains elusive, and definite proof that fats and cholesterol actually cause ischaemic heart disease seems unlikely to be forthcoming in the foreseeable future.

Certain facts have been established. During conditions of subnutrition associated with wartime, and in individuals with chronic wasting diseases, deaths from arteriosclerosis decrease. Fats and the related substance, cholesterol, are present in all arteriosclerotic deposits; this has been known for almost a hundred years. Patients with ischaemic heart disease tend, on the whole, to have higher than normal amounts of cholesterol in their blood. Studies mainly from the USA have purported to demonstrate that when diets rich in saturated fats – containing, for example, egg yolks, cream, butter, lard and fatty meats – are consumed, blood cholesterol levels rise. On the other hand, vegetable fats and oils, rich in polyunsaturated fats, tend to decrease blood cholesterol levels. In the euphoria following these discoveries, bodies as prestigious as the US Academy of Sciences proclaimed that the risk of coronary heart disease was 'positively correlated with the level of blood cholesterol'. Other authorities went even futher. Saturated fats were impugned as a major risk factor in relation to coronary heart disease and there was passionate advocacy in several quarters of an immediate change to diets rich in polyunsaturated fats.

Yet in spite of a plethora of literature citing cholesterol as the major culprit in ischaemic heart disease, doubts remained and anomalies persisted. Results varied greatly between ethnic groups and in different parts of the world; it also became increasingly difficult to separate blood cholesterol levels from other known risk factors, particularly high blood pressure, smoking, and disturbances of sugar metabolism. Also, even if the cholesterol thesis did have validity, important questions still remained to be answered. Why, for instance, did the lowering of cholesterol levels by diet or by the use of various drugs convey so little protection from subsequent attacks of coronary thrombosis?[1] Why, when blood fats and cholesterol were normal, was immunity not guaranteed from the disease?[2]

During the 1970s the cholesterol saga took a further twist. The discovery was made that a small part of the total cholesterol in blood – designated the high-density lipoprotein – was actually protective as far as coronary heart disease was concerned. This observation could be very important but at present its significance is difficult to assess in the absence of accurate methods of measurement and large scale epidemiological surveys.

The four established risk factors in relation to coronary heart disease are the height of the blood pressure, addiction to tobacco, blood cholesterol levels and a disorder of sugar metabolism.[3] Amongst others which may be important is obesity. This issue is very complex because of the varying criteria for the definition and measurement of obesity and the multifactorial origin of the condition. At present most authorities take the view that moderate obesity is not a strong risk factor in relation to coronary heart disease. However, weight reduction in such patients will frequently be desirable because it will tend to lower blood pressure and to counteract abnormally high blood fat and cholesterol levels.

Much has also been written about the relationship of physical activity to the occurrence of ischaemic heart disease. *Homo sedentarius* is said to be much more prone to the condition than his more active colleagues, and substantive evidence has been adduced that those in more active occupations tend to have a relatively low incidence of heart attacks. Again, however, the issue is clouded with uncertainties, the major difficulty being to determine whether sedentary living *per se* is responsible for ischaemic heart disease or whether it merely acts as a multiplier and intensifier of the three major risk factors discussed above.

The greatest change in Western diets which has occurred over the past one hundred years is probably the rise in sugar consumption. In Britain in 1880, sugar consumption per head per annum was 64 lbs; by 1974 it had risen to 105 lbs. Dietary habits involving the ingestion of refined sugar, particularly in the form of white bread, have been cited as causative in relation to coronary heart disease. At present, however, evidence to support this contention is not clear-cut.

Soft water has been much publicized as a risk factor in coronary heart disease. It is especially appealing to epidemiologists because, should it turn out to be the *deus ex machina*, it could be modified without the necessity for a complete change in life-styles. However, international evidence linking water composition to ischaemic heart disease is conflicting and many authorities remain sceptical that such an association does indeed exist.

Stress, diabetes and heredity have all been linked to coronary heart disease. The concept of stress is extremely difficult to define; what is stress for one person constitutes a challenge to another. Evidence culled from international sources tends to throw doubt on the hypothesis that stress is primarily responsible for the current epidemic of heart attacks. Rural Finns from Karelia – tranquil, stoical, eating a diet rich in saturated fats – have the highest incidence of the disease anywhere in the world. Yet in Japan's burgeoning, overcrowded and frenetic cities where the tempo of life is continually accelerating and where stress would seem to be maximal, the incidence of the malady remains relatively low.

Diabetes mellitus is an illness of great complexity. Arteriosclerosis is frequently associated with it, and diabetics are prone to develop it together with its complications, including those affecting the coronary arteries, at a relatively early age. Yet the precise biochemical mechanisms involved in the genesis of heart disease in diabetics remain to be elucidated and this whole field is likely to be a focus of increasing interest in future decades.

Family history in ischaemic heart disease is obviously important and at one time was regarded as crucial. But many authorities now give it a considerably lower ranking, stressing the importance of cultural and environmental, as opposed to genetic, factors in patients with the condition.

There seems little likelihood that major improvements in death rates and illness rates from ischaemic heart disease will be achieved by pouring funds into measures based on engineering medicine. Instead the emphasis must most decidedly be on prevention. And the inescapable corollary to such a conclusion is that radical change will be necessary – in governmental policies, in social mores and most important of all in personal life-styles.

Such alterations are likely to be increasingly urged during the final two decades of this century. So far, however, governmental reactions have been pusillanimous and few nations have been prepared to rise to the challenge. Norway is a notable exception. Its Parliament is now proposing to adjust the country's agricultural policy by providing subsidies designed to stabilize meat production, reduce food grain imports and encourage fish consumption. At the same time, state-sponsored propaganda in Norway is continuously alerting people to the health implications of their eating habits. In Sweden the Government has been urging for several years that people should smoke and drink less, exercise more and adopt a 'prudent' diet lower in calories, saturated fats and sugar. Judgement on the success or failure of the Scandinavian experiment cannot yet be given; but by the end of this century the evidence should be available and meanwhile the exemplar is being watched with great interest in other parts of the world.

The Greek word for 'crab' is *karkinos*. Hippocrates used it to describe a mysterious disease which seemed to grip the body with crab-like pincers. After ischaemic heart disease, cancer is the commonest cause of illness and death in the industrialized world. In the USA alone in

1975, 665,000 new cases were diagnosed and 365,000 people died from cancer, the latter figure being five times more than the American military personnel killed in the Vietnam and Korean Wars combined. In developed countries the rate of increase in cancer deaths is more rapid than that of the population and this is taking place in spite of any recent advances which have been made in diagnosis and treatment.

No age, sex or ethnic group is immune from cancer. In pregnant women the disease can be transmitted through the placenta to the foetus. Evidence for this came in the early 1970s when an association was found between the use of the hormonal substance stilboestrol by a group of pregnant diabetic women and the occurence of cancer of the vagina in their adolescent daughters some twenty years later. Cancer is a prominent cause of death amongst children, and there are several forms of the disease specific to this group. After the age of fifteen years, adult types of cancer increase in frequency and after forty, the rise is both awesome and spectacular.

In the Third World infectious diseases currently predominate as killers, especially amongst younger age groups. But as the population of developing countries ages, as described in Chapter 9, the incidence of cancer will assuredly rise, and by the end of the century it is likely to have become a major cause of death. Even now cancer is far from rare in this area, and in 1976 the highest incidence of malignant disease at all sites of the body in men was reported from the African population of Bulawayo in Rhodesia.

In a much quoted apophthegm, the British cancer authority, Sir Richard Doll, once declared: 'There is no cancer which occurs with even moderate frequency which occurs everywhere and always to the same extent.' Doll was stressing the quite remarkable variation which exists in cancer incidence within and between countries, and it is this evidence *par excellence* which places it within the category of an environmental disease. Indeed, the view is now generally accepted that in at least 80 per cent of human cancers environmental factors are of paramount importance.[4]

Cancer of the gullet (oesophagus) is probably the quintessential example of a type of malignancy demonstrating a huge geographical and spatial variation at the global level. Rates are highest in parts of Central Asia, particularly in the areas bordering on the Caspian Sea and in the Soviet State of Kazakhstan. The distribution of gullet cancer in Africa is bizarre. The disease is rare on the west coast of the continent, more frequent in parts of East Africa such as Mozambique, Uganda and Tanzania and most prevalent of all in areas of Rhodesia, South Africa and particularly in the Transkei where in certain localities it has attained almost epidemic proportions. Other parts of the world in which gullet cancer is quite common include Curaçao and some provinces of Brazil. The disease is relatively rare in Europe except in parts of France, notably Brittany.

Different environmental factors operate to produce gullet cancer in areas of high prevalence. Alcohol is probably important, especially when combined with cigarette smoking. In South-East Africa an association is believed to exist between the tumour and the use of maize in the preparation of alcoholic beverages, and in France the association also seems to hold particularly when alcohol is ingested in the form of Calvados.

Iran has the world's highest incidence of gullet cancer. The Caspian littoral is the area most affected, and as elsewhere, remarkable variations exist in the incidence of the disease over quite short distances. Prevalence is low in the western province of Gilian; this area is humid and densely forested, criss-crossed with paddy fields, tea estates and fruit farms and inhabited mainly by indigenous Iranians. The province of Mazandaran, where the incidence is very high, has quite different characteristics geographically and demographically. Rainfall is low, vegetation scanty, soil strongly salinic; the region is thinly populated by nomadic Turkomans, who grow wheat, barley and cotton and have as their principal livestock sheep and goats. Between the low and high incidence areas of Gilian and Mazandaran, there is a tenfold difference in the gullet cancer rate for men and a thirtyfold variation in the case of women.

Accurate and painstaking work by the Joint Iranian International Agency for Research on Cancer has delineated some of the environmental factors which may be responsible for the production of malignant disease of the gullet in this area of the country. Alcohol and tobacco – agents considered to be important in other parts of the world – seem to have little significance. On the other hand, a restricted diet low in total calories is important; so also is the heavy consumption of morphine by sections of the population. The ingestion of hot fluids, especially tea, in large quantities, may have played a subsidiary role.

The 'gullet cancer belt' in Asia extends from Iran into Central China. As mentioned previously, the highest rates here are in the

Soviet Republic of Kazakhstan, and the incidence in the city of Guruyev is reputed to exceed that anywhere in the world. It is interesting that gullet cancer seems to be commoner in Kazakhs than in Slavic Russians. Under the age of forty, the differential is sevenfold but after sixty, it falls to between two and fivefold.

Evidence relating the environment to gullet cancer has recently been forthcoming from the People's Republic of China. The building of a dam caused the relocation of 50,000 people from an area of high incidence to one of low prevalence. When the farmers migrated they left their chickens behind and on arrival, purchased new birds from cancer-free flocks. Soon, however, both the birds and the migrants themselves showed a raised incidence of gullet cancer. Environmental factors, probably associated with cooking habits, are thought to have been responsible. Table scraps form part of the standard chicken diet and a pickled vegetable mixture containing substances known as nitrosamines – already recognized to be carcinogenic in animals and capable of being formed in foods during storage and cooking – are currently under suspicion.

Spatial and geographical factors are also important in other types of malignant disease although the evidence is less dramatic than in the case of gullet cancer. Unusually high rates for stomach cancer arc found in Japan and European Russia; on the other hand rates for this disease are relatively low throughout North America. When Japanese people migrate to Hawaii or to the continental USA, their incidence of stomach cancer falls and eventually comes to approximate that of the indigenous population. This type of evidence in migrant populations has been much quoted and stresses the importance of environmental as opposed to genetic factors in the causation of stomach cancer.

Cancers of the bowel and female breast show a geographical distribution almost precisely opposite to that of stomach cancer. Rates for these diseases are highest in the Western USA and are much lower in Eastern Europe and Japan. Again, evidence from migrant populations supports the contention that environmental factors are significant. Thus Norwegian and Polish immigrants to the USA show higher rates of bowel cancer than would be expected had they remained in their country of birth; in the Poles both bowel and breast cancer rates rose following migration. Within the USA patterns of distribution for breast and bowel cancer are strikingly similar, suggesting that the two diseases have an environmental factor in common. However, at present the nature of such a factor has not been determined.

D. P. Burkitt and his associates believe that differences in dietary roughage content greatly affect the incidence of bowel cancer. African populations, eating large amounts of bran, with a rapid bowel action and large stools, have a low incidence of the condition. On the other hand, US citizens, whose diet tends to be low in fibre and who have a sluggish bowel action and small stools, show much higher rates. Burkitt's observations are of considerable interest. But they do not seem to hold up well at the international level, particularly in surveys which have compared diet and cancer rates in various populations and ethnic groups.

Cancer of the lung is the commonest form of malignancy in the Western World. Britain has especially unfavourable rates, and in Scotland the morbidity from the disease is amongst the highest in the world. The association between lung cancer and cigarette smoking is consistent in all countries which supply accurate data for morbidity and mortality. The epidemiological evidence for the relationship between tobacco smoking and malignant disease of the lung is now strong, specific and coherent, and the establishment of the link must rank as one of the foremost achievements of recent medical research.

Two other types of cancer merit attention in this context. Primary liver cancer is rare but has a notable geographical distribution. Its highest incidence is amongst Africans in Bulawayo but it is also quite prevalent in Chinese both in Singapore and in the Bay Area of San Francisco. On the other hand the condition is infrequent throughout Europe and most of North America. Dietary factors are almost certainly important in liver cancer and substances known as aflotoxins are strongly suspected of being a major cause. A tumour termed Burkitt's lymphoma is probably also a product of the environment. It is almost unknown outside of Africa and Papua New Guinea and is never encountered when the temperature falls below 16°C and the annual rainfall is less than 76 centimetres.

A huge literature now exists on occupational cancer. This is not the place to review it,[5] but various estimates indicate that in industrialized countries like the USA, between 5 to 15 per cent of all cancer deaths in men are occupational in origin. Lung cancer is found in asbestos workers, uranium miners and those exposed to the chemical bischloromethyl ether, much used in the manufacture of resins. Skin cancer is most frequent in people working out of doors, particularly farmers, labourers and seamen; it is also prevalent in shale oil workers. Organic chemists are prone to contract cancer of the pancreas, while those involved in the production of the substance vinyl chloride are at risk from liver cancer. Malignant disease of the bladder is frequent in workers in the aniline dye and rubber industries. Beryllium is suspected to be an occupational carcinogen in relation to bones and lungs, lead to kidneys, chloroform, DDT and carbon tetrachloride to the liver, arsenic and benzene to lymphatic tissue.

People whose occupations bring them into contact with ionizing radiations have been shown to be more susceptible to certain forms of cancer than the general population. Hospital radiologists are especially prone to develop cancer of the skin and leukaemia; painters of clock and watch faces who use luminous paints containing radium and thorium tend to develop bone cancer; a form of lung cancer known as 'mountain sickness' was once prevalent in pitch-blende miners in the eastern part of Germany and was traced to the radioactive gas, radon. The literature on occupational exposure to ionizing radiations is already vast and the controversy surrounding the maximum dosages which are permissible for industrial workers is one of the most acrimonious in the whole of modern science.[6] The only point which requires emphasis here is that willy-nilly our civilization seems destined to become increasingly involved with radioactivity as its use in industry and medicine proliferates and as nuclear reactors permeate the universe. In *The Death of Tomorrow* I expressed my conviction that as regards ionizing radiations the generation to which I belong has undoubtedly grasped 'the iron broom of history'. What would be the opinion of posterity on our activities, I wondered. Would it bless us for our percipience or would it curse us for nursing into life a serpent with the capacity to sting mankind to death?

Cancer, like ischaemic heart disease, is now being increasingly recognized as a malady in which behavioural patterns and personal life-styles are of transcendent importance. Amongst such socio-economic factors, the subject of tobacco has been most thoroughly researched. A number of points have now been definitely clarified. They include the penchant for cigarette smoking to increase the risk not only of cancer of the lung, but also of other malignancies including those of the mouth, larynx, bladder and pancreas. In smokers other environmental factors have been shown to produce a multiplier effect. Thus lung cancer incidence rises markedly in smokers who are also exposed to asbestos; malignant diseases of the mouth, gullet and liver flourish inordinately in smokers who are also heavy consumers of alcohol; bladder cancer has a specially high rate in smokers exposed to hydrocarbon chemicals in the course of their work. Cancer risks with forms of tobacco other than the cigarette are also well recognized. Thus betel chewers in India and Sri Lanka are prone to mouth cancer; in Kashmir and parts of Central America, chutta smoking – placing the burning end of a cigar in the mouth – is widely practised and the effects of tobacco and burning combine to produce a spectacular increase in cancers of the mouth, tongue and palate.

One of the most worrisome current trends in this field is the rapid spread of cigarette smoking to Third World countries. The global tobacco business is, of course, controlled by multinational corporations and the developing world has now become their most important area for expansionist policies. Most smokers in the poor countries receive much less information about the hazards of tobacco than is standard in industrialized nations, and the point is frequently made that smoking-related diseases are not a major health problem in the Third World at present. The economic case is also argued strongly. Governments of such countries derive finacial benefit from tobacco, and the latter can still be a profitable crop for the peasant farmer living close to subsistence level. But two factors make it imperative that a surcease be imposed on this trend with maximum speed. The first is that tobacco uses scarce land resources in poor countries which would be much better employed growing food or less dangerous cash crops. The second is the certainty that Nemesis cannot be long delayed and that given a continuation of current policies an epidemic of tobacco-related diseases will be raging in Third World countries well before 2000 AD.

Contraception now plays a major role in people's life-styles. Since the Pill was introduced over twenty years ago in Puerto Rico and Haiti it has become exceedingly popular and at the end of the 1970s, some 80 million women around the world are taking it. Acceptance rates for the Pill are likely to increase in the future as preparations with fewer side-effects and better menstrual control come on the market. But the popularity of oral contraception poses considerable health problems mainly because a potent drug is being administered to healthy young women over long periods of time. In no area are anxieties greater than in that involving possible carginogenic effects.

In 1978, the World Health Organization confronted this issue.[7]

Apropos of breast cancer in women no clear evidence was forthcoming that the Pill had either an adverse or a beneficial effect; it was, however, emphasized that the period of study had been relatively short and that at present valid conclusions about really long-term effects could not be drawn. On the other hand, breast tumours which did not show malignant change appeared to be less prevalent in Pill users than in the general population.

Cancer of the body of the womb under the age of forty is a rare disease, and Pill preparations in common use do not seem to affect its incidence. With cancer of the ovary, the Pill might even confer some slight degree of protection. Evidence in relation to cancer of the neck of the womb is confused and difficult to interpret. Long-term use might be associated with increased risk, but again the WHO could not give a definite opinion because of the necessity to take into account other variables including socio-economic development and marital status, sexual mores and previous reproductive history. Only with a rare and non-malignant tumour of the liver is there definite proof that the incidence rises in Pill users, and that the hazard is greater the longer the duration of the medication. Overall risk remains low, however. In women over thirty, the WHO found that it was three per hundred thousand Pill users and in older subjects it was only slightly greater.

With both ischaemic heart disease and cancer, time is of the essence, and the period between the initiation of the maladies and the presentation of the patient to the doctor may span several decades. In his treatment, therefore, the doctor has to bear this in mind, and the analogy of locking the stable door not only after the horse has bolted but after he has been grazing the pasture for many years seems apposite. William Farr, writing in 1872, proclaimed that the exact determination of evils is the first step towards their remedies. The evils responsible for coronary heart disease, cancer and other environmental maladies are many and varied. The whole subject is still in its infancy. Yet it is crucial to the well-being of mankind and it desperately requires research, innovation and massive funding on a global scale. The unravelling of the complicated web of factors responsible for environmental diseases will be a task of great complexity. But undoubtedly it represents one of the greatest challenges facing medical practitioners of the future.

NOTES AND REFERENCES

[1] The recent large-scale long-term trial of lowering blood cholesterol levels with the drug Clofibrate in Britain showed no change in mortality but a reduction in non-total heart attacks.

[2] The prestigious British cardiologist Sir John McMichael ('For Debate: Fats and Atheroma: An Inquest', *British Medical Journal*, January 20, 1979) has recently concluded that all *well-controlled* trials of cholesterol-reducing diets and drugs have failed to reduce mortality from coronary heart disease. McMichael points out that Israelis and urban Bedouins who consume a diet relatively high in polyunsaturated fats have a high incidence of coronary heart disease. He goes on to suggest that 'official medical endorsement of cholesterol-reducing measures should be withdrawn', and that commercial, professional and governmentally-sponsored propaganda in this direction should cease.

[3] These risk factors account for only 50 to 70 per cent of cases of coronary heart disease. Others therefore remain to be discovered.

[4] See also R. W. Armstrong (1979) for a wide-ranging review.

[5] A good recent article in this field is by Samuel S. Epstein (1977).

[6] See, for example, R. D. E. Rumsey (1973), 'Radiation and Health Hazards', in G. M. Howe and J. A. Loraine (eds.), *Environmental Medicine*, Heinemann Medical Books, London, p. 25, for a discussion of this issue.

[7] See World Health Organization (1978), *Steroid Contraception and the Risk of Neoplasia.*

Epilogue

In May 1984, sixty years after I was born, the zoo animals mentioned in Chapter 2 met to discuss the future of the world. The elephant was in the chair. He hoped that the meeting would not become too polemical. But he had his doubts.

The dolphin spoke first. He had always been a great admirer of Herman Kahn and he was very optimistic. *Le belle époque* envisioned by Kahn was in the process of dawning; things were definitely going well; a spendid future was opening up for mankind. It was true that economic growth had slowed in the 'seventies and was zero in the 'eighties. But this was only a temporary setback. Quite soon people all over the world would be fabulously rich, prosperity and plenty would be universal. The USA was the paradigm *par excellence*; American values and attitudes extolling the 'good life' should be adopted throughout the world.

The dolphin saw technological fixes for everything. They would protect the environment from depredation; they would greatly lower energy costs; they would ensure adequate diets for all by the provision of synthetic foods; they would maintain long-term political stability; they would even prevent war.

Super-industrial societies currently in the making would soon give way to post-industrial states. The dolphin predicted that before the end of the century the commanding heights of science, biology, medicine and psychology would have been scaled. Talk of a finite planet with limits to economic growth was ridiculous. The earth's resources were boundless; all that was necessary was that they should be managed in a proper manner.

The post-industrial society would be affluent and supremely technological, with the majority of the people working in service industries. The production of the necessities of life would have become trivially easy. People would be living to great ages, and middle-class individuals all over the world would be emulating the life-styles of the aristocracy of the Victorian era in England. The emphasis would be on education and culture; people would live in huge baronial mansions and entertain lavishly therein.

Only one fear existed. To those of a dynamic, thrusting and ambitious temperament the post-industrial society might seem rather
dull and tame. But this could be readily countered. For one thing the
massive development of nuclear power as an energy source would be
both exciting and challenging. But pride of place would definitely go
to space colonization. Extra-terrestial activities would become the
focus for vigorous and sustained endeavour. Soon there would be
large and virtually autonomous colonies in many parts of space.
People living there would process their own raw materials, supply
energy for themselves and for the remaining inhabitants on planet
earth, and enjoy a quality of life undreamt of even by the greatest
optimists of previous generations. How ridiculous it was in 1984 to
talk of a population problem on earth when the transfer of multitudes
of people to outer space would offer a simple and ready solution!

The dolphin's speech had a mixed reception and the elephant had
some difficulty in keeping order. Vipers, cobras and an assortment of
snakes began a sustained hissing; the polar bear, obviously very angry,
swung his head and stamped his feet. The wild cat bared his claws;
frogs croaked, 'Limits to growth, limits to growth;' two sea lions
honked, 'Solar good, nuclear bad'. Even the hippopotamus stirred
himself out of his lethargy to register his disagreement.

Only the cheetah and the red kangaroo seemed to support the
dolphin. The cheetah adored speed. She could run at sixty miles an
hour and the idea of fast travel in unlimited space was irresistible.
The kangaroo for his part revered Lenin. He had been a fluent
Russian speaker since his youth and had read all the Marxist-Leninist
literature on futures, especially the writings of people like Modrzhinskaya, Kosolapov, Zagladin and Frolov. Jostling other would-be
speakers aside the kangaroo bounded to the rostrum.

He began by saying that the future of the world had never been
brighter. To talk of a shortage of raw materials was ridiculous; unlimited energy would soon be produced from nuclear fusion. Everyone could be fed to satiety and there was no problem about turning
deserts into flowering orchards. Overpopulation was nothing but an
artifact, a mere symptom of societal malaise and one which could be
easily rectified.

It was a coruscating irony, the kangaroo said, that the post-
industrial society had not by now become a reality. There could be a
paradise on Earth; self-esteem and self-fulfilment could be ubiquitous; the average life span could be a hundred years or more; by 2030

rail transport could be established on the moon. But it went without saying that such a post-industrial society could only be socialist. Capitalist and imperialist forms of economic growth must cease immediately. The earth's technological capability could readily transform mankind's lot for the better. It was the *system* which must be changed and for the kangaroo a communist utopia was the only answer.

During the kangaroo's speech there had been mounting uproar and cries of dissent. When he finished pandemonium erupted as animal after animal headed for the podium. But the elephant's choice of speaker was preordained. Pride of place must be given to the lion.

The lion, having reached the platform, roared his condemnation of Herman Kahn and the Marxist-Leninists. He agreed with the French ecologist René Dumont that many of their views were 'semi-lunatic'. And what an egregiously bad prophet Kahn had proved to be so far. He had failed to forecast the humiliation of the USA in South-East Asia and its virtual withdrawal from that continent. He had failed to predict the emergence of OPEC as a powerful global force with resurgent Islam rampant and with its finger on the jugular of the West. In his book *The Year 2000* he had not even forecast the economic recession of the 'seventies and 'eighties, much less the emergence of a strong environmentalist movement with a significant political clout. *La belle époque* was a travesty; instead the world seemed to be entering *la mauvaise époque*. Surely now after such an abysmal record a period of silence from the Hudson Institute would be much appreciated.

The lion went on to berate the dolphin, the cheetah and the red kangaroo for their quite unjustified optimism. He then proceeded to outline *his* view of the world's future in the years immediately following 1984.

Even though population growth rates had slowed slightly in the 'seventies and the trend was continuing in the 'eighties, the planet was still grossly overcrowded. Massive overbreeding had been permitted to occur, particularly since the end of World War II, and as a result the people of the earth were manifestly out of tune with their indigenous resources. The Western world had been outrageously profligate with its most precious patrimony – energy derived from fossil fuels. The USA was especially culpable and what right, the lion demanded, did that country have, with only four per cent of the earth's population, to continue to consume more than forty per cent of its energy?

Ecological collapse at the global level was drawing even closer; the environment found itself increasingly unable to cope with burgeoning and baneful industrialization. The traditional horsemen of the apocalypse – war, famine, disease and death – had so far been content to remain in the wings but were now preparing to move to the centre of the stage.

But it was when he turned to the relationships between developed and developing countries that the lion was most scathing. Who had ordained that the industrialized nations, occupying about one-fifth of the earth's territory, should utilize over eighty per cent of its natural resources and squander three-quarters of its wealth? Was it not shameful in 1984 that millions of people in the Third World should toil all their days in penury and misery while Westerners were concerned only with increasing their personal affluence and boosting their already over-luxurious life-styles? And was it not an inequity on a gargantuan scale that multinational agribusiness corporations working in collaboration with Western Governments should through their arcane and malign manipulations dictate that the poor of the earth remain forever hungry?

It was a powerful speech with an outstanding peroration. The elephant, whose sense of history was deeply ingrained, compared it with Gladstone during the Midlothian campaign, Lloyd George at Limehouse, Lenin at the Finland Station in St Petersburg, Churchill in 1940, Aneurin Bevan in full flow, and Castro at his most ebullient. The audience found the lion's arguments convincing and fell silent. Who would be prepared to take the platform next? Eventually the rhinoceros, having indicated that he wanted to talk about the threat of war, lumbered up to the dais.

The rhinoceros had no cause to love the human race. For years they had been intent on exterminating him and his ilk for the basest motives of greed and profit. Now he had a chance to retaliate and he did so with all the force and eloquence at his disposal.

War was his obsession. Man was preparing for it with frenzied speed; and one of the symptoms of his mania was that the whole mass of technological weaponry was advancing at a rate infinitely faster than the fragile and often specious negotiations being conducted between nation states ostensibly to foster disarmament. Man could and probably would wipe himself off the face of the earth through a nuclear holocaust. The rhinoceros would shed no tears for that. Indeed it would be good riddance to bad rubbish, for the earth would be all the better without man's propensity for pillage, rapine and despoilation. But why, in God's name, should animals be forced to share in the imbroglio? *They* had not invented the atom; *they* were not responsible for the suicidal invocation much in vogue in the 'eighties of 'mutual assured destruction'. *They* would not have defiled space by transforming it into a military jungle. *They* would not have permitted a situation in which spending on nuclear and conventional weapons was equivalent to the combined Gross National Products of about one hundred countries in Africa and Latin America, where it topped the total worldwide governmental expenditure on education, where it was about three times the total expenditure on health care, and where it was twenty times the value of total governmental aid to the poorer countries of the world.

In his youth the rhinoceros had been as pugilistic and combative as any of his species. Now his apostasy was complete and he had become deeply pacific. The Gadarene descent of planet earth to oblivion must at all costs be prevented. The atom should be banned immediately, the poisoned chalice of nuclear proliferation eschewed, the doctrine of war preparedness – a crude cloak for extreme militarism – finally jettisoned. Instead, disarmament must rapidly become Sir Galahad's Holy Grail, the pot of gold over the rainbow. Since humans had failed to do any of these things, it was up to the animals to take over, rescue mankind from his madness and inculcate some sanity into the situation.

The reception for the rhinoceros was rapturous. The lion roared his approval. Peacocks and parrots joined the sea lions in chanting 'solar good, nuclear bad'; the python, who had once eaten a man whole, was the focus for adulation and congratulation. The dolphin, the kangaroo and the cheetah slunk disconsolately away.

It was left to the elephant to sum up. He was well aware that he must avoid heady rhetoric; he must at all costs try to remain cool and dispassionate. He agreed with the lion that Herman Kahn and the staff of the Hudson Institute had given the impression that they were naïve and rather simple-minded optimists, although he did point out that in their most recent book, *The Next 200 Years*, their optimism had been tempered with at least a modicum of realism, particularly about the menace of nuclear proliferation. The elephant gave short shrift to the Marxist-Leninists. They were inhabiting a cloud-cuckoo-land espousing an anachronistic ideology, and even now in 1984, after all the upheavals of the past five years, they gave no indication of their preparedness to abandon it. But the elephant was also unimpressed with avowed doomsters like the Ehrlichs, Barry Commoner, Robert Heilbroner and the Meadows School which purported to speak for the Club of Rome. They had been guilty of gross exaggeration amounting at times to misrepresentation. By their penchant for hyperbole they had come near to inflicting mortal damage on a sagacious and prescient environmental movement.

The elephant could not resist reminding his audience of some previous bad guesses – Jan Smuts in 1926: 'We are all satisfied with South Africa now'; Adolf Hitler in 1934: 'We are winning international respect'; the Yorkshire miners' leader, Joseph Jones, in 1938: 'The strike weapon is out of date'; Richard Nixon in 1962: 'This is my last Press Conference'; Robert McNamara in 1965: 'We have stopped losing the war in Vietnam'. Perhaps the future *was* unpredictable. But as least humans could try to avoid howlers of this magnitude.

What then were the major perils affecting planet earth, asked the elephant. He was in total agreement with the rhinoceros that the threat of war must take pride of place over anything else. Vengeance would not limp, and the military build-up of both nuclear and conventional weapons during the 'eighties had been awesome. SALT had always been and remained a shambles; it was an anaemic instrument continuously being overtaken by the passage of events, and the recent acquisition of a nuclear weapons capability by countries like South Africa, Pakistan, Iran and Israel would have profound historical implications. It was only a matter of time before a leader appeared on the world stage with the mentality of Adolf Hitler in his infamous Berlin bunker of thirty-nine years ago. Given the presence of the atom, what would *his* reaction have been to nuclear proliferation?

But the elephant was also concerned about energy. It could prove to be the Achilles heel of the world. Profligacy with oil continued unabated; US imports were escalating and the value of the dollar was plummeting dangerously. Henry Kissinger, who would be influential in the new Republican administration elected in 1984, was declaiming *ad nauseum* that the only solution was for the Marines to seize Arab oil wells. The new Soviet Politburo, constituted after Leonid Brezhnev's death – younger, thrusting, no longer imbued with the caution which flows from a gerontocracy – was growling its disapprobation. OPEC governments, with a resurgent and increasingly militaristic form of Islam at their helm, were much more intransigent than in the past. The whims and caprices of conventional Western leaders – tethered to their Procrustean bed of economic growthmanship, eulogizing the God of Mammon, pathetically proselytizing for consumerism *à toute outrance* – were being increasingly neglected. *La belle époque* of Herman Kahn was undoubtely a chimera; instead the weather was likely to get rougher and rougher.

As the elephant came to the end of his summing up the animals heard a noise. At first it was faint, then louder, more obtrusive, more minatory. It was the tramp of feet and soon a serried phalanx of keepers appeared. Those in the lead were bearing a heavy canister on which the letter 'P' was emphatically emblazoned. Long ago the animals had recognized that plutonium was their arch-enemy. But still they would have their last moment of defiance and in unison they shouted with fervour and conviction, 'Solar good, nuclear bad.' The elephant vacated the chair and the meeting rapidly dispersed. It seemed unlikely that it would reconvene until the early years of the twenty-first century.

Select Bibliography

CHAPTER 1: RETROSPECT ON THE SEVENTIES

Brown, Lester R. (1978), *The Twenty-Ninth Day*, Norton, New York.

Higgins, Ronald (1978), *The Seventh Enemy: The Human Factor in the Global Crisis*, Hodder & Stoughton, London.

Loraine, John A. (1975), 'Overpopulation, Underdevelopment and Poverty – the Main Issues of World Population Year', *International Journal of Environmental Studies*, Vol. 8, p. 83.

Loraine, John A. (1977), 'Doctors and the Global Population Crisis', *British Medical Journal*, Vol. 2, p. 691.

Loraine, John A. (1977), *Syndromes of the Seventies*, Peter Owen, London.

People (1978), 'Unmet Needs', Vol. 5, No. 3.

People (1978), 'India After the Emergency: 2. Strategy for Development', Vol. 5, No. 4.

Pirages, Dennis Clark (ed.) (1977), *The Sustainable Society*, Praeger, New York.

Population Reference Bureau (1978), 'World Population Data Sheet', May.

Royal Commission on Environmental Pollution (1976), *Sixth Report: Nuclear Power and the Environment*, HMSO, London.

Shanks, Michael (1978), *What's Wrong With the Modern World?: Agenda for a New Society*, The Bodley Head, London.

SIPRI Yearbook (1978), *World Armaments and Disarmament*, Taylor & Francis, London.

Tinbergen, Jan (co-ordinator) (1976), *Reshaping the International Order: A Report to the Club of Rome*, Hutchinson, London.

The Windscale Inquiry (1978),Report by the Hon. Mr Justice Parker, Vol. I, HMSO, London.

United Nations World Population Conference (1975), *Action Taken at Bucharest*, Centre for Economic and Social Information.

Westoff, Charles F. (1978), 'Marriage and Fertility in the Developed Countries', *Scientific American*, Vol. 239, No. 6, p. 35.

CHAPTER 2: THE NUCLEAR IMBROGLIO

Barnaby, Frank (1977), 'World Arsenals in 1977', *Bulletin of the Atomic Scientists*, Vol. 34, No. 5, p. 10.

Epstein, William (1976), *The Last Chance: Nuclear Proliferation and Arms Control*, Collier Macmillan, London.

Feld, Bernard T. (1976), 'The Consequences of Nuclear War', *Bulletin of the Atomic Scientists*, Vol. 32, No. 6, p. 10.

Hackett, General Sir John and Others (1978), *The Third World War, August 1985*, Sidgwick & Jackson, London.

Hussain, Farooq (1978), 'Unknown Effects of Neutron Bombs', *New Scientist*, 23 February.

Kaplan, Fred M. (1978), 'Enhanced Radiation Weapons', *Scientific American*, Vol. 258, No. 5, p. 44.

Kistiakowsky, George B. (1978), 'The Folly of the Neutron Bomb', *Bulletin of the Atomic Scientists*, Vol. 34, No. 7, p. 25.

Loraine, John A. (1977), 'Time for Doctors to Take a Stand on Nuclear Proliferation', *Bulletin of the Atomic Scientists*, Vol. 33, No. 8, p. 6.

Loraine, John A. (1977), 'Nuclear Clouds on the World Horizon', *The Scotsman*, 23 December.

Lovins, Amory B. (1977), *Soft Energy Paths: Toward a Durable Peace*, Penguin Books, Harmondsworth.

Purple, Robert A. (1978), 'U.S. Nuclear Policy and the European Energy Market', *Energy Policy*, Vol. 6, No. 4, p. 277.

Scoville, Herbert Jr. (1977), 'Slowing the Arms Race', *Bulletin of the Atomic Scientists*, Vol. 33, No. 7, p. 4.

SIPRI (1977), *World Armaments: The Nuclear Threat.*

SIPRI (1977), *Weapons of Mass Destruction and the Environment*, Taylor & Francis, London.

SIPRI Yearbook (1978), *World Armaments and Disarmament*, Taylor & Francis, London.

Warnke, Paul C. (1978), 'Arms control; a global imperative', *Bulletin of the Atomic Scientists*, Vol. 34, No. 6, p. 32.

Wohlstetter, Albert (1977), 'Racing Forward, or Ambling Back?', in *Defending America*, Basic Books Inc., New York.

Zhelezhov, R. (1977), 'Atomic Power and Non-Proliferation of Nuclear Weapons', *International Affairs*, Vol. 2, p. 46.

CHAPTER 3: OPEC IN THE SADDLE

Cleron, Jean Paul (1978), *Saudi Arabia, 2000: A Strategy for Growth*, Croom Helm, London.

Energy Policy, A Consultative Document (1978), HMSO, London.

Financial Times Survey (1978), 'Bahrain', 3 April.

Financial Times Survey (1978), 'Saudi Arabia', 20 March.

Flower, Andrew R. (1978), 'World Oil Production', *Scientific American*, Vol. 238, No. 3, p. 42.

Frazer, Frank (1978), 'United Arab Emirates, using oil wealth to build a modern welfare state', *The Scotsman*, 4 December.

Frazer, Frank (1978), 'Qatar', *The Scotsman*, 27 February.

Johnson, R. W. (1978), 'The oil crisis re-visited', *New Society*, 16 November.

Loraine, John A. (1978), 'Energy Policies around the World', *Contemporary Review*, Vol. 233, No. 1352, p. 129.

Mangone, Gerard J. (ed.) (1976), *Energy Policies of the World*, Elsevier Scientific Publishing Company, New York, Oxford, Amsterdam.

McDermott, Anthony and Whitley, Andrew (1979), 'Iran without the Shah', *Financial Times*, 17 January.

Resources for the Future (1977), 'The Future of OPEC', No. 54, January/March.

The Times (1978), 'Kuwait', 12 June.

The Times (1978), 'Venezuela', 17 March.

Willrich, Mason (1975), 'World Energy Policy; a Global Framework', *Annals of the New York Academy of Science*, Vol. 261, p. 186.

World Energy Outlook (1977), Organization for Economic Co-operation and Development, Paris.

CHAPTER 4: NORTH AMERICA AT THE CROSSROADS

An Energy Strategy for Canada: Policies for Self-Reliance (1976), Issued under the authority of the Minster of Energy, Mines and Resources, Ottawa.

Berman, Sam M. (1979), 'An American View of Energy Strategies', Paper read at meeting of Parliamentary Liaison Group for Alternative Energy Strategies, London.

Clark, Wilson (1977), 'Renewable Energy Sources and a Conservation Economy', *The Ecologist*, Vol. 7, No. 7, p. 283.

De Carmoy, Guy (1978), 'The USA Faces the Energy Challenge', *Energy Policy*, Vol. 6, No. 1, p. 36.

Financial Times Survey (1978), 'Canada', 19 December.

Fishlock, David (1978), 'Energy from the Grass Roots', *Financial Times*, 22 August.

Gallois, Ramues (1978), 'What Price Oil Shales?', *New Scientist*, 23 February.

Goldstein, Walter (1978), 'The Politics of US Energy Policy', *Energy Policy*, Vol. 6, No. 3, p. 180.

Griffith, Edward D. and Clarke, Alan W. (1979), 'World Coal Production', *Scientific American*, Vol. 240, No. 1, p. 28.

Hayes, Denis (1978), 'The Solar Energy Timetable', *Worldwatch Paper 19*, April.

Loraine, John A. (1978), 'Energy Policies around the World', *Contemporary Review*, Vol. 233, No. 1352, p. 129.

Lovins, Amory B. (1977), *Soft Energy Paths: Toward a Durable Peace*, Penguin Books, Harmondsworth.

Martin, William F. (ed.) (1977), *Energy Supply to the Year 2000: Global and National Studies*, MIT Press, Cambridge, Mass. and London.

Oil Fields as Military Objectives, A Feasibility Study (1975), Special Sub-committee on Investigations by the Committee on International Relations, Library of Congress, August.

Orr, David W. and Phillips, Cecil R. (1977), 'Towards a Sustainable Energy Society', *The Ecologist*, Vol. 7, No. 7, p. 294.

Pimentel, David (1977), 'America's Agricultural Future', *The Ecologist*, Vol. 7, No 7, p. 254.

Rao, S. Ramachandra (1978), 'Oil Sands Put Canada on Firmer Ground', *New Scientist*, 17 August.

Ridpath, Ian (1978), 'Sunny Future for Power Satellites', *New Scientist*, 25 May.

Rose, David J. and Lester, Richard K. (1978), 'Nuclear Power, Nuclear Weapons and International Stability', *Scientific American*, Vol. 238, No. 4, p. 45.

Tuve, George L. (1976), *Energy, Environment, Population and Food*, Wiley, New York, London, Sydney and Toronto.

World Energy Resources 1985-2020 (1978), Report to Conservation Commission of the World Energy Conference, IPC Science & Technology Press, London and New York.

CHAPTER 5: ENERGY FUTURES IN SCANDINAVIA

Blegaa, S., Josephesen, L., Meyer, N. I. and Sorensen, B. (1977), 'Alternative Danish energy planning', *Energy Policy*, Vol. 5, No. 2, p. 87.

Financial Times Survey (1978), 'Norway', 17 May.

Financial Times Survey (1978), 'Finland', 19 June.

Frazer, Frank (1977), 'Norway Thinking Again about Oil Policy', *The Scotsman*, 25 October.

Hinrichsen, Don (1977), 'The Scandinavian Energy Race', *New Scientist*, 16 December.

Johansson, Thomas B. and Steen, Peter (1977), *Solar Sweden – An Outline to a Renewable Energy System*, Secretariat for Future Studies, Stockholm.

Kininen, Olli (1977), 'Finland', *The Times*, 5 December.

Lönnroth, Möans, Steen, Peter and Johansson, Thomas B. (1977), *Energy in Transition*, Secretariat for Future Studies, Stockholm.

Martin, William F. (ed.) (1977), *Energy Supply to the Year 2000: Global and National Studies*, MIT Press, Cambridge, Mass. and London.

Norway Information (1975), 'The Future Development of Energy Supplies in Norway', Royal Norwegian Ministry of Foreign Affairs.

Norway Information (1976), 'Petroleum and Norwegian Foreign Policy', Royal Norwegian Ministry of Foreign Affairs.

Norway Information (1977), 'Norway and North Sea Oil', Royal Norwegian Ministry of Foreign Affairs.

Norway Information (1977), 'The Northern Region in relation to Norwegian Foreign Policy', Royal Norwegian Ministry of Foreign Affairs.

Taylor, Gordon (1978), 'Sweden Strides Towards a Solar Society', *New Scientist*, 24 August.

The Times (1977), 'Norway', 30 November.

CHAPTER 6: ENERGY FUTURES FOR BRITAIN, FRANCE AND
FEDERAL GERMANY

Angelmayer, David (1978), 'West Germany's Nuclear Dilemma', *New Scientist*, 13 July.

Bugler, Jeremy (1977), 'The Nuclear Politics of France', *New Statesman*, 26 August.

Coal Technology: Future Developments in Conversion, Utilisation and Unconventional Mining in the United Kingdom (1978), Department of Energy, London.

Denton, Richard (1977), 'Energy Futures for the Federal Republic of Germany: Three Scenarios', *Energy Policy*, Vol. 5, No. 1, p. 35.

Dryburgh, Peter (1979), 'Peat: A Missing Contribution', in Allan Scott and John A. Loraine (eds.) *Here Today – World Outlooks on Energy, Pollution, Medicine and Population*, Edinburgh University Student Press, p. 32.

Energy Policy, A Consultative Document (1978), HMSO, London.

Fells, Ian (1977), 'The energy future of West Germany', *Energy Policy*, Vol. 5, No. 4, p. 341.

Financial Times Survey (1978), 'Managing Energy', 10 October.

Fishlock, David (1978), 'Why the French are setting the pace', *Financial Times*, 26 August.

Flowers, Brian (1978), 'Nuclear Power: A Perspective on Risks, Benefits and Options', *Bulletin of the Atomic Scientists*, Vol. 34, No. 3, p. 21.

Foley,Gerald and Van Buren, Ariane (1978), *Nuclear or Not? Choices for our energy future*, Heinemann, London.

France and the Oil Problem (1977), printed by Manton Ltd., London.

Leach, Gerald, Lewis, Christopher, Romig, Frederic, Van Buren, Ariane and Foley, Gerald (1979), *A Low Energy Strategy for the United Kingdom*, Science Reviews, London.

Patterson, Walter C. (1978), 'The Windscale Report: A Nuclear Apologia', *Bulletin of the Atomic Scientists*, Vol. 34, No. 6, p. 44.

Patterson, Walter C. (1978), 'Energy Conservation: "Not doing without but doing more" ', *Bulletin of the Atomic Scientists*, Vol. 34, No. 10, p. 6.

Royal Commission on Environmental Pollution (1976), *Sixth Report: Nuclear Power and the Environment*, HMSO, London.

Ryle, Martin (1977), 'Economics of Alternative Energy Sources', *Nature*, Vol. 267, p. 111.

Select Committee on Science and Technology (1977), *The Development of Alternative Sources of Energy for the United Kingdom*, HMSO, London.

Shaw, Walter (1978), 'Is Energy Policy Right?', *Business Finance*, April.

Sweet, William (1977), 'The Opposition to Nuclear Power in Europe', *Bulletin of the Atomic Scientists*, Vol. 33, No. 10, p. 40.

Taylor, Peter (1977), 'The Struggle against Nuclear Power in Central Europe', *The Ecologist*, Vol. 7, No. 6, p. 217.

The Windscale Inquiry (1978), Report by the Hon. Mr Justice Parker, HMSO, London.

CHAPTER 7: PERSPECTIVES ON THE SOVIET UNION

Aganbegyan, A. (1978), 'Exploiting Siberia's Natural Resources', *Social Sciences*, Vol. 9, No. 2, p. 116.

Eason, Warren W. (1976), *Demographic Problems, Fertility and the Soviet Economy in a New Perspective*, Compendium of papers submitted to the Joint Economic Committee, Congress of the United States, p. 155, October.

Erickson, John (1977), 'The Soviet Union, the Future and Futures Research', *Futures*, Vol. 9, No. 4, p. 335.

Fesbach, Murray and Rapawy, Stephan (1976), *Soviet Population and Manpower Trends and Policies*, Compendium of papers submitted to the Joint Economic Committee, Congress of the United States, p. 113, October.

Fyodorov, Yevgeny (1978), 'Growth Will Go On', *Development*, No. 3, p. 1, April.

Heer, David M. (1977), 'Three Issues in Soviet Population Policy', *Population and Development Review*, Vol. 3, No. 3, p. 229.

Hingley, Ronald (1974), *Joseph Stalin: Man and Legend*, Hutchinson, London.

Kennan, G. F. (1978), 'A Last Warning', *Encounter*, Vol. 51, No. 1, p. 15.

Labedz, Leopold (1978), 'The Two Minds of George Kennan', *Encounter*, Vol. 50, No. 4, p. 78.

Leddy, Frederick A. (1973), *Demographic Trends in the USSR: Soviet Economic Prospects for the Seventies*, Compendium of papers submitted to the Joint Economic Committee, Congress of the United States, p. 428, June.

Loraine, John A. (1978), 'Population Patterns in Eastern Europe', *Coexistence*, Vol. 15, No. 2, p. 232.

McLellan, David (1973), *Karl Marx: his life and thought*, Macmillan, London.

NATO – Directorate of Economic Affairs (1975), *Economic Aspects of Life in the USSR*, Brussels, January.

Papp, Daniel S. (1977), 'Marxism-Leninism and Natural Resources: The Soviet Outlook', *Resources Policy*, Vol. 3, No. 2, p. 134.

Papp, Daniel S. (1977), 'Soviet Resources Policy: Foreign Investment, Resources and the Tenth Five Year Plan', *Resources Policy*, Vol. 3, No. 3, p. 195.

Pipes, Richard (1978), 'Mr. X Revises', *Encounter*, Vol. 50, No. 4, p. 18.

Sacks, Michael Paul (1976), *Women's Work in Soviet Russia: Continuity in the Midst of Change*, Praeger, New York.

Smith, Henrick (1976), *The Russians*, Sphere Books, London.

Ulam, Adam B. (1965), *Lenin and the Bolsheviks*, Secker & Warburg, London.

Zagladin, V. and Frolov, I. (1977), 'The Global Problems of Our Times', *Social Sciences*, Vol. 8, No. 4, p. 66.

CHAPTER 8: FOOD PROSPECTS FOR THE NEXT TWENTY YEARS

Abbott, John C. (1977), 'Food and Agricultural Marketing in China', *Food Policy*, Vol. 2, No. 4, p. 318.

Allaby, Michael (1977), *World Food Resources: Actual and Potential*, Applied Science Publishers, London.

Bhattacharjee, J. P. (1976), 'Population, Food and Agricultural Development – A Medium Term View', *Food Policy*, Vol. 1, No. 3, p. 179.

Brown, Lester R. (1978), 'The World-wide Loss of Cropland', *Worldwatch Paper 24*, October.

Ehrlich, Paul (1968), *The Population Bomb*, Sierra Club/Ballantine, New York.

Enzer, Selwyn, Drobnick, Richard and Alter, Steven (1978), 'Neither Feast nor Famine: World Food 20 Years On', *Food Policy*, Vol. 3, No. 1, p. 3.

Food and Agriculture (1976), *Scientific American* Book, Freeman, San Francisco.

George, Susan (1976), *How the Other Half Dies: The Real Reasons for World Hunger*, Penguin Books, Harmondsworth.

Green, Maurice B. (1978), *Eating Oil: Energy Use in Food Production*, Westview Press, Boulder, Colorado.

Hardin, Garrett (1968), 'The Tragedy of the Commons', *Science*, Vol. 162, p. 1243.

Hay, Roger W. (1978), 'The Statistics of Hunger', *Food Policy*, Vol. 3, No. 4, p. 243.

Ishikawa, Shigeru (1977), 'China's Food and Agriculture – A Turning Point', *Food Policy*, Vol. 2, No. 2, p. 90.

Josling, Tim (1975), 'The World Food Situation – National and International Aspects', *Food Policy*, Vol. 1, No. 1, p. 3.

Loraine, John A. (1970), *Sex and the Population Crisis*, Heinemann Medical Books, London.

New Internationalist (1977), 'Food First: Beyond the Myth of Scarcity', September.

Paarlberg, Don (1975), 'The World Food Situation – A Consensus View', *Food Policy*, Vol. 1, No. 1, p. 15.

Paddock, William and Paddock, Paul (1968), *Famine 1975!*, Weidenfeld & Nicolson, London.

Rojko, Anthony S. and O'Brien, Patrick (1976), 'Organizing Agriculture in the Year 2000', *Food Policy*, Vol. 1, No. 3, p. 203.

Rush, Howard, Marstrand, Pauline and Gribbin, John (1978), 'World Food Futures – Growth with Redistribution', *Food Policy*, Vol. 3, No. 3, p. 114.

Sai, Fred T. (1977), *Food, Population and Politics*, International Planned Parenthood Federation, London.

Tudge, Colin (1977), *The Famine Business*, Faber & Faber, London.

Tuve, George L. (1976), *Energy, Environment, Population and Food*, Wiley, New York.

Wynne-Tyson, Jon (1976), *Food for a Future*, Abacus Books, London.

CHAPTER 9: POPULATION STILL DOMINANT

Beattie, Walter M. (1978), 'Ageing: A Framework of Characteristics and Considerations for Co-operative Efforts between the Developing and Developed Regions of the World', Background paper for UN meeting in New York, April.

Benjamin, Bernard (1978), *The Decline in the Birth Rate: Towards a Better Quality of Life*, Birth Control Trust, London.

Bouvier, Leon F. with Shypock, Henry S. and Henderson, Harry W. (1977), 'International Migration: Yesterday, Today and Tomorrow', *Population Bulletin* (Population Reference Bureau), Vol. 32, No. 4, September.

Care of the Elderly in Great Britain (1977), HMSO, London.

Cartwright, Ann (1978), *Recent Trends in Family Building and Contraception*, HMSO, London.

Central Policy Review Staff (1977), *Population and the Social Services*, HMSO, London.

Day, Lincoln, H. (1978), 'What Will a ZPG Society Be Like?', *Population Bulletin* (Population Reference Bureau), Vol. 33, No. 3, June.

Ehrlich, Paul R., Ehrlich, Anne H. and Holdren, John P. (1977), *Ecoscience: Population, Resources, Environment*, Freeman, San Francisco.

Goldsmith, Edward (1978), 'The Ecological Approach to Unemployment', *The Ecologist Quarterly*, No. 1, Spring, p. 32.

Harrison, Richard (1976), 'The Demoralising Experience of Prolonged Unemployment', *Department of Employment Gazette*, April, p. 339.

Hawkes, Nigel and Hamilton, Adrian (1978), 'Silicon Chips with Everything', *Observer*, 16 July.

Hines, Colin (1978), 'The "Chips" Are Down. A Discussion Paper', Earth Resources Research, April.

Loraine, John A. (1972), *The Death of Tomorrow*, Heinemann, London.

Loraine, John A. (1977), *Syndromes of the Seventies*, Peter Owen, London.

Loraine, John A. (1977), 'Doctors and the Global Population Crisis', *British Medical Journal*, Vol. 2, p. 691.

Loraine, John A. (1977), 'Twenty-Five Years of the World Population Crisis', *Contemporary Review*, Vol. 231, No. 1341, p. 208.

Loraine, John A. (1977), 'A Terrifying Society?', *Populi*, Vol. 4, No. 4, p. 12.

Loraine, John A. (1978), 'The Changing Face of Britain', *Update*, Vol. 16, No. 1, p. 65.

McNamara, Robert S. (1977), *Address to the Massachusetts Institute of Technology*, MIT, Cambridge, Mass.

Maddock, Sir Ieuan (1978), 'Beyond the Protestant Ethic', *New Scientist*, 23 November.

Maudlin, W. Parker (1977), 'World Population Situation: Problems and Prospects', *World Development*, Vol. 5, p. 395.

Nortman, Dorothy (1977), 'Changing Contraceptive Patterns: A Global Perspective', *Population Bulletin* (Population Reference Bureau), Vol. 32, No. 3.

People (1976), Special issue on human settlements, Vol. 3, No. 2.

Population and the American Future (1972), The Report of the Commission on Population Growth and the American Future, Library of Congress Catalog No. 72/77389.

Population Reference Bureau (1978), 'World Population Data Sheet', May.

Ray, G. F. (1978), 'UK Productivity and Employment in 1991', *Futures*, Vol. 10, No. 2, p. 91.

Tsui, Amy Ong and Bogue, Donald J. (1978), 'Declining World Fertility: Trends, Causes, Implications', *Population Bulletin* (Population Reference Bureau), Vol. 33, No. 4, October.

Williamson, J. (1979), 'Old Age', in G. M. Howe and J. A. Loraine (eds.), *Environmental Medicine*, 2nd Edition, Heinemann Medical Books, forthcoming.

CHAPTER 10: THE PROGNOSIS FOR BIRTH CONTROL

Black, T. R. L. (1976), 'Community-based Distribution: The Distributive Potential and Economics of a Social Marketing Approach to Family Planning', in R. V. Short and D. J. Baird (eds.), *Contraceptives of the Future*, The Royal Society, London, p. 199.

Gillett, Peter G. (1977), 'Immunologic Control of Fertility: Search for a Contraceptive Vaccine', *Clinical Obstetrics and Gynaecology*, Vol. 20, No. 3, p. 705.

Harkavy, O., Jaffe, F. S., Koblinsky, Marjorie A. and Segal, J. J. (1976), 'Funding of Contraceptive Research', in *Contraceptives of the Future*, The Royal Society, London, p. 37.

Hearn, J. P. (1976), 'Immunisation against Pregnancy', in *Contraceptives of the Future*, The Royal Society, London, p. 149.

Kretsler, D. M. De (1976), 'Towards a Pill for Men', in *Contraceptives of the Future*, The Royal Society, London, p. 161.

Loraine, John A. (1978), 'Abortion: The World Scene', *Contemporary Review*, Vol. 232, No. 1345, p. 92.

Loraine, John A. and Bell, E. T. (1968), *Fertility and Contraception in the Human Female*, Livingstone, Edinburgh and London.

Pilsworth, Robert (1978), 'Problems with pregnancy vaccination', *New Scientist*, 9 March.

Potts, D. M. (1976), 'The Implementation of Family Planning Programmes', in *Contraceptives of the Future*, The Royal Society, London, p. 213.

Potts, Malcolm, Diggory, Peter and Peel, John (1977), *Abortion*, Cambridge University Press, London, New York and Melbourne.

Stevens, Vernon C. (1978), 'Aspects of Contraception: Research for the Development of Anti-fertility Vaccines', I and II, *British Journal of Sexual Medicine*, August and September.

Short, R. V. (1976), 'The Evolution of Human Reproduction', in *Contraceptives of the Future*, The Royal Society, London, p. 3.

Tietze, Christopher (1977), 'Induced Abortion', *Report on Population/Family Planning*, No. 14, December.

Vessey, M. P. (1978), 'Contraceptive Methods', *British Medical Journal*, 9 September.

Vessey, M. P., Wright, N. H., McPherson, K. and Wiggins, P. (1978), 'Fertility After Stopping Different Methods of Contraception', *British Medical Journal*, 4 February.

World Health Organization (1977), *Special Programme of Research, Development and Research Training in Human Reproduction*, Sixth Annual Report, November.

World Health Organization (1978), *Induced Abortion*, Report of Scientific Group, Geneva.

World Health Organization (1978), *Research in Human Reproduction: Strengthening of Resources in Developing Countries*, Report of Study Group, Geneva.

CHAPTER 11: THE PARAMOUNTCY OF ENVIRONMENTAL MEDICINE

Armstrong, R. W. (1979), 'Environmental Influences in Cancer Aetiology', in G. M. Howe and J. A. Loraine (eds.), *Environmental Medicine*, 2nd Edition, Heinemann Medical Books, London, forthcoming.

Blackburn, Henry (1974), 'Progress in the Epidemiology and Prevention of Coronary Heart Disease', in Paul N. Yu and James S. Goodwin (eds.), *Progress in Cardiology*, Vol. 3, p. 1.

British Medical Journal (1978), 'Clofibrate and the primary prevention of Ischaemic heart disease', Leading article, 9 December.

Burkitt, Denis P. (1977), 'Are Our Commonest Diseases Preventable?' *Preventive Medicine*, Vol. 6, p. 556.

Dever, G. E. Alan (1977), 'The Pursuit of Health', *Social Indicators Research*, Vol. 4, p. 475.

Eckholm, Erik P. (1977), *The Picture of Health: Environmental Sources of Disease*, Norton, New York.

Epstein, Samuel S. (1977), 'Cancer and the Environment', *Bulletin of the Atomic Scientists*, Vol. 33, No. 3, p. 22.

Fox, Renée C. (1977), 'The Medicalization and Demedicalization of Society', *Daedalus*, Vol. 106, No. 1, p. 9.

Gillis, C. R. (1977), 'Malignant Neoplasms', in G. M. Howe (ed.), *A World Geography of Human Diseases*, Academic Press, London, New York and San Francisco, p. 507.

Horrobin, David (1978), *Medical Hubris: A Reply to Ivan Illich*, Churchill Livingstone, Edinburgh.

Howe, G. M., Burgess, L. and Gatenby, P. (1977), 'Cardiovascular Disease', in G. M. Howe (ed.), *A World Geography of Human Diseases*, Academic Press, London, New York and San Francisco, p. 431.

Illich, Ivan (1974), *Medical Nemesis*, Calder & Boyars, London.

Lancet (1978), 'Cancer Clues from Chinese Chickens', Leading article, 28 January.

Lewin, Roger (1978), 'Cancer: Detecting the Chemical Culprits', *New Scientist*, 13 July.

Loraine, John A. (1979), 'Health Care in a More Sustainable Society', in Allan Scott and John A. Loraine (eds.), *Here Today – World Outlooks for Energy, Pollution, Medicine and Population*, Edinburgh University Student Press, p. 108.

Muller, Mike (1978), *Tobacco and the Third World: Tomorrow's Epidemic?*, War on Want, London.

Pedoe, H. Tunstall (1977), 'Atheroma: Prevention of Atheroma', *British Journal of Hospital Medicine*, Vol. 18, No. 4, p. 317.

Powles, John (1977), 'Have Health Services Reduced Mortality?', *The Ecologist*, Vol. 7, No. 8, p. 303.

Shapiro, Jean and Garth, Susan (1978), 'Heart Disease: Is Cholesterol Really the Culprit?', *Good Housekeeping*, July.

Symington, T. and Carter, R. L. (eds.) (1976), *Scientific Foundations of Oncology*, Heinemann Medical Books, London.

Taylor, Stanley H. (1977), 'Atheroma: Clinical Aspects of Atheroma', *British Journal of Hospital Medicine*, Vol. 18, No. 4, p. 317.

Waterhouse, J., Muir, C., Correa, P. and Powell, J. (1976), *Cancer Incidence in Five Continents*, Volume III, IARC Scientific Publications No. 15, Lyon.

Woolf, Neville (1977), 'Atheroma: Aspects of Atherogenesis', *British Journal of Hospital Medicine*, Vol. 18, No. 4, p. 286.

World Health Organization (1978), *Quarterly Report; Project on Cancer in the Caspian Littoral in Iran*, January/March, Tehran.

World Health Organization (1978), *Steroid Contraception and the Risk of Neoplasia*, Technical Report Series, Geneva.

EPILOGUE

Boucher, Wayne (ed.) (1977), *The Study of the Future: An Agenda for Research*, National Science Foundation, July.

Commoner, Barry (1976), *The Poverty of Power: Energy and the Economic Crisis*, Jonathan Cape, London.

Ehrlich, Paul R. and Ehrlich, H. (1972), *Population, Resources, Environment: Issues in Human Ecology*, 2nd Edition, Freeman, San Francisco.

Fowles, Jib (ed.) (1978), *Handbook of Futures Research*, Greenwood Press, Westport, Connecticut, and London.

Freeman, Christopher and Jahoda, Marie (eds.) (1978), *World Futures, The Great Debate*, Blackwell, Oxford.

Heilbroner, Robert L. (1974), *An Inquiry into the Human Prospect*, Norton, New York.

Kahn, H. and Wiener, A. (1967), *The Year 2000*, Macmillan, London.

Kahn, Herman, Brown, William and Martel, Leon (1977), *The Next 200 Years*, Associated Business Programmes, London.

Kennet, Wayland (1976), *The Future of Europe*, Cambridge University Press, Cambridge, London, New York and Melbourne.

Marien, Michael (1977), 'The Two Visions of Post-Industrial Society', *Futures*, Vol. 9, No. 5, p. 415.

Meadows, Donella H., Meadows, Dennis L., Randers, Jorgen and Behrens, William W. III (1972), *The Limits to Growth*, Earth Island, London.

Mesarovic, M. and Pestel, E. (1974), *Mankind at the Turning Point*, Dutton/Reader's Digest Press, New York.

Modrzhinskaya, Y. and Stephanyan, C. (1973), *The Future of Society*, Progress Publishers, Moscow.

Robertson, James (1978), *The Sane Alternative: Signposts to a Self-fulfilling Future*, published by the author.

Index

abortion, 19, 122, 175-7, 185, 186
Abu Dhabi, 53
Accra, 168
Acheson-Lillienthal Report, 45
Africa, age structure in, 16; agricultural production in, 140; breastfeeding in, 135; desertification in, 148; labour force in, 171; land distribution in, 135; population of, 156; sex education in, 15; women's rights in, 21
agriculture, 30, 136-44
Alaska, 71
Alcan pipeline, 71, 83
Algeria, 16, 156, 162, 171
Amin, Idi, 18
amniotic sac, 176
anaemia, 24
angina pectoris, 191
Argentina, 46, 136, 161
Armenia, 119
arteriosclerosis, 191, 193
Asia, age structure in, 16; agricultural production in, 140; atomic reactors in, 34; desertification in, 148; labour force in, 171; population of, 156, 158; sex education in, 15
Asmara, 168
Athabasca River Valley, 71, 81
Atommash reactor, 126
atomic fission, see nuclear fission
atomic reactors, see nuclear reactors
Australia, 27, 154, 161, 192
Austria, 16, 28, 157, 164
Azerbaijan, 119

Bahrain, 52, 53
Baikal-Amur railway, 125
Baker Nun Camera, 39
Baltic Sea, 190

Bangkok, 185
Bangladesh, 134, 140, 156, 181
Barbados, 155
barefoot doctors, 19, 186
Baruch, Bernard, 41, 45
'bazaar economy', 169
Belgium, 16, 157, 164, 167
Belo Horizonte, 168
Belorussia, 119, 126
Benn, Tony, 107
beryllium, 201
Bevan, Aneurin, 208
'biodegradable delivery system', 179
biomass, 77, 83, 89, 95
birth control, 15, 19, 21, 122, 164, 175-87, 202
bischloromethyl ether, 200
Bogota, 168
Bolivia, 137
Bombay, 168
Bonn, 26, 113
Botswana, 16
Boumedienne, Houari, 162
Boyd Orr, Lord, 150
Brazil, 26, 46, 156, 161, 168, 171
Brenner, Dr Harvey, 173
Brest Litovsk, Peace of, 24
Brezhnev, Leonid, 117, 118, 125, 129, 210
British Commonwealth, 155
Brokdorf, 113
Brown, Lester, 143
Bucharest, 17, 121
Bulawayo, 197, 200
Bulgaria, 16, 118, 127, 164, 172
Burkitt, D. P., 200

Cairo, 168
Calcutta, 168, 185
Canada, 38, 71, 81-5, 97, 161, 192

227